AF594093

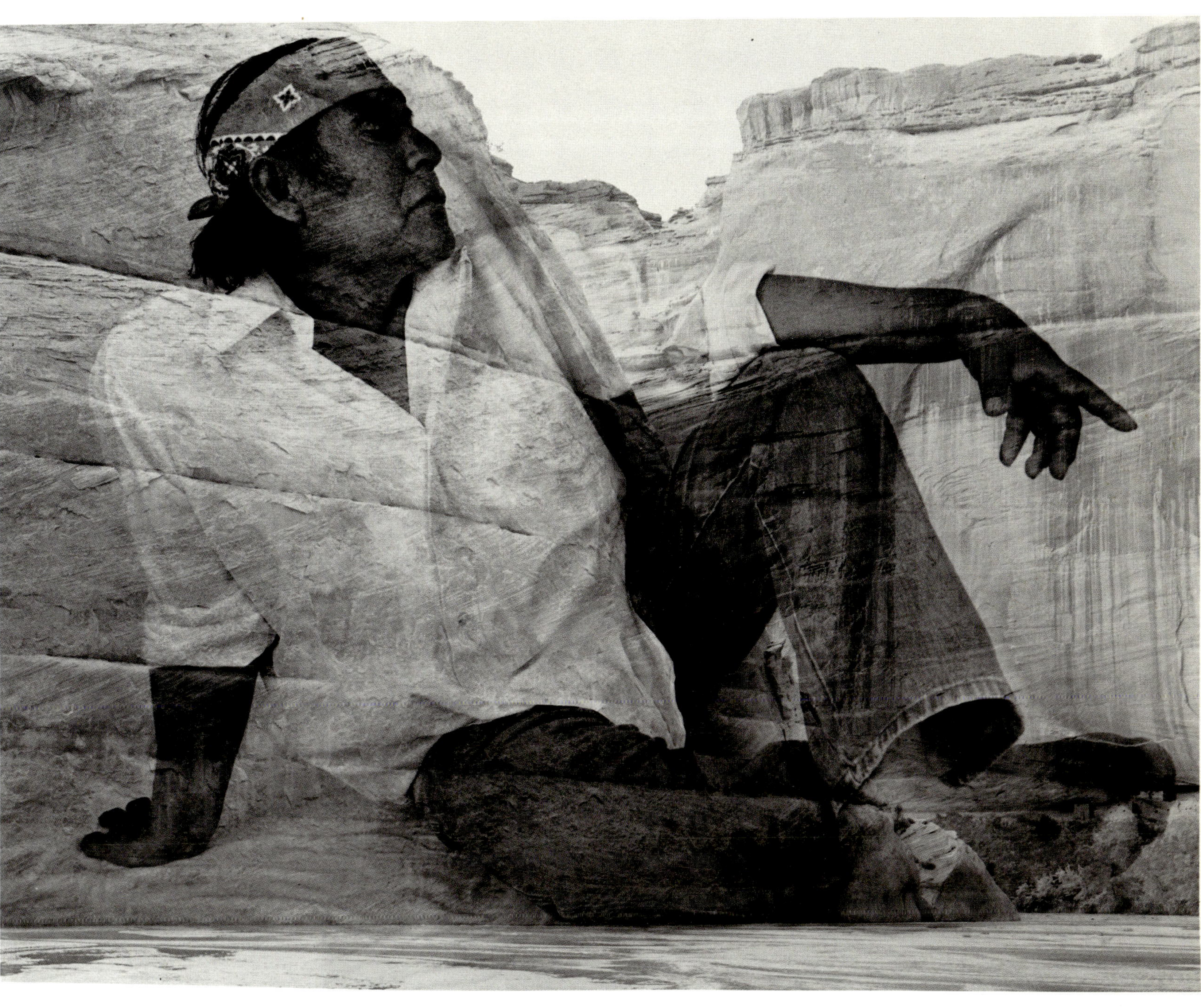

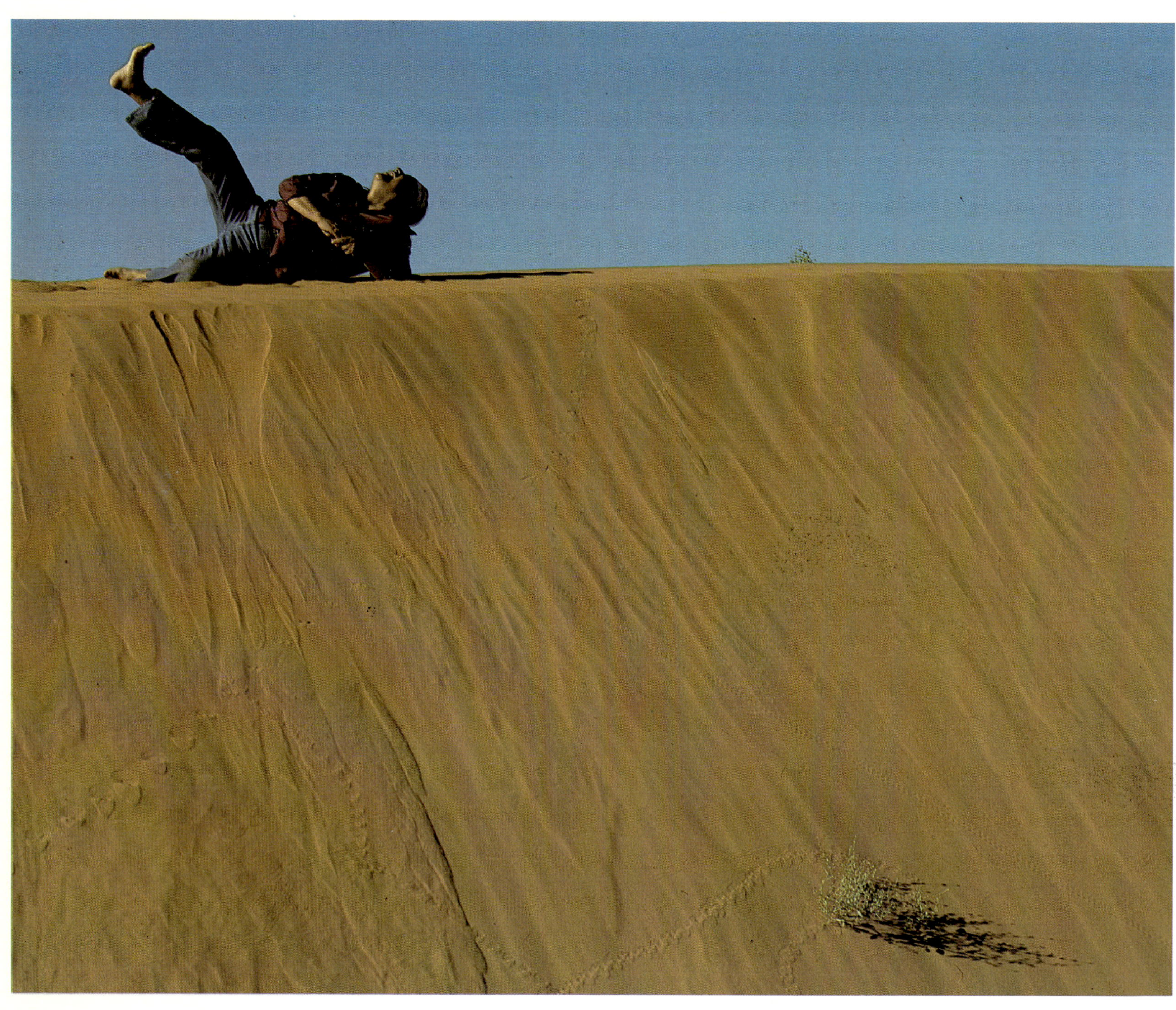

Gorman in the dunes near Chinle,
Arizona, 1981

R. C. GORMAN

A Portrait

Photographs by Chuck Henningsen

Text by Stephen Parks

A New York Graphic Society Book

Little, Brown and Company • Boston

Library of Congress Cataloging in Publication Data

Henningsen, Chuck.
R. C. Gorman, a portrait.

"A New York Graphic Society book."
1. Gorman, R. C. (Rudolph Carl), 1932–
2. Artists—United States—Biography. 3. Navaho Indians
—Biography. I. Parks, Stephen, 1944– . II. Title.
N6537.G66H46 1983 709'.2'4 83-9829
ISBN 0-8212-1537-X

New York Graphic Society books are published by Little, Brown and Company.
Published simultaneously in Canada by Little, Brown and Company (Canada) Limited.

First edition

Printed in Italy

To Mary Jean, Curtis, and R. C., for the love and laughter

—C. H.

To my wife and son, Sam and Dylan

—S. P.

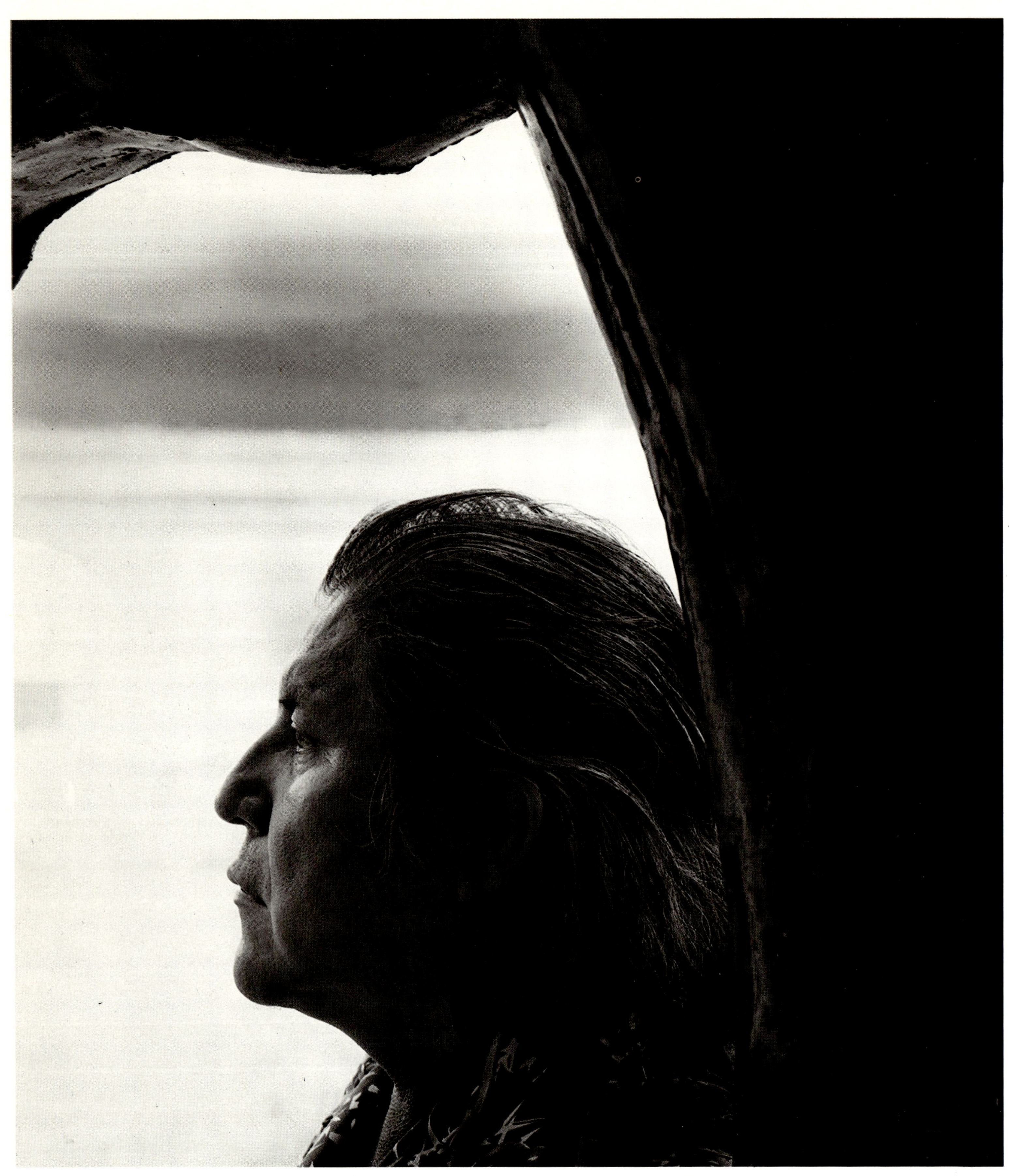

R. C. Gorman,
Taos, New Mexico, 1980

R.C. GORMAN

A Portrait

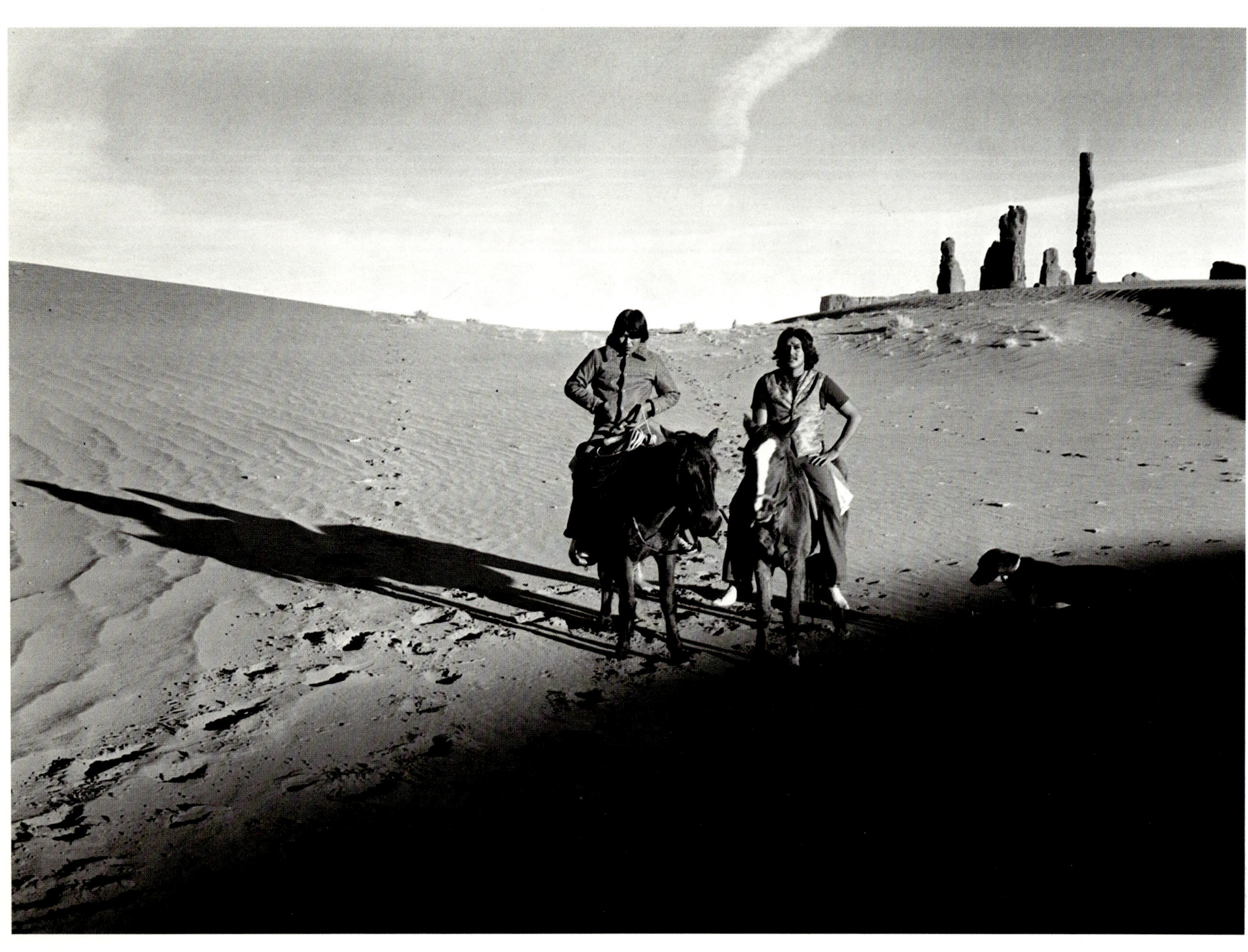

Navajo sheepherders,
Monument Valley, Arizona, 1976

Preface

My odyssey began years back. I was in the beautiful sand dunes of Monument Valley with the array of equipment necessary to shoot a photographic essay on Southwest Indians and landscapes. I watched shadows slowly fill concave spaces, the light getting longer, adding hundreds of feet to the sandstone towers. I idly fiddled with *f* stops and film holders, feeling the panorama soften, the glorious images dance and change, waiting to be photographed.

Suddenly apparitions materialized: dogs, horses, Navajo sheepherders unflocked. They cluttered my beautiful dunes, their feet tracked unbroken sand seas. I was swept backward hundreds of years to the end of the Anasazi, the beginning of the Navajo. Sheepherders, horses, and dogs stopped, frozen in time. I fumbled with light meters, shutter speeds, dark cloths, focal planes; my intrusion in their place had left me self-conscious and slowed me. View cameras were not meant to record ancient men fading into another time. Still, nothing moved. Finally, the shutter softly signaled an image—a record of this mirage. Then, as quickly as they had come, dogs darted, horses and men slipped into the long shadows. Had I imagined it all? Was I discovered in their world or were they trapped in mine?

Years and a thousand images later, I met R. C. Gorman, at first just another of the hundreds of Indians I had photographed along my journey. But, like my sudden apparitions, I was jolted. Gorman was different. Not silent and sullen as some, not secret and guarded as many, not tottering on the edge of extinction as the white man attempts to weave new ways into the old. Gorman is an artist not just recording, but exalting, celebrating, bathing in the Indian ways. He is a Renaissance man enjoying all worlds, all time, and savoring each as no man I had met from either place. I had been a wandering sightseer in the Navajo experience, attempting to capture the spirit of a land and a race. However, Gorman gave my images focus and emotional texture. He is a creative hero who has journeyed out from the hogan, and across many layers of cultural experience, without moving from the roots of his inspiration.

So these photographs and Steve Parks's words are our record of R. C. Gorman, his friends, his people, his land, and most of all, his art. We are pleased to share it with you.

Chuck Henningsen

Who Is R. C. Gorman?

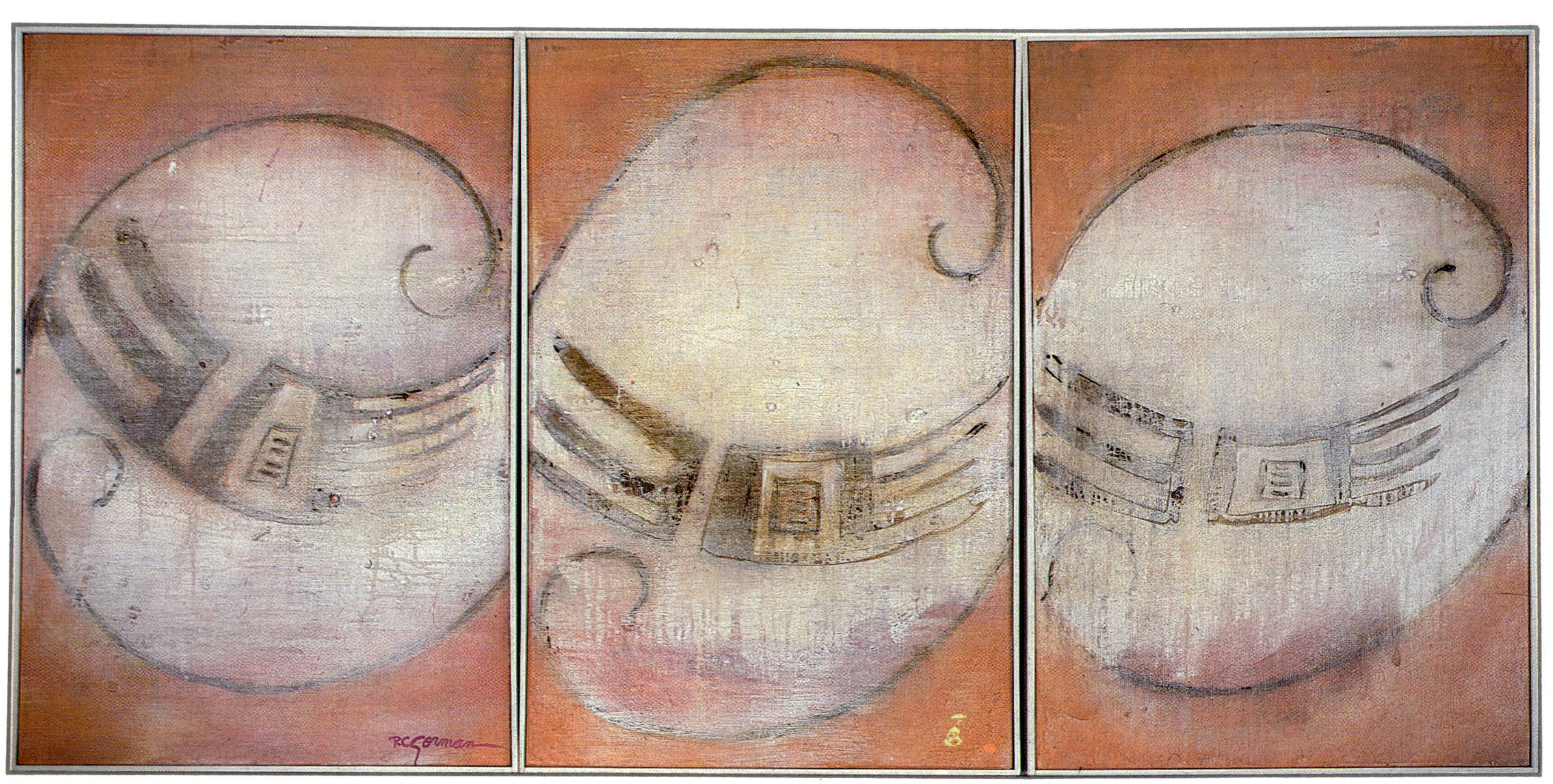

Pottery Triptych,
acrylic on canvas, 1978

"Who is R. C. Gorman?" ask the bumper stickers and billboards scattered about the Southwest. To tens of thousands of people, R. C. Gorman is the world-famous Navajo artist whose paintings and lithographs of Indian women grace the walls of their homes and offices. To millions of others, he is the quick, engaging, and often outrageous celebrity they have seen on *Good Morning, America* and read about in *People* magazine. He is the Indian jet-setter of Taos who wears Brooks Brothers suits and a headband.

Gorman himself has carefully cultivated this free-for-all persona. And while it is a true expression of his fun-loving self, it reveals only one side of the man, a fraction of what he thinks and feels, where he is from and headed. The jet-setter image obscures the heritage, the depth of experience and sensitivity, that finally are responsible for the beauty and grace of his work and for its immense popularity.

"Who is R. C. Gorman?" The answer is intriguingly complex. He is *the* American Indian who has cashed in on the American Dream, the underprivileged kid from the Arizona reservation who wanted so badly to burst from the religious, economic, and psychological strictures of his ancestral home. He wanted to wear fine clothes rather than hand-me-downs, eat and drink whatever he wanted rather than what was available. He had a glittering vision of the outside world as a place of bright lights and beautiful people, and he wanted to be right in the midst of it. With his talent, determination, faith in his vision and potential, he has succeeded.

As a consequence of this Indian's achievements in the white man's world, some of the stereotypes and deep-seated prejudices the nation has held about its original citizens have been challenged. We secretly harbor the childish notion that Indians have a native kind of intelligence that comes in handy when stalking game and sneaking up on white settlers. Gorman's native intelligence, however, is exemplified in his negotiations with art dealers and corporate executives. And he has never been known to sneak in anywhere. He comes through the front door, always. Many like to think that art produced by Indians is carved on canyon walls or concerned only with rendering cute Bambi deer. Gorman makes art with the sophisticated aesthetic of the Romantic European academies. He is an anomaly, an

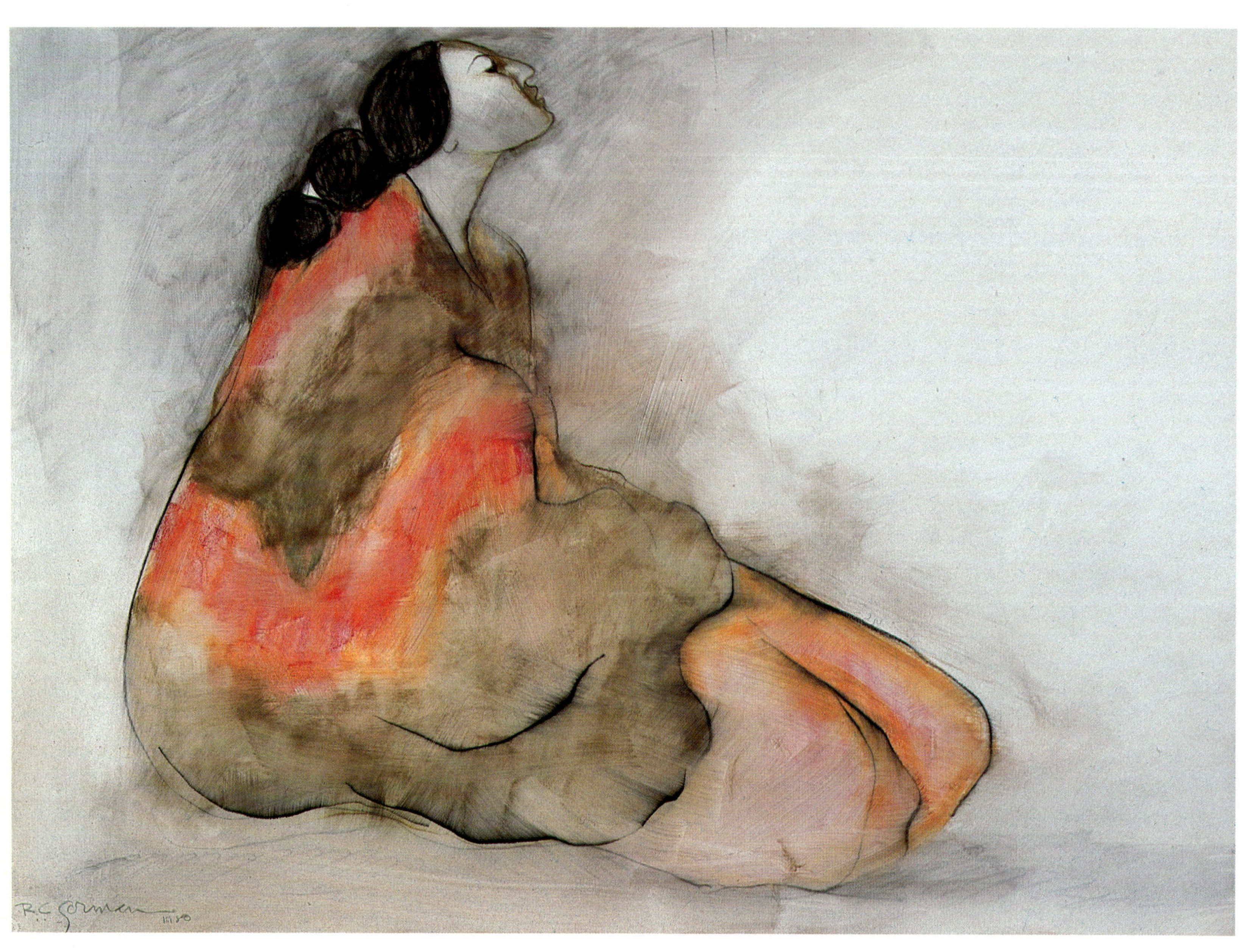

Seated Woman,
oil pastel drawing, 1980

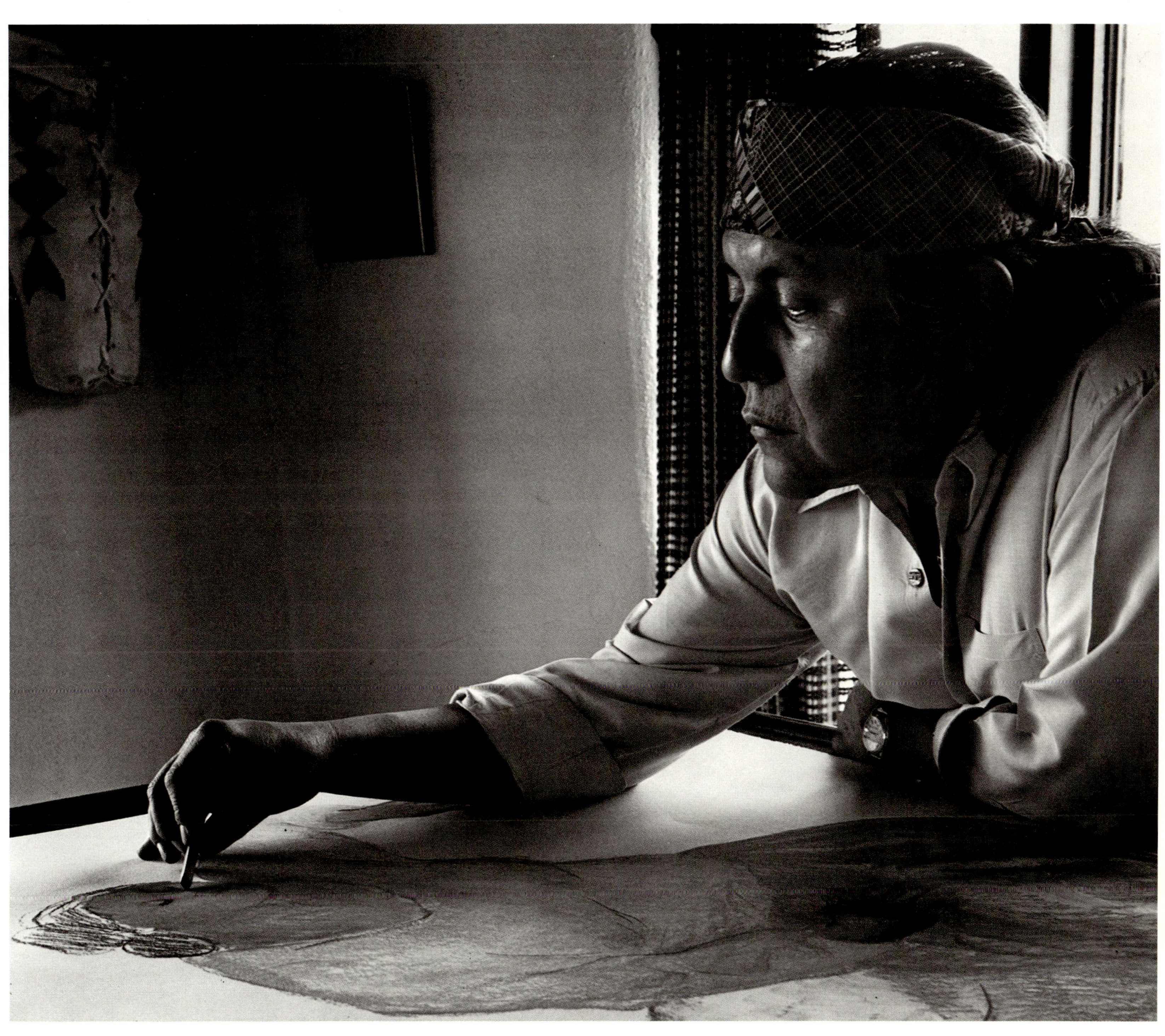

R. C. Gorman at work,
Taos, 1980

Indian individual, a man of the world who puts on a headband the first thing every morning.

By his example, he has encouraged scores of young Indian artists, shown them how they too can express themselves without forsaking their essential Indianness.

Gorman has become famous for his tranquil images of Indian women in soft, earth-colored robes, cradling children in their arms, quietly glowing with peace and pride. They are strong women, used to hard work, but always with a youthful spirit. Inextricably connected with the earth, they clearly symbolize an archetypal ideal of woman. Gorman's women harken back to simpler times, of course, but the artist's vast popularity indicates that he has also tapped into a very contemporary yearning for strength, serenity, and the shining sort of beauty that has characterized the female spirit through the ages.

Art is only one part of the artist's life, to be sure, and drawing conclusions about Gorman's personality from viewing his work is probably a misleading and specious exercise. The man who paints desert madonnas could hardly himself be described as a saint. In fact, many people regard him as a high-living, heavy-drinking sybarite, and there is a ribald, Falstaffian side to the man. Those close to Gorman also know him as exceedingly generous, cultured, dedicated to his work, and almost completely without guile. As active as he is, and as much as he loves to talk and party, he is a private man. He reveals little of the Navajo that lies beneath the garish headband, at the center of his being. Except to the handful of people who know him best, his private expression is reserved for his art.

Only by spending a great deal of time with Gorman can one expect to catch those bright, brief bursts of understanding that occasionally flash in everyday activities and casual conversations and, like epiphanies, reveal essential truths. In the hope of gaining a deeper understanding of the artist and his art, we persuaded Gorman to go along on a trip to the Navajo heartland in Chinle and Canyon de Chelly, Arizona. We were not disappointed.

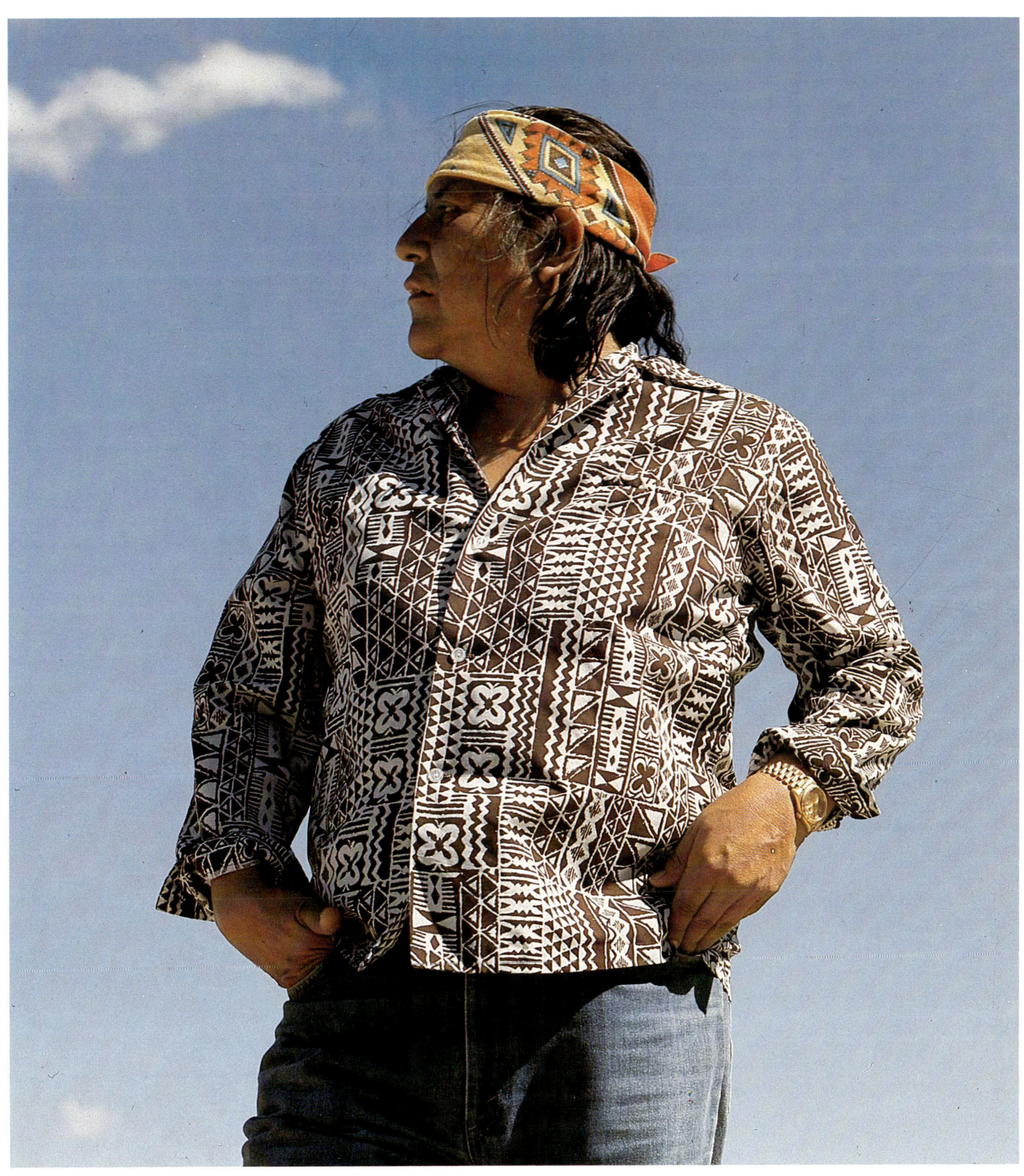

Gorman at Black Mountain,
Arizona, 1981

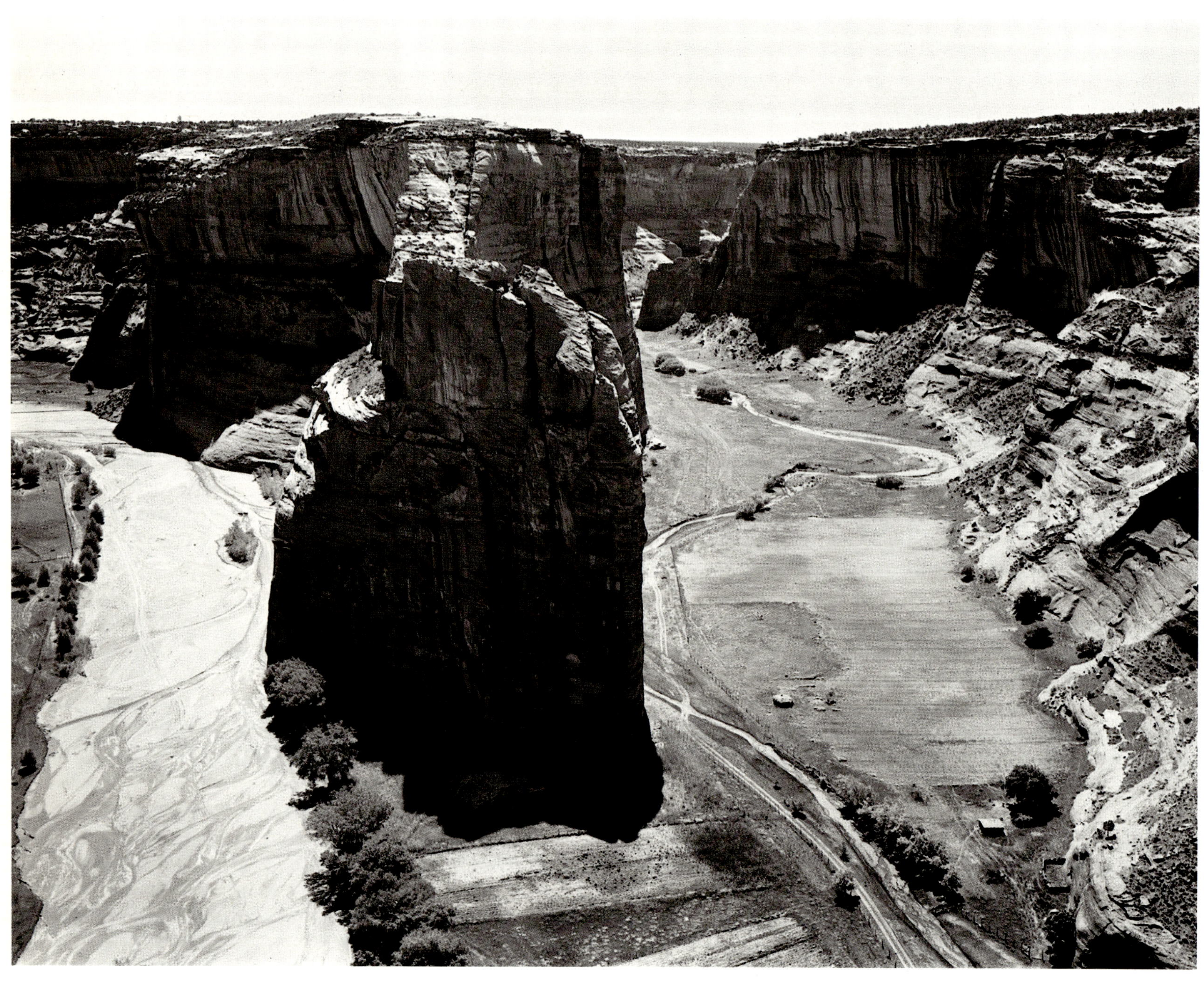

Junction of Canyon de Chelly and Canyon del Muerto,
Arizona, 1979

The Roots:

Canyon de Chelly and Black Mountain

Gorman was ambivalent about going to Chinle and the famous Canyon de Chelly. Though he had been born there, and his art was firmly rooted in the place, he seldom visited Chinle and, in fact, had not been in the canyon in the nearly forty years since he left. The man obviously felt a tension between the idealized vision of the beauty of the reservation's land and people that constitute a prime theme in his art, and his memories of childhood poverty, loneliness, and deprivation. Perhaps Gorman was not sure he wanted to be reminded of such realities.

There was also some protective resistance from members of Gorman's entourage who wanted him to stay home and rest or paint. He sometimes works and parties to excess, and there had been concern about his health. Gorman, however, laughs off such worry. "The doctors should worry, no one else. I'm like a piece of ivory, valuable when new, but worth more when old. Though I'm degenerating, I'm more valuable. My friends, neighbors, priests, bankers and lawyers, cats and dogs, shouldn't worry—these people I feed."

He looks to be forty or so, admits to being fifty, though some put the figure a few years higher.

Throughout most of our trip, Gorman was subdued. Though he was cheerful and his humor was as raucous as ever, there wasn't the same driving level of prodigious energy that characterizes his life in Taos. Perhaps it was because there were fewer people to entertain. Perhaps he felt humbled by the fact that on the reservation his gold Mercedes-Benz was regarded as a sign of unimaginable wealth, while in Taos some of his less gifted and less successful artist contemporaries regard such trappings with a mixture of scorn and envy. And, too, there is the feeling that in Chinle you are in an ancient land, watched and judged by its harsh though ultimately benevolent spirit. Gorman seemed very aware of the presence of that spirit.

We met Gorman and Curtis Grubbs, his studio assistant, long-time friend, and usual traveling companion, in Window Rock, the capital of the Navajo Nation. It is a dusty town filled with gas stations and pickup trucks. Gorman was tired. He'd spent ten exhausting days skipping between Taos, Albuquerque, Window Rock,

Phoenix, Tucson, Wichita, and Houston, promoting his art and working on lithographs with various printers. His feet hurt. One of his great pleasures is to have his feet massaged, and Grubbs obliged Gorman's instructions: "Do the toes . . . harder there . . . wonderful."

Not surprisingly, they are the same feet one sees rendered so prominently in his representations of women. They are pudgy but strong and sensuous. They seem to have an inherent significance, a mysterious independence like that of eyes, as if they had a mind and soul of their own. Like the feet of the women in his paintings, Gorman's feet are symbolic of a connection with the earth, a grounding.

As Grubbs massaged, he and Gorman gossiped some about Gorman's family. They discussed the English slang employed by certain nieces and nephews, and whether one teenager was really benefitting from the piano lessons Gorman was paying for.

It was a relaxing evening. We drank a bottle of wine, and the two friends began to talk about food, beginning with the quality of the *posole* (high) that was served in the motel's restaurant. Gorman recounted, with either a remarkable memory or ready ability to conjure up fictional detail, the most memorable meals eaten during his wide travels. "Remember, Curtis, the floating restaurant in Aberdeen, near Hong Kong, the one Queen Elizabeth Taylor ate in? I had the crab. It was green and hairy and the shell was as hard as porcelain. I don't know how to describe the taste . . . gamey. Virginia [Virginia Dooley, director of his Navajo Gallery in Taos] had a huge fish. You had shrimp. That's your Baptist upbringing —no fun."

The next morning, we drove the back road from Window Rock to Chinle. Gorman was quiet as we drove past Ganado Lake, through the shanty town of Nazlini, and over a moonlike landscape. When asked what he was thinking about, he replied lightly but with a hint of something held back, "Nothing." The only life along the road was sparse juniper or piñon trees, a dog, a herd of sheep. He pointed out a small, conical pile of rocks by the road. "That's a prayer pile. Good luck."

We passed two women sitting in the shade of a large bush. "Oh, stop! It's bad luck to pass them. One of them might be a witch." We backed up and they climbed into the car. They were perhaps forty and fifty years old, though it was impossible to tell. They might have been thirty and sixty. The elder one wore glasses and her hair pulled back tight against the head; the other, the quiet one, had a permanent. Gorman's spirits picked up immediately. Highlighting their conversation for me in English, he chatted in Navajo with them, the words coming out flat and staccato from deep in the throat. The women pointed out landmarks to the Indian who hadn't been on the road since his childhood. "Nazlini—that means 'bend in the water.' Over there is Crow Springs."

"Oh, pick up that man," teased the elder as we passed a young Navajo in a cowboy hat and plaid shirt. "He can sit on my lap. We're not like other ladies, we like to joke." They giggled loudly with their eyes nearly closed, looking very Oriental. Only when they were silent were their eyes fully open, gazing out at the land. They were going to Chinle; one to the Social Security office, the other wouldn't say where. "Maybe to find a boyfriend," her friend said, laughing. We passed a lone goat foraging in the sparse grass, watched by a dog. "You two herd the sheep," the talkative one said. "We'll take the car."

We dropped them in Chinle, and Gorman pointed out the hill on which his boyhood home had stood. The top of the hill had been leveled and a new police station built on the site. At the Canyon de Chelly Motel, owned by his cousin, Rosetta Gorman ha font, we drank a glass of wine, then drove a few miles to the mouth of the canyon itself. Suddenly, as if on cue, two women appeared, standing on top of a rocky hill, wearing traditional velvet garb. "There they are," Gorman exclaimed. "Two Gorman models. See the pinks and blues in their clothes? The clouds?"

There was an air of expectation as we approached this beautiful and powerful place, home of the ancient Anasazi, for centuries the Navajo refuge from Indian, Spanish, and finally Anglo invaders, and their fertile summer home where squash, beans, corn, and fruit are grown. "Here's where I'd love to build the Gorman Museum," he said as we stopped on the little hill above the canyon's mouth. Should Gorman ever decide to build such a museum, this would be a perfect place for it. Stretching away from one side of the hill is the empty high desert circled by deso-

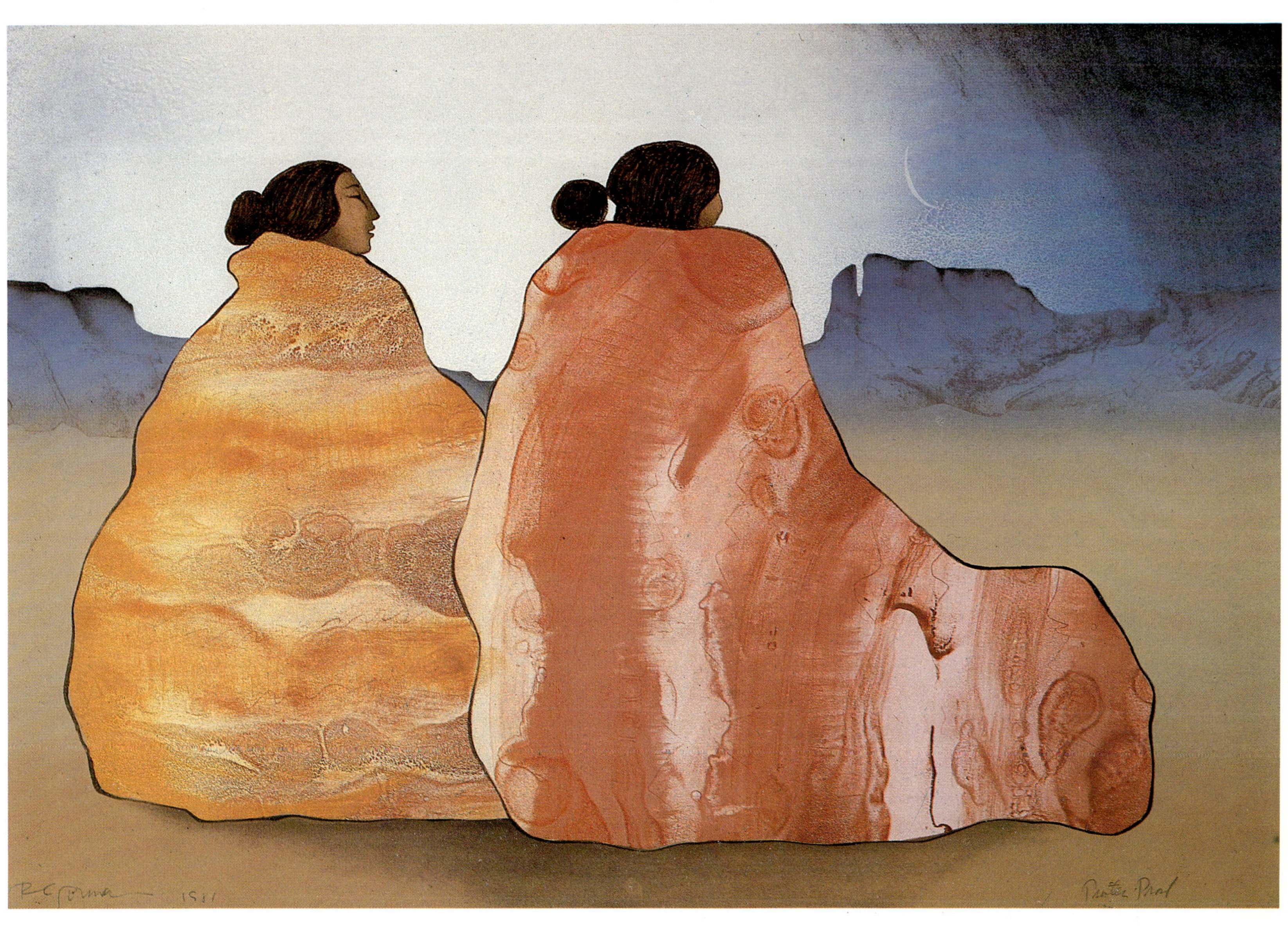

Summer Storm,
lithograph, Origins Press, 1981

late mountains, the plain where Gorman, like his ancestors before him for hundreds of years, grazed his sheep, where his family, like those ancestors, built its hogans and eked out a slim victory over hunger and cold. To the other side of the hill is the canyon, the traditional summer home, the place of plenty, of magic, and of power. The earth is fertile up the canyon's two arms—de Chelly to the right, del Muerto to the left. The sheer, glistening rock faces and monolithic shafts rise straight up, nearly a thousand feet in places. The canyon has been the creative inspiration for Gorman's work, but it was the harsh life on the empty plain that drove him from the reservation and continues to urge him toward the top of the art world.

At the entrance to the canyon, we met Chauncey Naboia, a short, bowlegged, ageless Navajo (he appeared to be an agile seventy-five) who was to be our guide. It seemed silly that the tribe required that we hire a guide when we were in the company of one of its favorite sons, but policy is policy in Navajoland as every-

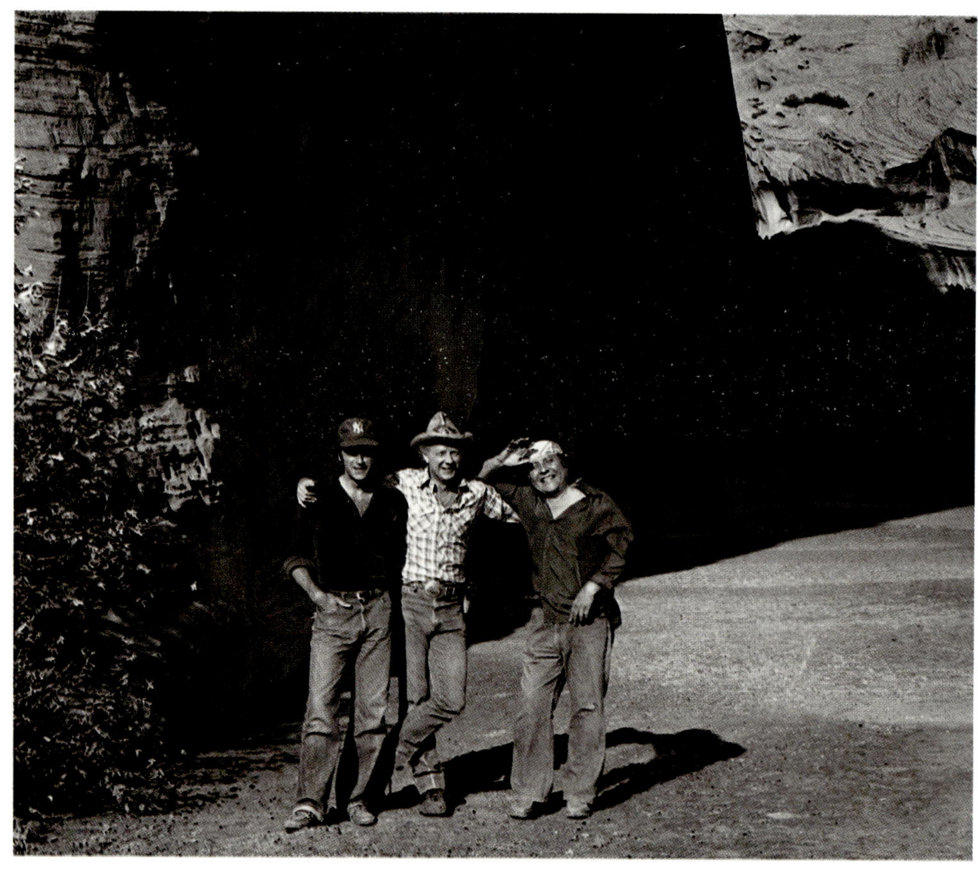

The writer, the photographer, and the artist, Canyon de Chelly, 1981

where else, and we were soon grateful that it was so. The roads through de Chelly and del Muerto are treacherous, pocked with areas of quicksand and broken shoulders. Chauncey, it turned out, had been a member of the famed Navajo Code Talkers in the Pacific during World War II, as was Gorman's father, Carl. He was well versed in the legends and history of the canyons, pointing out Fortress Rock upon which in 1864 a small band of his people had managed to hold out against Kit Carson and thus escape the murderous Long Walk into exile in Bosque Redondo, New Mexico. He showed us many ancient petroglyphs carved impossibly high on sheer sandstone walls by the canyons' first residents, the Anasazi, a Navajo word meaning "The Ancient Ones." "The legend is," Chauncey quipped, "that the Ancient Ones had claws instead of hands."

When we stopped for photographs, particularly when he was to be the subject, the famous Gorman banter began. "Do you hear the crows? They're saying 'Galth, galth, galth,' which in Navajo means 'coming, coming, coming.' My grandmother used to tell me they were warning each other, saying 'somebody's coming . . . coming.'

"This is the cliff dwelling my mother climbed up just before I was born. She couldn't get back down. It's so beautiful here when it rains and the water comes crashing over the cliffs. . . . Do you know what the difference is between the Navajos and the Anasazi? They came from Kyoto. We came from Peking. . . . Smell the sheep? I love the smell of sheep dung."

In his quiet moments, Gorman is serious and secretive. It's possible that at these times his mind is empty of thought, functioning like a camera that captures images and emotions unfettered by logic. There was a note of sadness late in the afternoon as we left the canyon. Driving out through Canyon del Muerto, Gorman pointed to the family farm, owned most recently by an uncle but now lying fallow, the peach trees burned stumps. "I used to run all the way up here. There was corn, beans, fruit . . . now there's nothing. My cousins fought over who should get it, and they were so busy fighting that they let it die."

We said goodbye to old Chauncey, who, as he does daily, then walked the ten miles back up the canyon to his hogan.

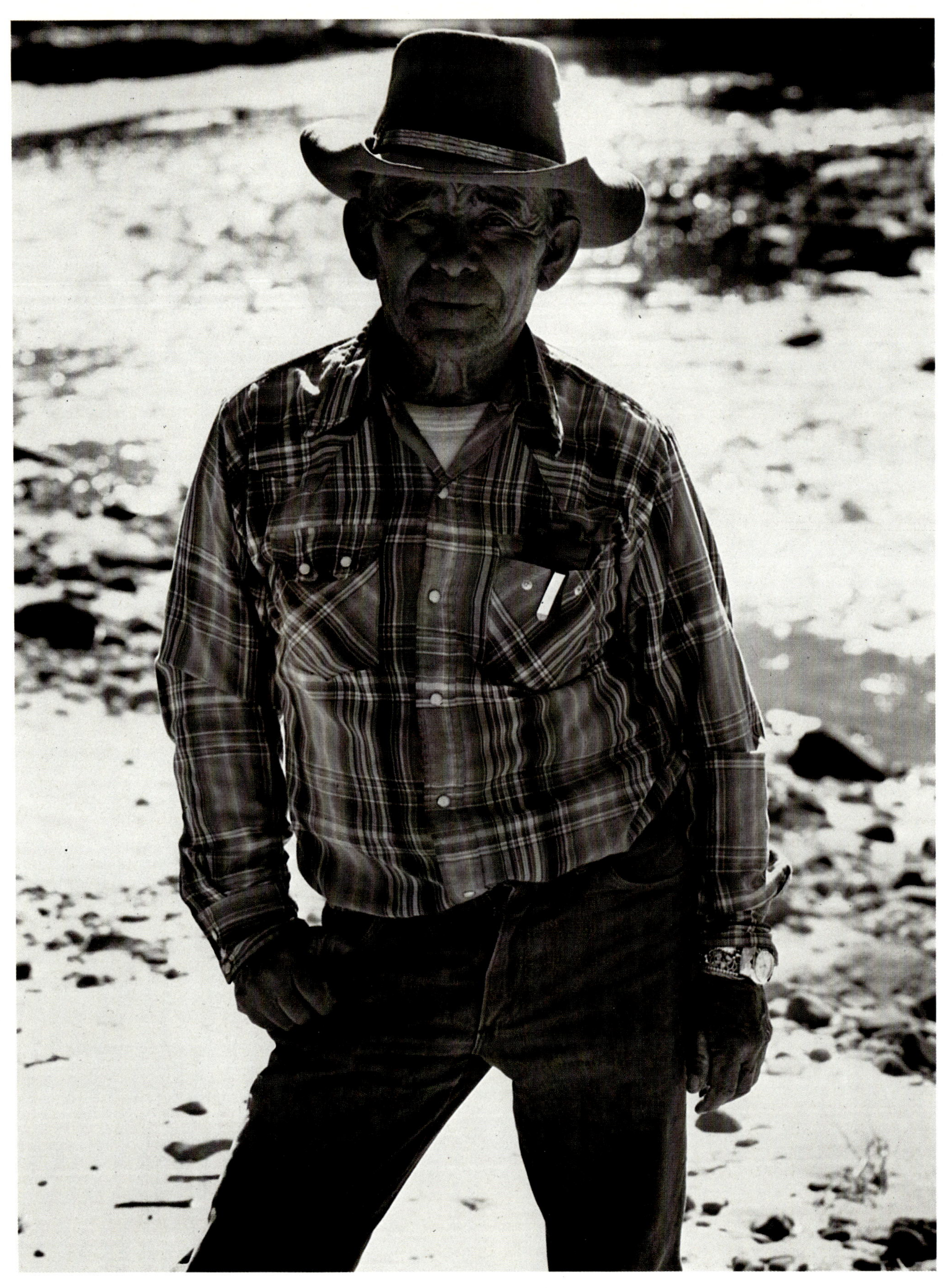

26 Chauncey Naboia, Navajo guide,
Canyon de Chelly, 1978

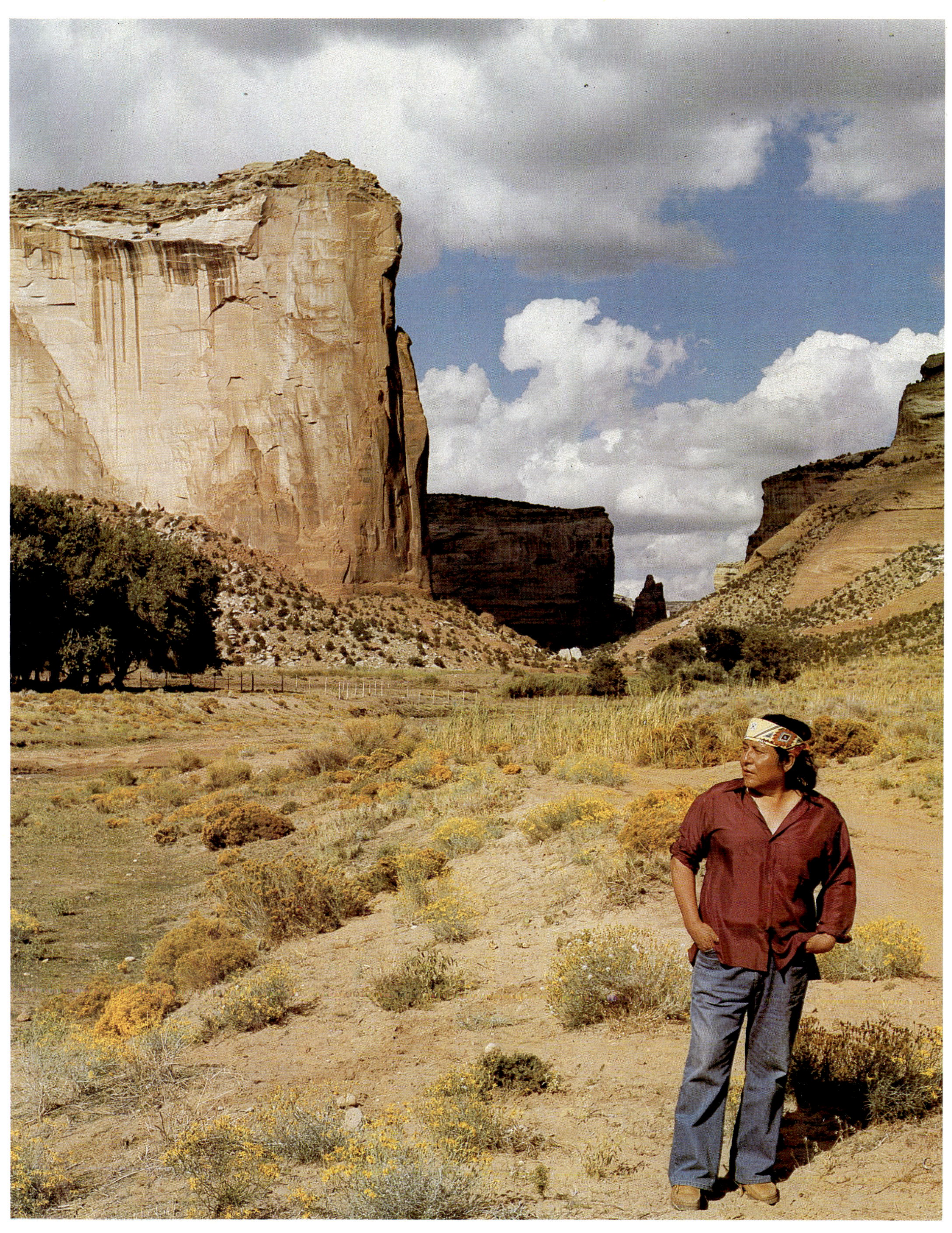

The artist in his boyhood home,
Canyon de Chelly, 1981

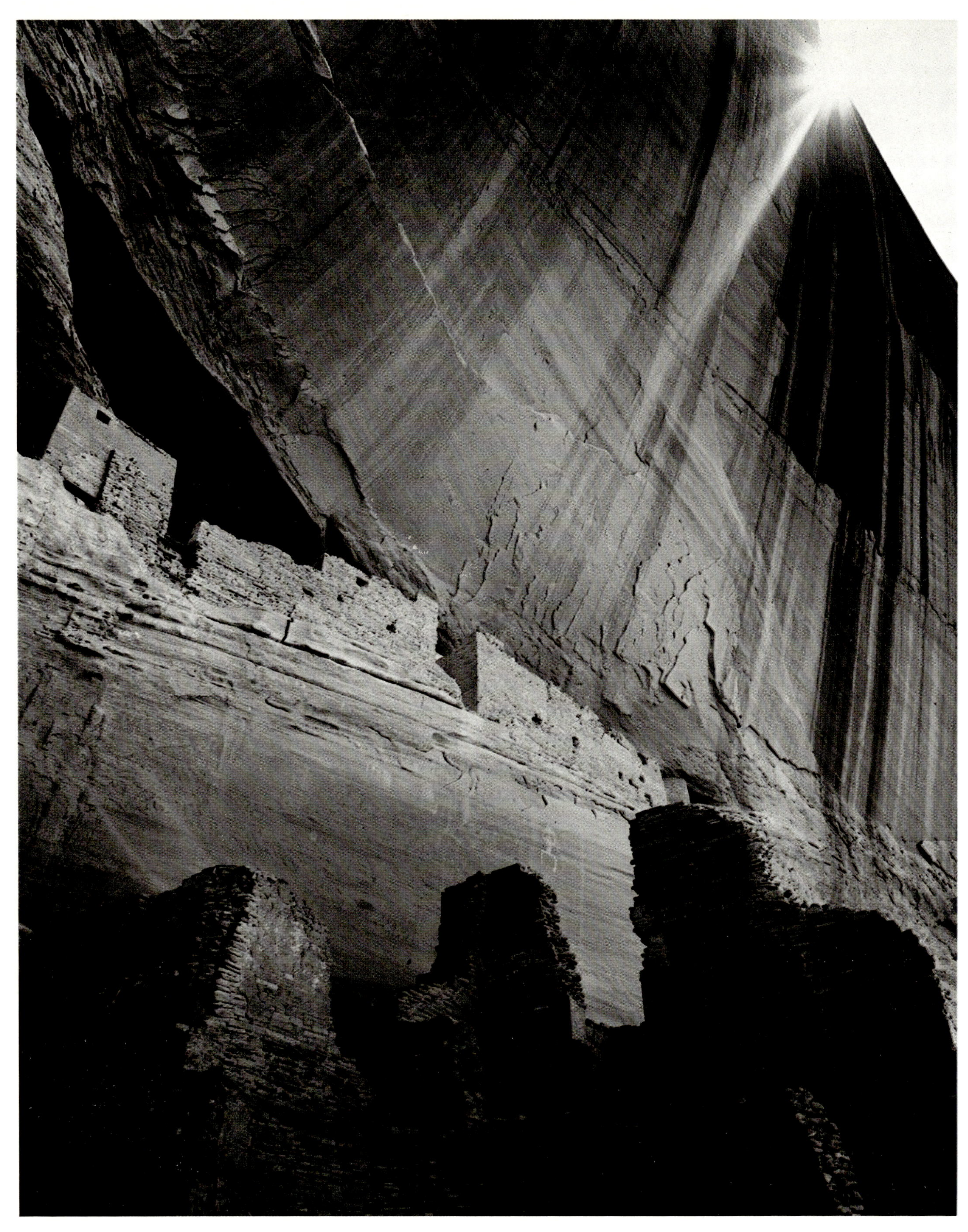

28 Sunrise over White House Ruins,
Canyon de Chelly, 1979

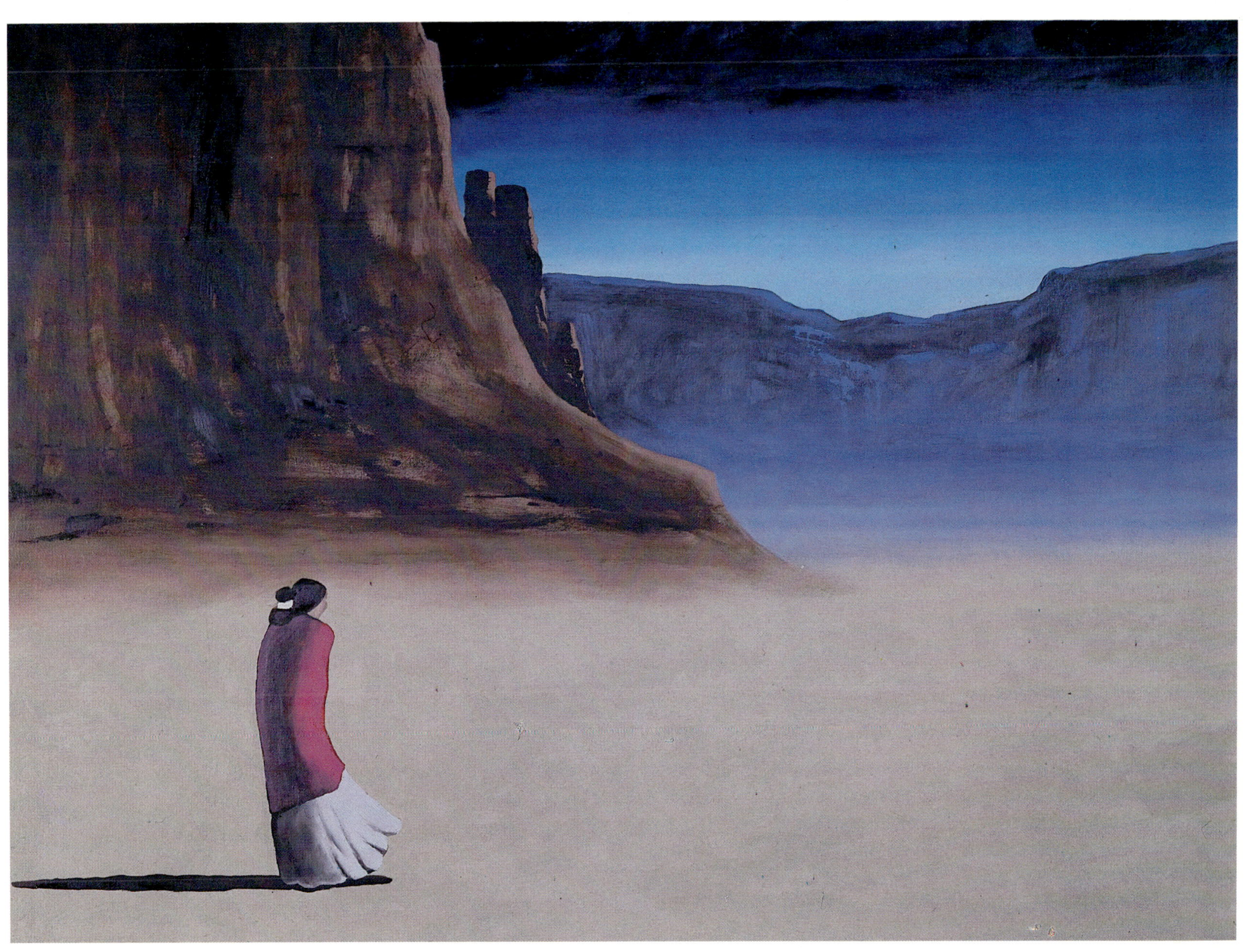

The Spirit of the Foothills,
oil on canvas, 1982.
Collection of Goldwater's Department Store, Tucson

At breakfast the next morning, we were met by Gorman's father, Carl, and stepmother, Mary. The two of them, father and son, are proud, handsome men. Carl looked quite patrician with his long silver hair pulled back and bound at the back with the *chongo*, a whipped knot of white yarn worn by married Navajos, both male and female. The headband, worn as a proud badge by R. C., is the style of the unmarried male. There seems a complex mixture of respect and old hurt between the two of them. Carl left the family and went to war when Gorman was young. He served with the Navajo Code Talkers, an elite Marine unit that used the Navajo language for sending messages and baffled the Japanese during the last years of the war.

R. C. was left with much of the responsibility for caring for his brothers and sisters. Yet it was the father, himself a respected artist, who encouraged his son and first drew him away from the reservation and exposed him to the sophisticated world of the white man.

Carl was stationed in Barstow, California, during the early years of World War II. R. C. visited him occasionally, and it is the restaurants, the glitter, and the glamour of Los Angeles that he remembers vividly. He felt for the first time in his life like a foreigner, and he loved the freedom of the feeling.

What Carl remembers fondly are the origins of his son's career. "R. C. always carried a tablet and drew, wherever we were," Carl remembered. "We were dipping sheep once, and he got a little girl to model for him. A white man working with us saw the drawing, got me, and said, 'Look. Someday he's going to be a great artist.' And it's true. He was less than ten years old at that time. I never held his hand, or led him like a teacher. His eyes were his teachers." R. C. himself thinks he acquired his drawing talent from his father's genes.

"Art is the gift of Talking God," Carl continued, illustrating how close he has remained to his Navajo roots, "and must be used unto his glory. The Navajo religion is called the Blessing Way and is much more powerful than what those missionaries have tried to shove down our throats. There are twelve holy people. Each of them is in charge of a different thing—rain, sun, planting, and so on. Talking God is the boss. His power is given to him by the Unknown Power."

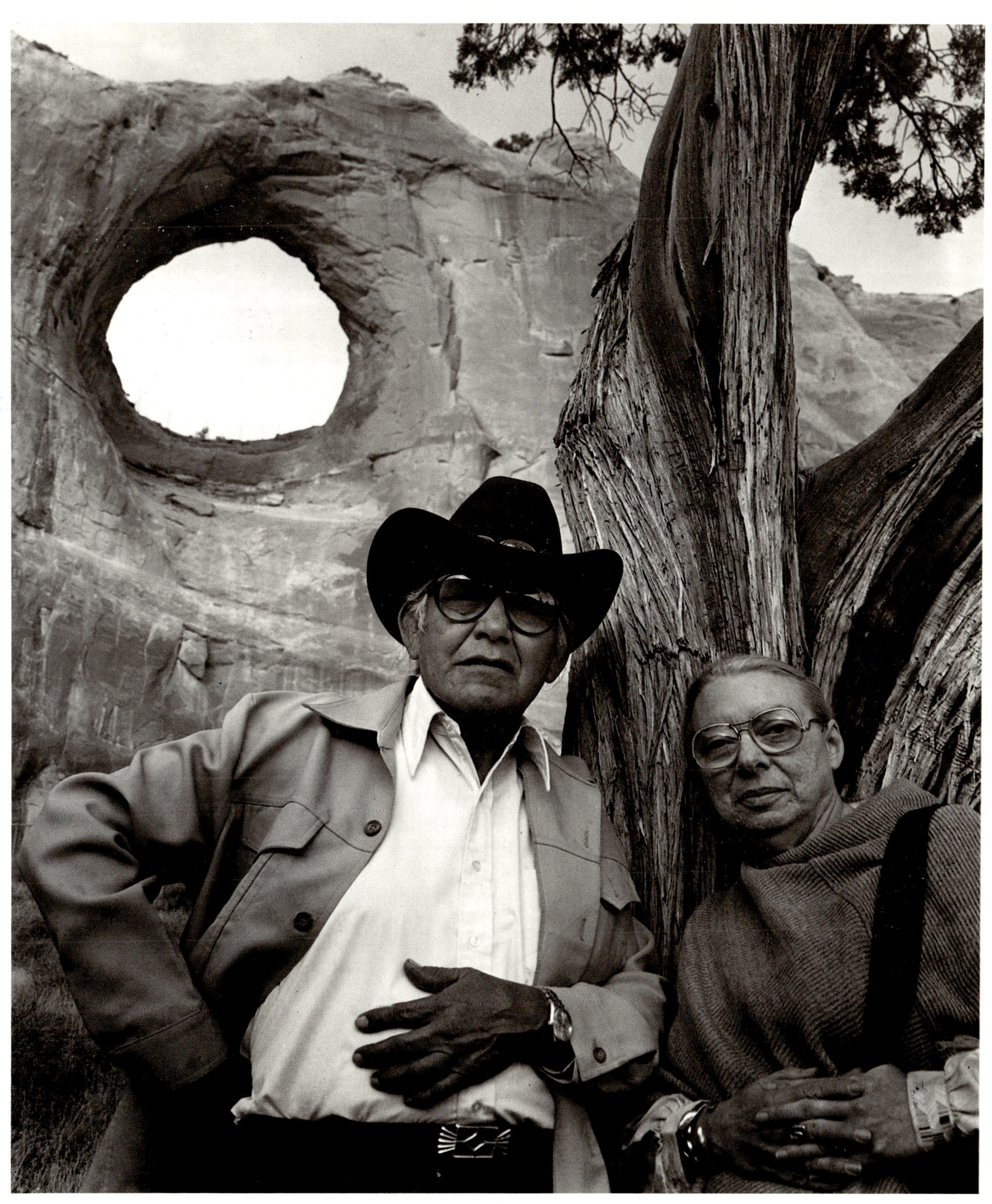

Carl and Mary Gorman,
Window Rock, Arizona, 1981

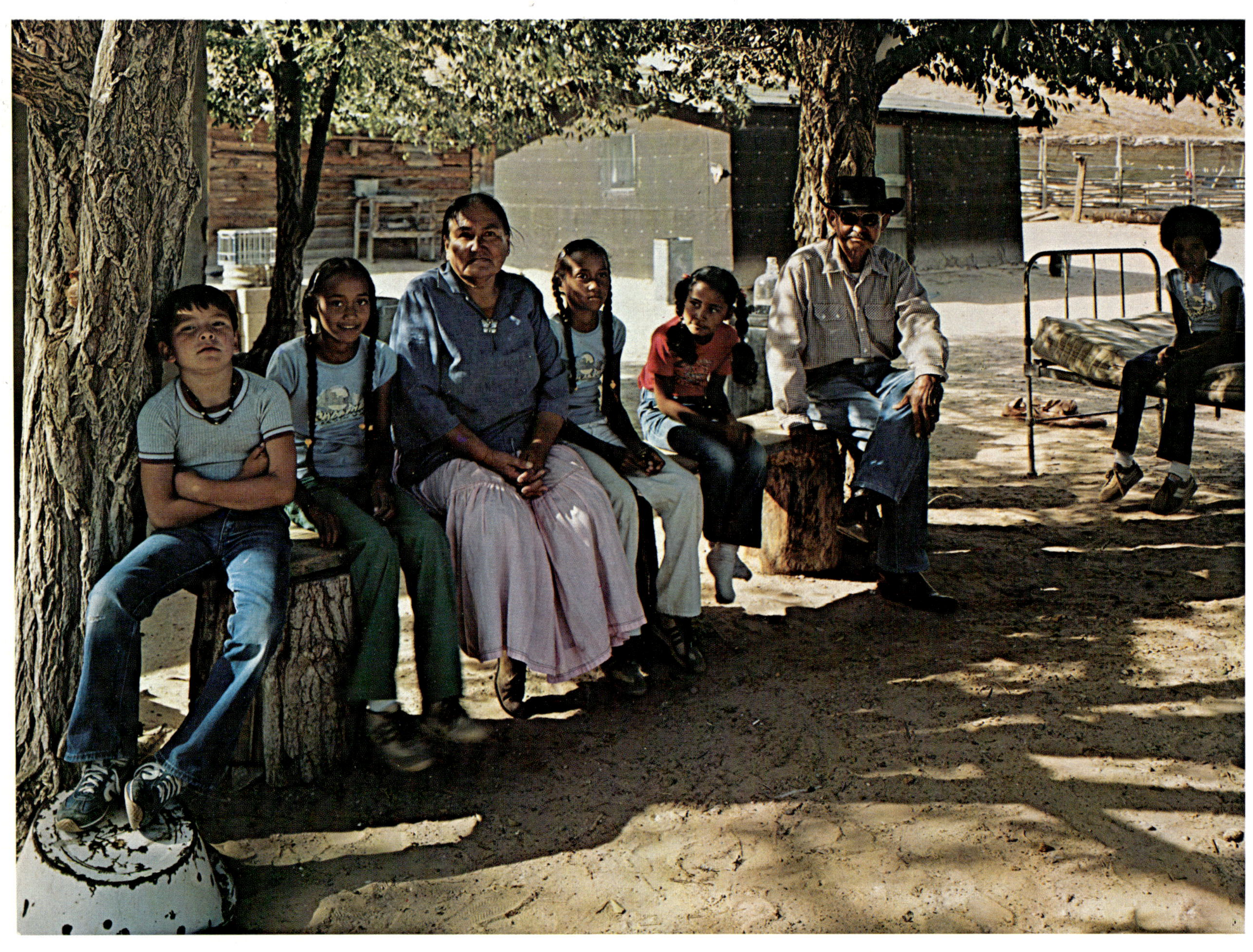

Aunt Mary, Uncle Joe, and their grandchildren,
Black Mountain, 1981

Carl Gorman is a very proud man, proud of his son, proud of his heritage, proud of his own artistic achievements and his informal but prominent status within the tribe as a learned man of Navajo history, religion, and culture. He loves to tell stories: "My father went to the first government school at Fort Defiance. There was an army camp there, watching the Navajos, probably afraid of an uprising or something. He went to this school with a friend, and when they arrived they were met by this army guy who had a roster of the men in the camp, and was issuing names from that list to the Navajo kids as they came in. He wrote the names on tags and put them around their necks. Nelson Carl Gorman was the name my father got, and his friend got the next one on the list, John Gorman. His relatives and mine kept the names, and people have thought we were related ever since."

In late morning we packed food and equipment into a van. Carl and his wife came along on the drive to Aunt Mary's, some twenty miles south of Chinle. Gorman talked about his young adulthood—his years in the navy aboard the USS *Oriskiny* and then his move in the 1950s to San Francisco, where for some years he made a living as a male model, entering the city's art community. One of the first exhibitions of his work was at the Coffee Gallery. "It was at the end of the beatnik era," he said. "Lawrence Ferlinghetti and Allen Ginsberg often came into the place, and that's where I met Cynthia Bissel. I was doing the same kind of art everybody was doing in San Francisco in those days, phony abstract." He didn't begin serious figure painting until a trip in the early 1960s to Mexico, where he saw Orozco's paintings. "That's what started me painting figures." Later, back in San Francisco, a woman named Margaret Dutton encouraged him to paint Indians, and the Indian woman became the subject of his art. Except for a few later excursions into abstraction and an occasional painting of a male, his work is still devoted to portrayals of Navajo women.

Aunt Mary has always been one of the pivotal women in his life. Since the death of his mother in 1972, she has been perhaps the strongest family influence he has had. As we approached her house, he recognized places where, as a young boy, he herded her sheep. "This land is all clay, not sand like Chinle. When it rained, Aunt Mary and I would make little sculptures in the mud."

When we arrived, Aunt Mary, who speaks but a few words of English, had warm embraces for everyone, though she was somewhat embarrassed at being unprepared for our visit. A stout woman with a rolling kind of grace, she has a big smile and infectious manner that warms and softens everyone around her. She was dressed in sandals, striped knee socks, pink skirt, and a blue denim blouse closed at the neck with a silver butterfly brooch. With her husband, Joe Tsosie, and a brood of four grandchildren whom she has informally adopted, she lives in a primitive house with neither plumbing nor electricity. A calendar picture of Christ with a crown of thorns was pinned to the wall, along with color Polaroids of children and grandchildren. A Bible translated into Navajo was open on a bureau. The sheep were in a corral near the house. Several abandoned automobiles lay rusting out back.

Gorman regards his Aunt Mary as a queen, and the rest of us quickly came to regard her with the same reverence. He whispered some concern about how she would react to the wine we had brought to drink with the lunch she was preparing. Grubbs, who is close to the family and has spent more time on the reservation during the last decade than Gorman, tested the waters by opening a bottle and drinking the first glass. When Aunt Mary raised no objections, the rest of us had ours.

Lunch was to be Navajo fry bread, salad, lamb and vegetables boiled in a thin broth, and a blood sausage made by Gorman's sister, Donna, of meat, blood, potatoes, and grain, packed in a lamb's stomach and boiled. While the women cooked, the men left the house to walk in the juniper-dotted hills nearby, tell stories about days long ago, and exchange bits of Navajo lore. Gorman pointed out a plant the name of which aptly described its use—plant-for-brushing-off-cactus-spines. It grows next to prickly pear cactus, and the Navajo use it to clean the spines from the cactus fruit, which, when peeled, is as sweet and sumptuous as strawberries.

As if to regain a connection with his childhood, Gorman scavenged in the hills for relics of the life he had lived. "Look what I found, Curtis. A part of a wagon wheel. Let's take this home with us. I think I'll take this bucket, too." Its handle was gone and there was a hole in the bottom, but it just might have been something he had touched or used as a child, and the possibility was enough. He found

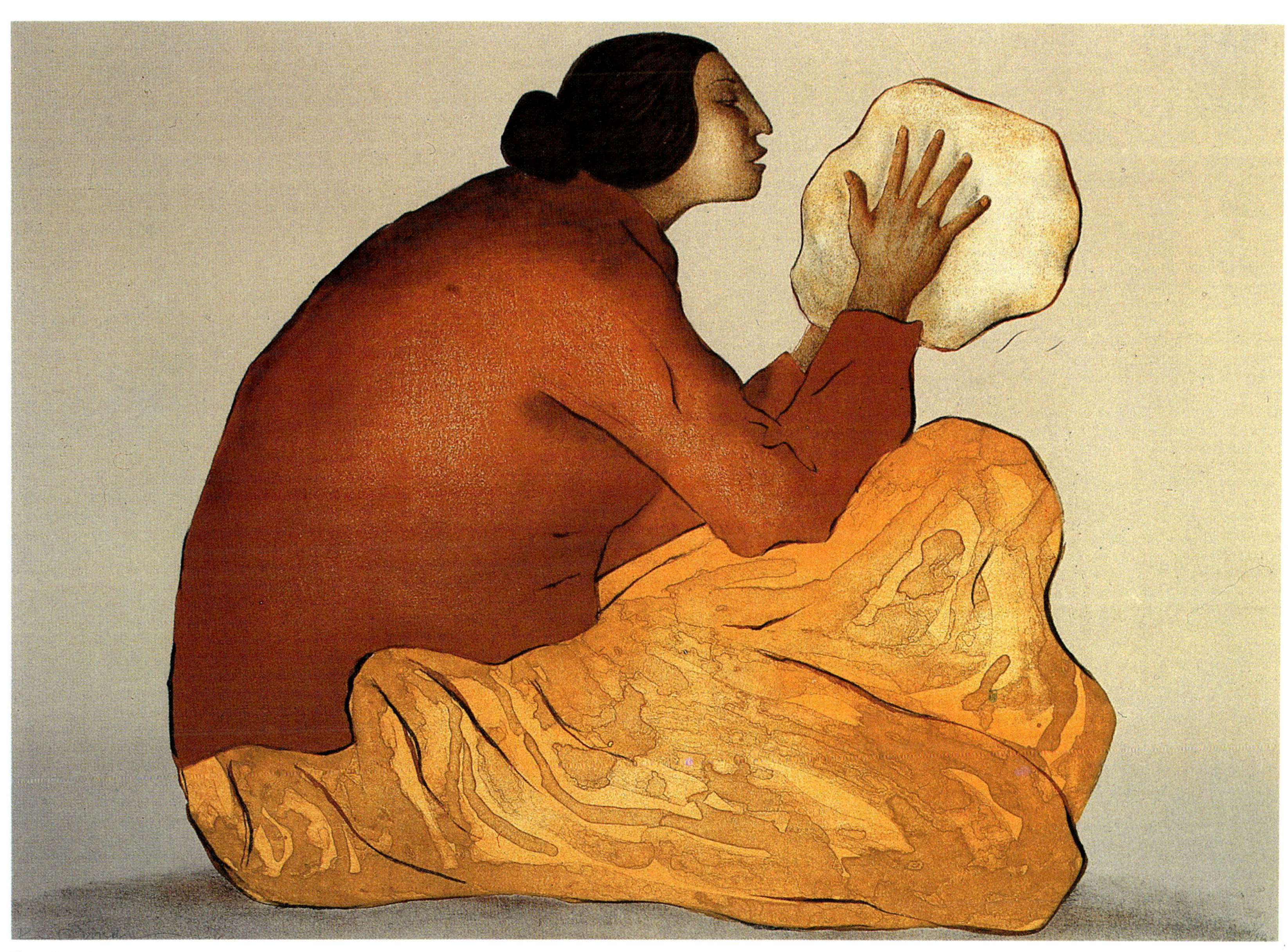

Tortilla Maker,
lithograph, Origins Press, 1978

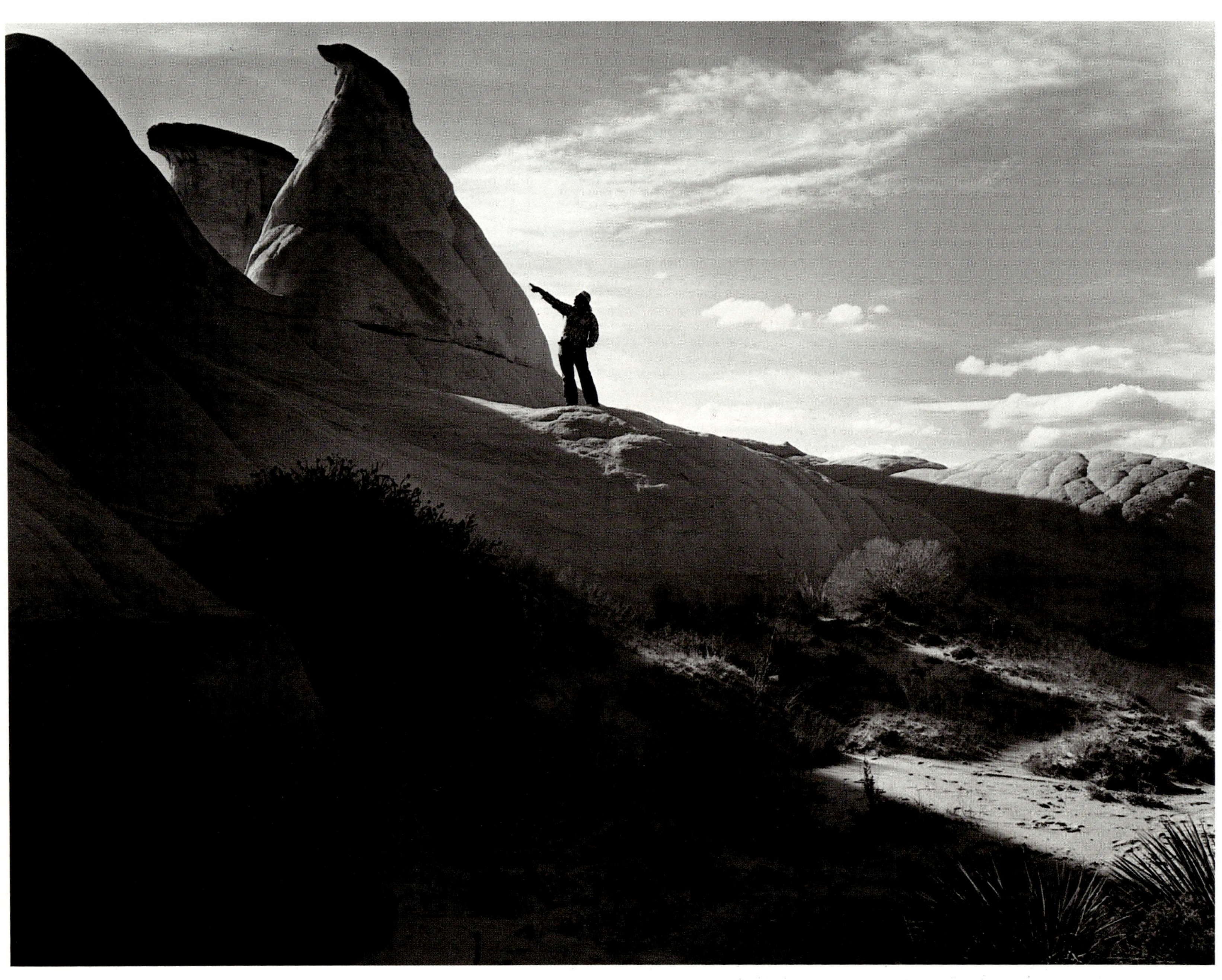

The artist as model on sandstone hills,
Black Mountain, 1981

an old wood trough carved from a log near the well where the sheep are watered. It had been carved for his grandmother. "I want to take it home. I can serve salad out of it when I give big parties." When we returned for lunch, Grubbs asked Aunt Mary if Gorman might have the trough. "Take it," she said. "I was going to chop it up for firewood. It must be a hundred years old."

Lunch was pleasant and relaxed. The Anglos present, with the exception of Gorman's stepmother and Grubbs, ate the blood sausage somewhat tentatively. No one questioned the propriety of our consuming two bottles of fine Riesling, which probably cost as much as Aunt Mary's weekly groceries.

Gorman enjoyed the day. "I felt so at home here. But it was cleaner then. We lived in a stone hogan. There weren't any cars junking up the yard."

From Black Mountain, Gorman and Grubbs were scheduled to drive back to Albuquerque, and a few days later the artist was off on a month-long work and pleasure trip to Spain and Portugal. But before leaving, we took a last short walk in the lonely, desolate, silent hills. Canyon de Chelly is outrageously splendid. It induces whoops of joy or whispers of respect, but Black Mountain discourages all sound but the wind. "This is where my life was," Gorman commented as we left Aunt Mary's. "In Canyon de Chelly, it's too much like Hollywood."

"The forms of the earth rubbed off on me. It's not a case of my getting inspiration from *Arizona Highways*, the *National Geographic*, or Edward S. Curtis. That's all right, but it's not my direction. These forms became loaves of bread. Muddy water became chocolate milk. As I got older, the rocks became people. The canyon was filled with images. The impressions never left me."—R.C.G.

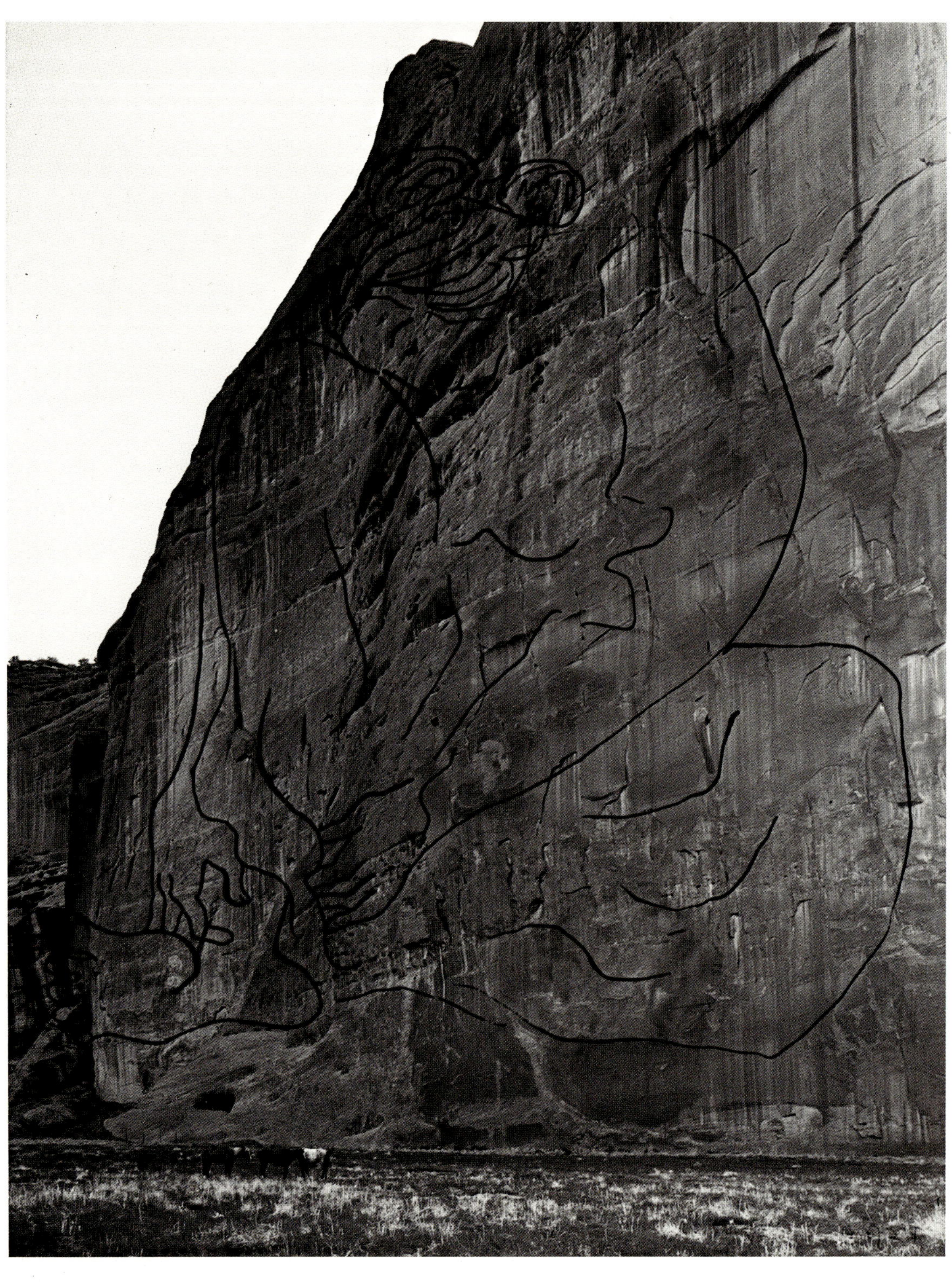

Gorman silkscreen figure and rock wall,
Canyon de Chelly. Silkscreen by Editions Press, 1979

The Navajo

As harsh as the land of northeast Arizona is, it possesses an awesome beauty that has held Indian people to its breast for millennia. Wind-carved rocks stand as spiritual sentinels over the immense, empty quiet. There is the feeling that God is near, that the sun and wind are holy. Love of the land's beauty, as expressed in the *Beautyway Chant*, is the substance of the Navajo's soul:

I will be happy forever, nothing will hinder me.
I walk with beauty before me, I walk with beauty behind me,
I walk with beauty below me, I walk with beauty above me,
I walk with beauty around me, my words will be beautiful . . .

Archaeologists believe the Anasazi were a peaceful, industrious people who first entered the four-corners region of New Mexico, Arizona, Utah, and Colorado about the time of Christ. Over the next thousand years, they slowly developed techniques for growing crops, making baskets and pottery, and building the magnificent cliff dwellings that still stand as monuments to their civilization in Mesa Verde, Betatakin, Canyon de Chelly, and many other sites. But by A.D. 1300 the Anasazi had disappeared from their cliff cities, driven out by drought or perhaps by marauding Shoshones. They resettled in what are now the pueblos of the Rio Grande. The mysterious petroglyphs left on the canyon walls above their homes are evidence of the Anasazi's deeply religious and artistic natures. They shouted out with the primal cry of all artists from all times, "I am here. I matter. What I believe is important enough to scratch into the walls of the earth!"

Canyon de Chelly lay silent for several hundred years until the nomadic Navajos arrived from the north and took up residence in the land of the Ancient Ones. They raised sheep and horses plundered from the Spanish settlers who entered the region from Mexico in the 1540s. They lived not in the cliff dwellings, but in hogans built near their fields along the river in the canyon's belly. The Navajos prospered, and by the nineteenth century they were acknowledged masters of weaving, which they learned from Indians in the pueblos to the east, and silver jewelry-making, learned from the Mexicans.

Though the Navajos have always been perhaps the most clever tribe at adopting the ways of outsiders, there is still a great gulf between the Navajo Way and that of the predominant Anglo culture of this continent. The instinctual characteristic that has defined the development of the Navajos and other tribes is their connection to, and regard for, the land. The earth is the mother, that ancient and most powerful of symbols. The people come from her, she nurtures them, and at death they return to her womb. They regard it not as myth, but as everyday reality. The Navajo universe is not man-centered or God-centered, but earth-centered.

The great spirit guide and goddess of the Navajos is a delightful, inventive old crone, Spider Woman, who lives in a cave beneath the earth. Several of Gorman's lithographs have dealt with the Spider Woman theme, and indeed a connection with the earth is everywhere evident in Gorman's art. His women are the sacred providers, the source of life and inspiration, beauty and grace incarnate. What differentiates them from the women rendered by most American Indian artists is the emotion that he imbues them with. In their happiness, serenity, or anguish, they are fully human, at once mythic in their meaning and ordinary in their humanity. He paints an ancient, universal theme with the tools of contemporary aesthetics.

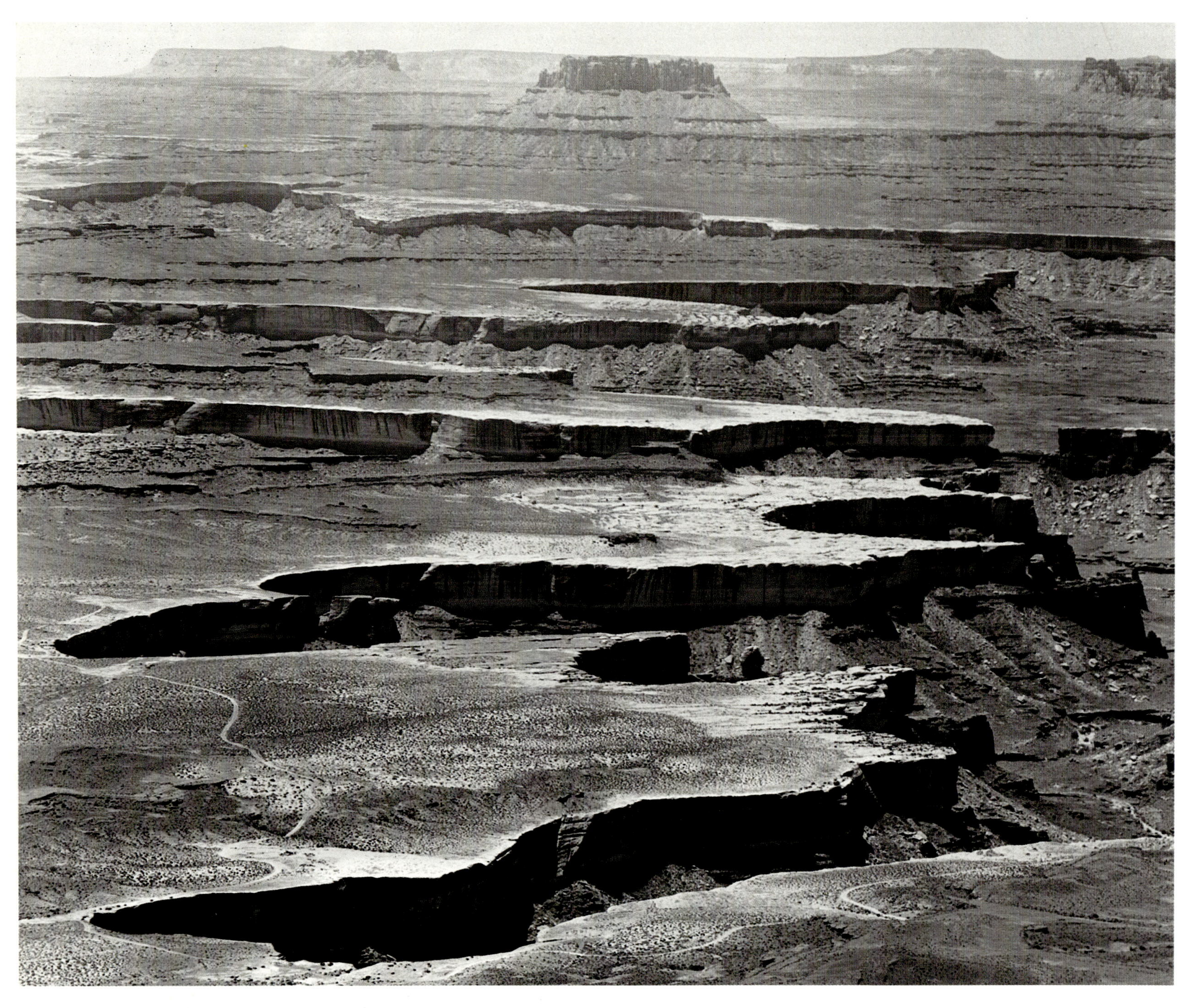

Canyon Lands overlook,
Utah, 1980

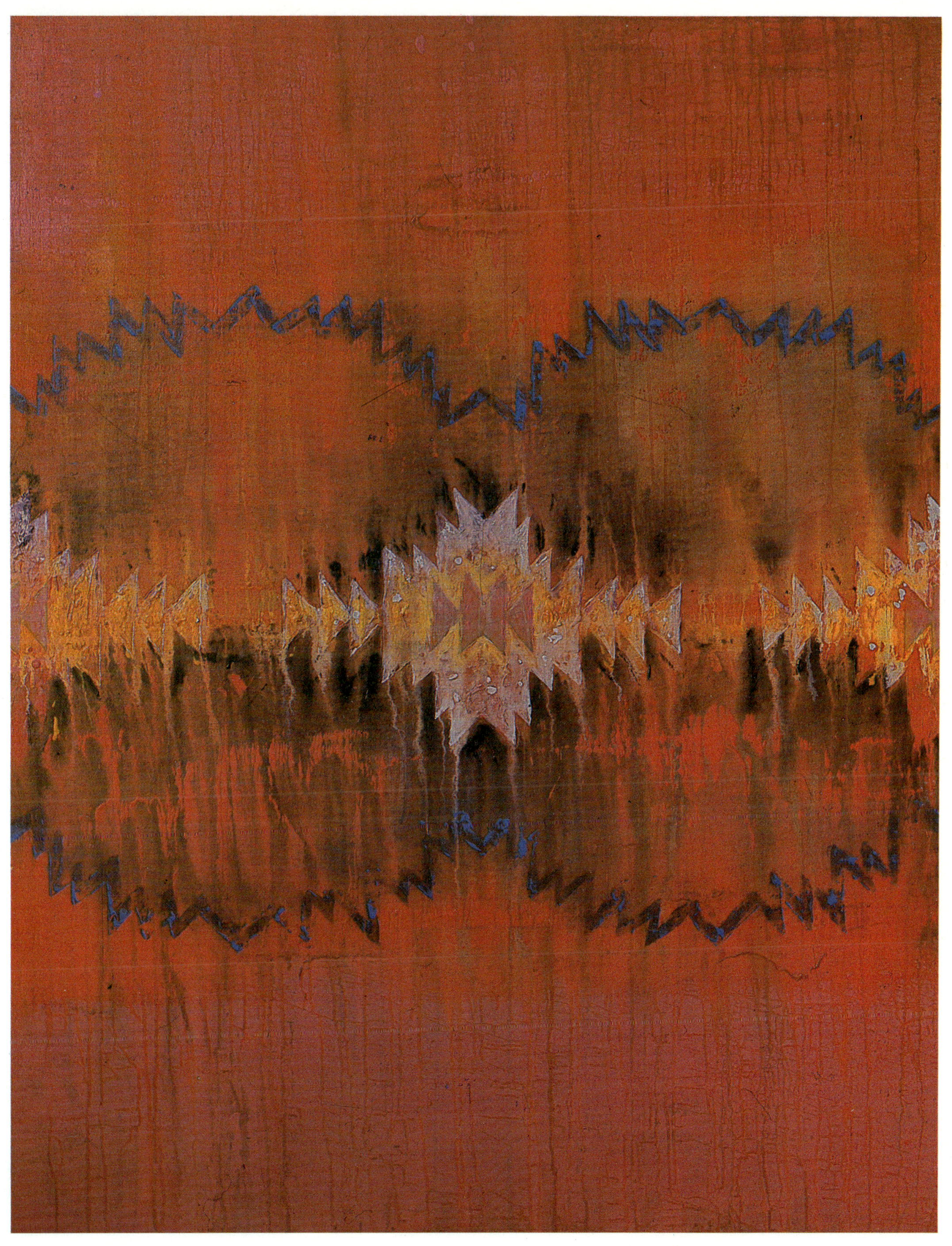

Red Rug Motif,
acrylic on canvas, 1973

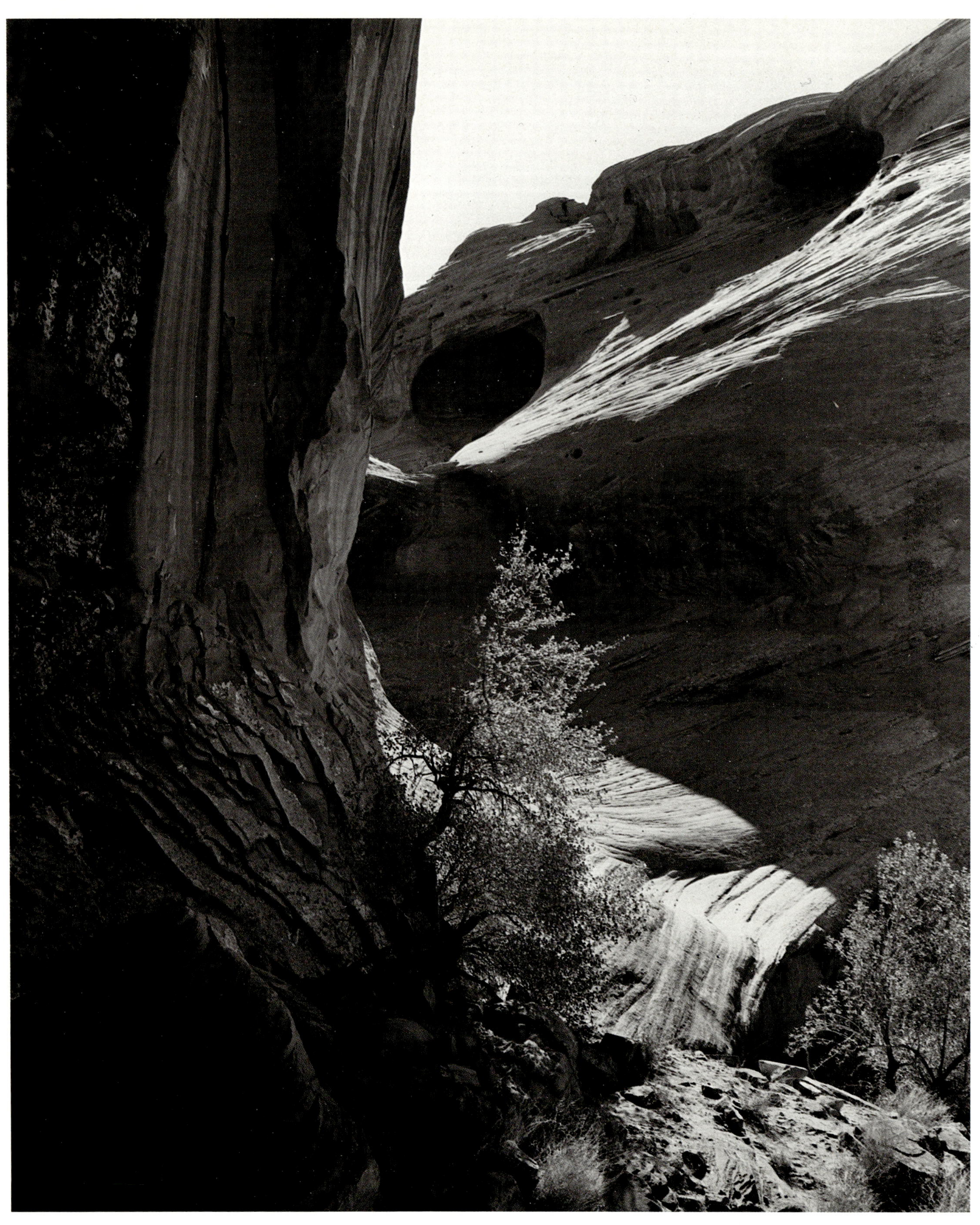

44 Rock walls,
Monument Valley, 1981

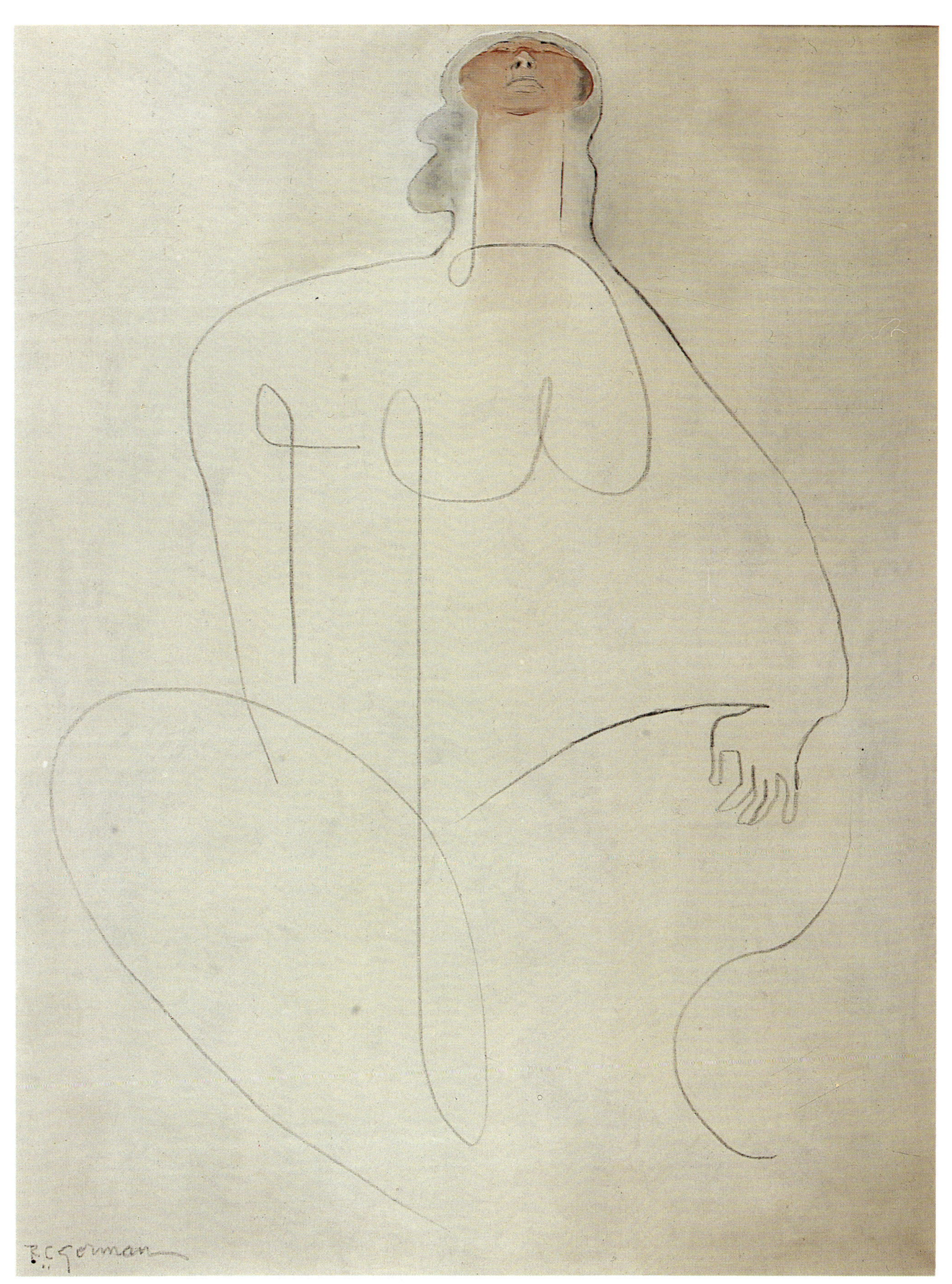

Ceremonial Woman,
acrylic, 1982, Gallery Mack, New York

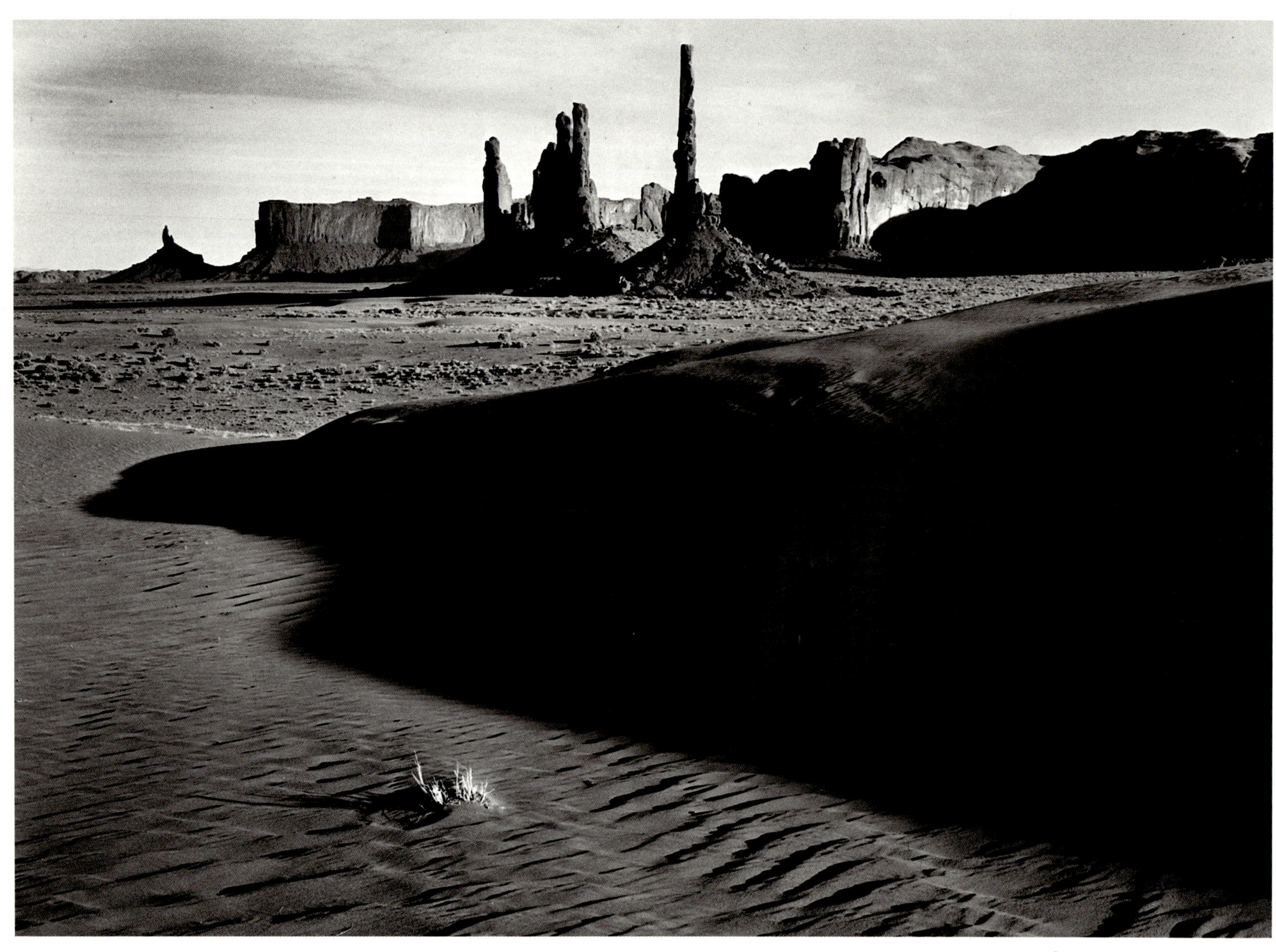

Shadow on sand,
Monument Valley, 1976

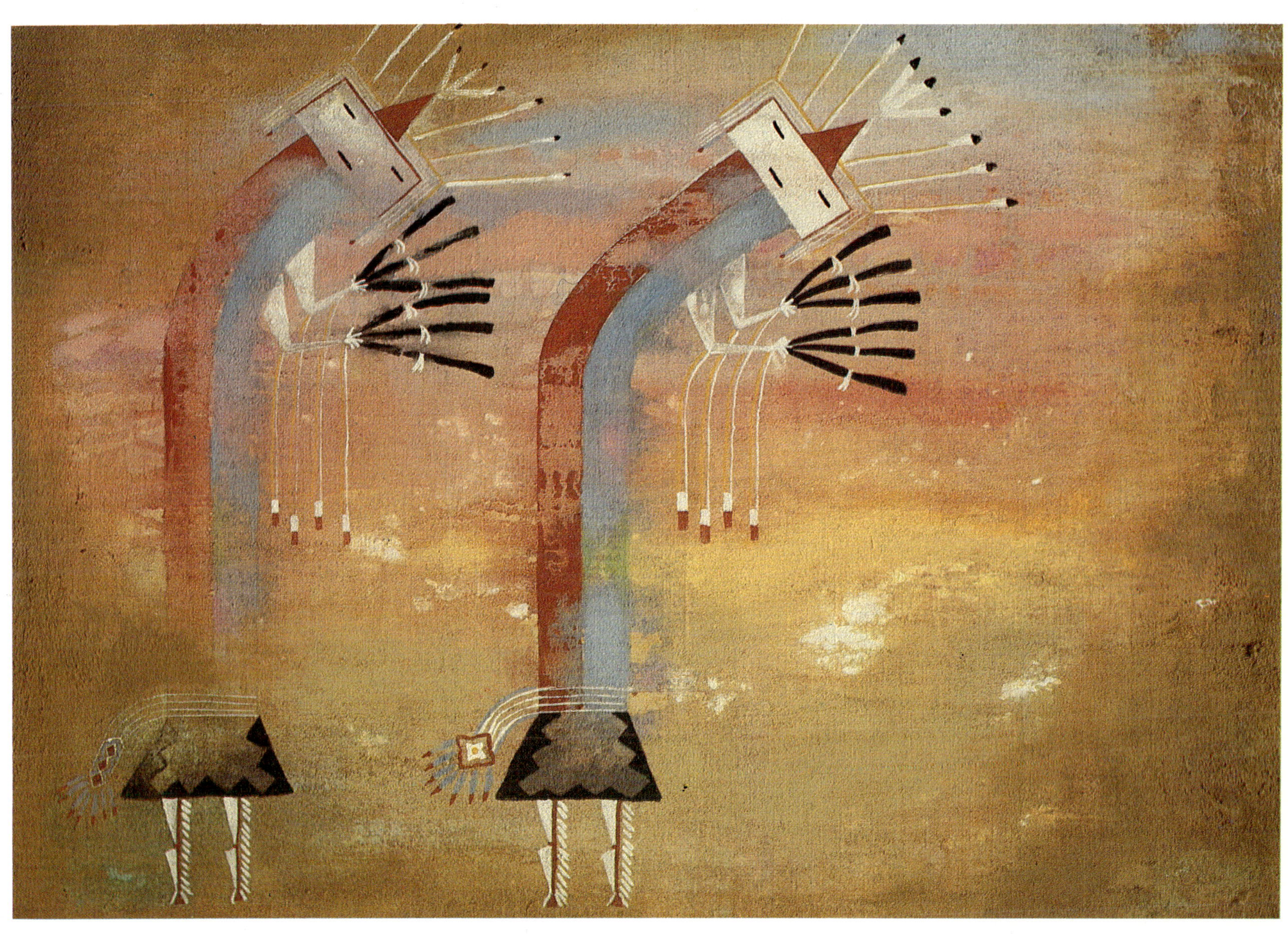

Rainbow Yei-Bi-Chai,
acrylic on canvas, 1967

"These are children in their summer home in Canyon de Chelly. The biggest boy makes me think of me at that age."—R.C.G.

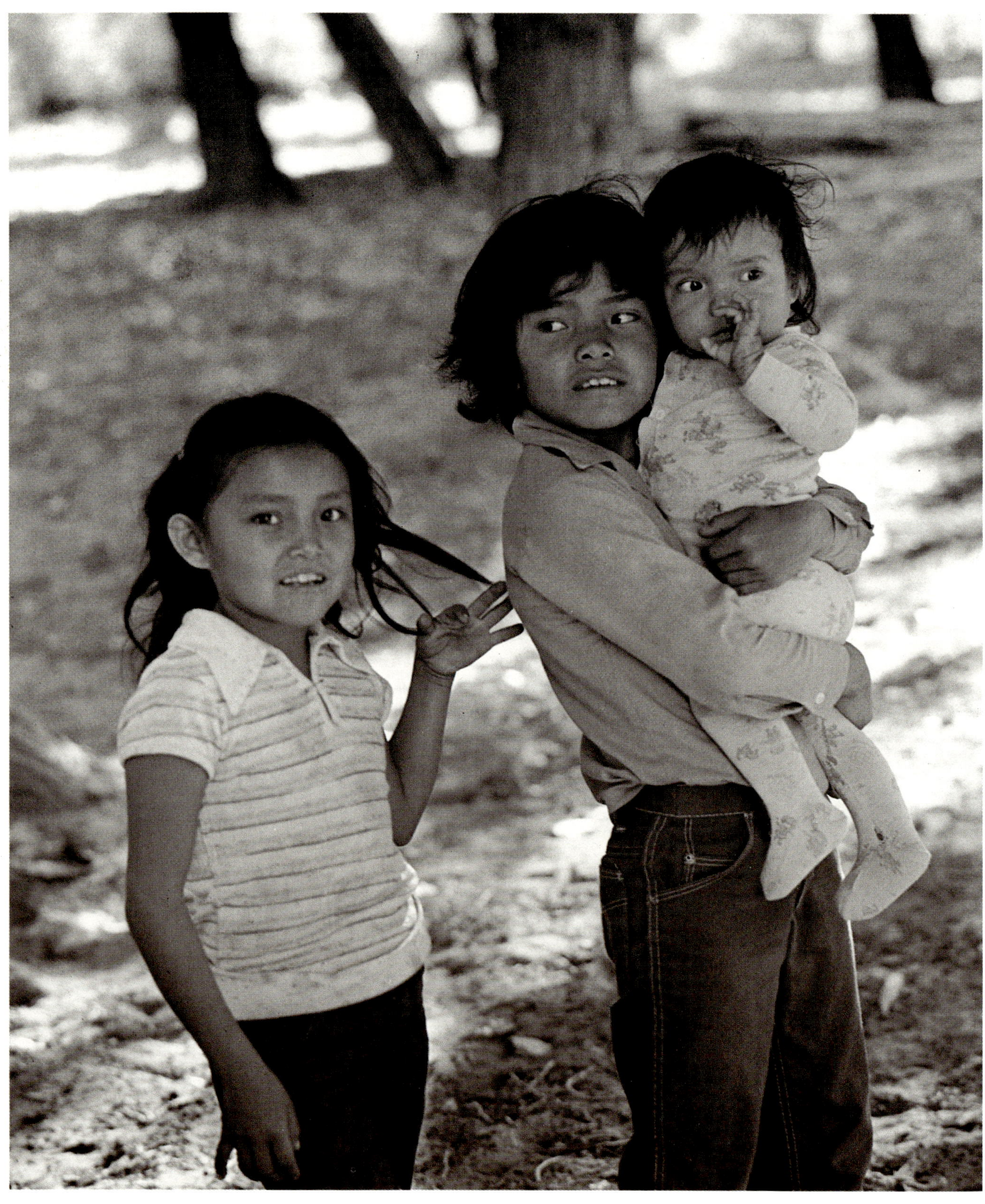

Navajo children,
Canyon de Chelly, 1979

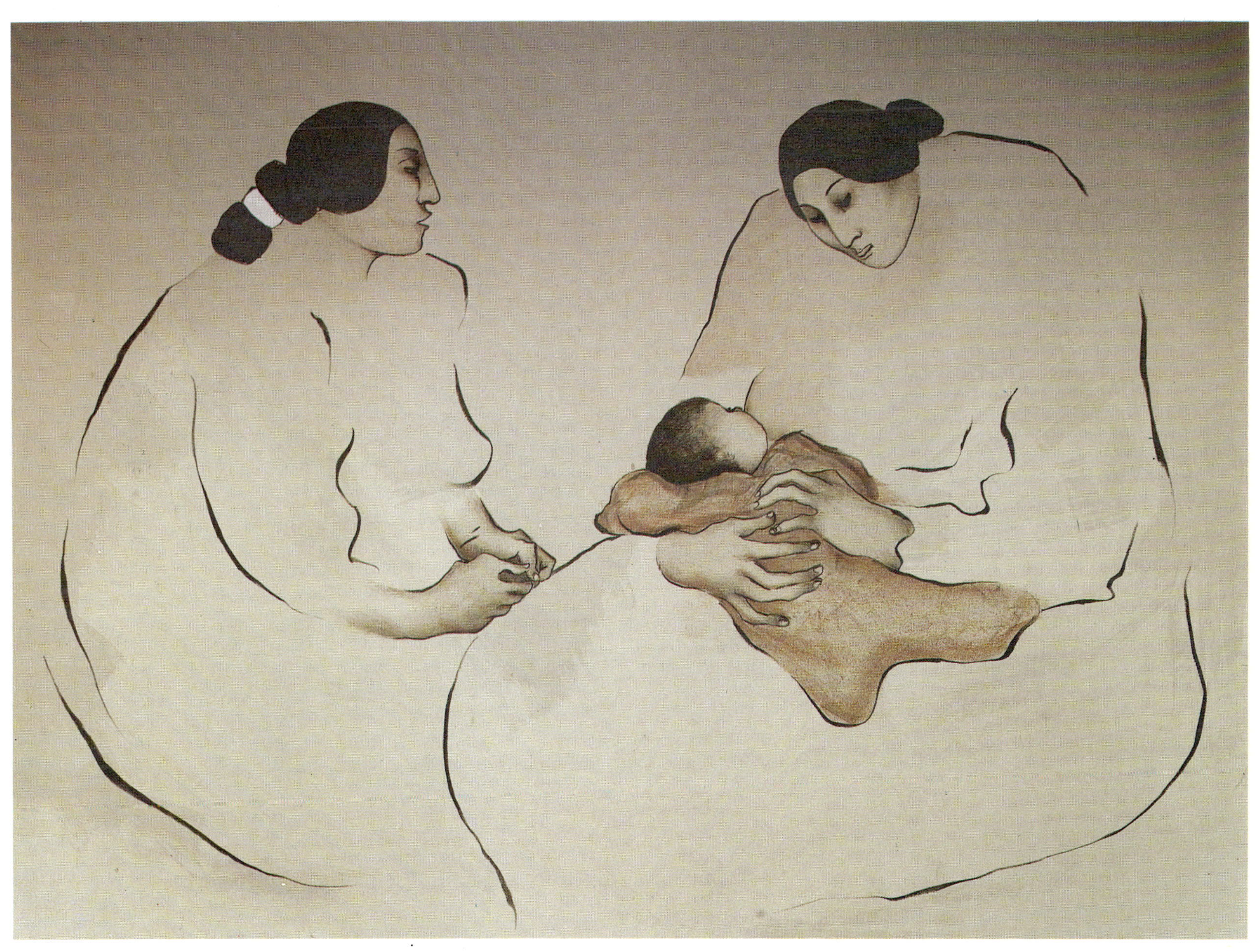

The Visitors,
lithograph, Origins Press, 1981

"She's beautiful. She doesn't look like a woman who diets or goes to the spa every day. She's just beautiful. We should all be so beautiful. She's strong. It's the same kind of beauty I strive to capture."—R.C.G.

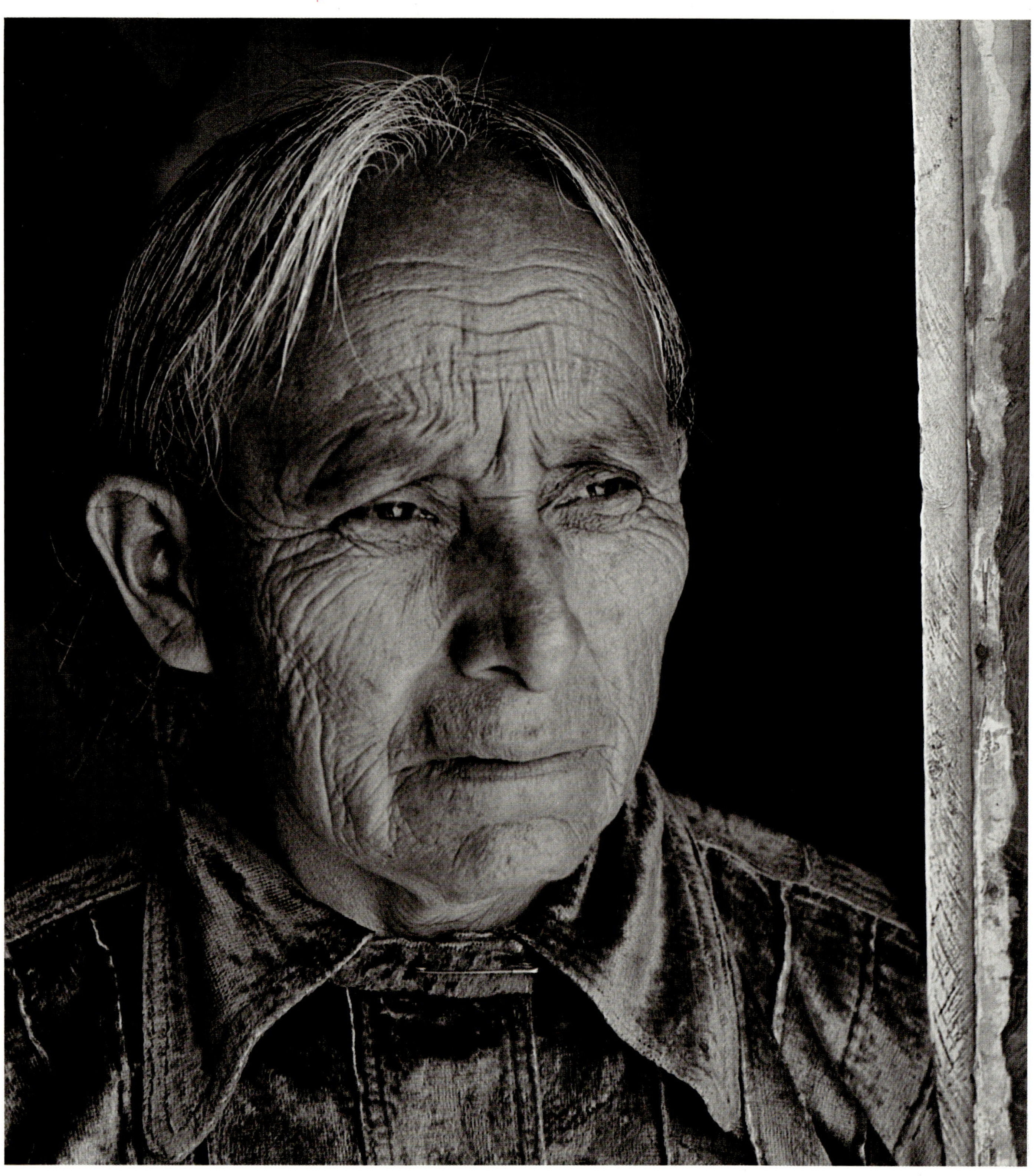

Dorothy Naboia,
Canyon de Chelly, 1979

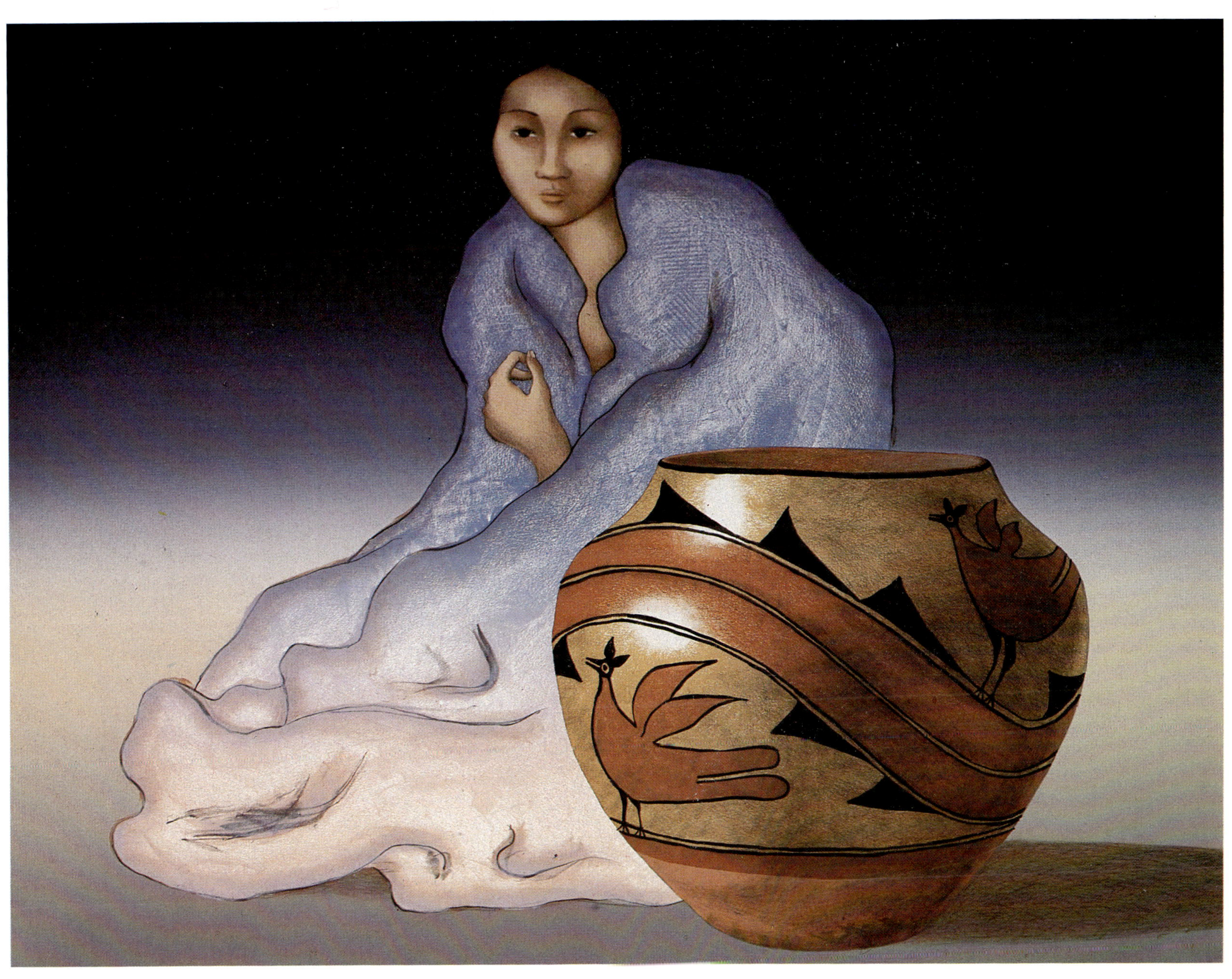

Rainbow Jar,
lithograph, Houston Fine Arts Press, 1982

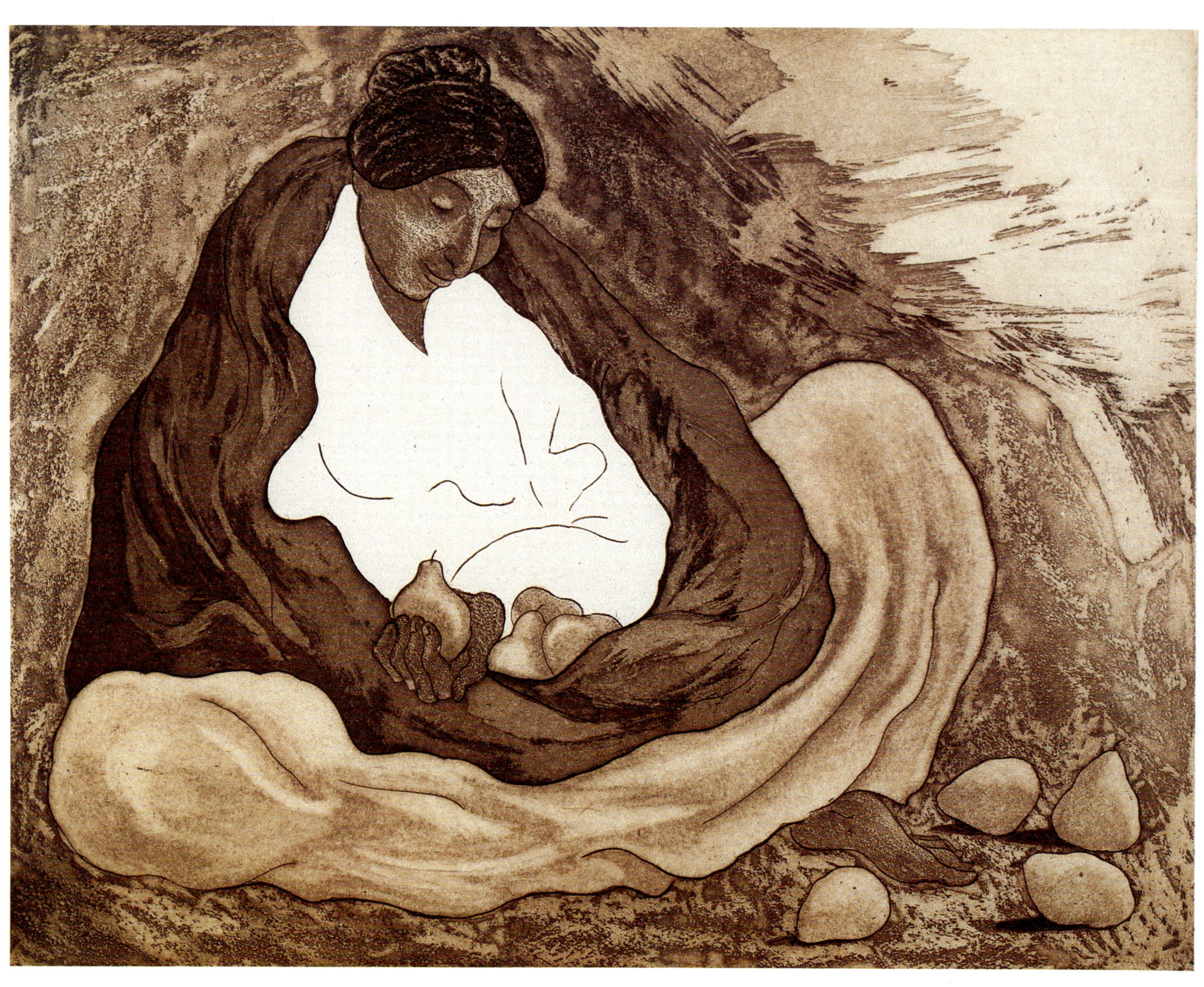

Woman with Pears,
lithograph, Hand Graphics, Ltd., 1978

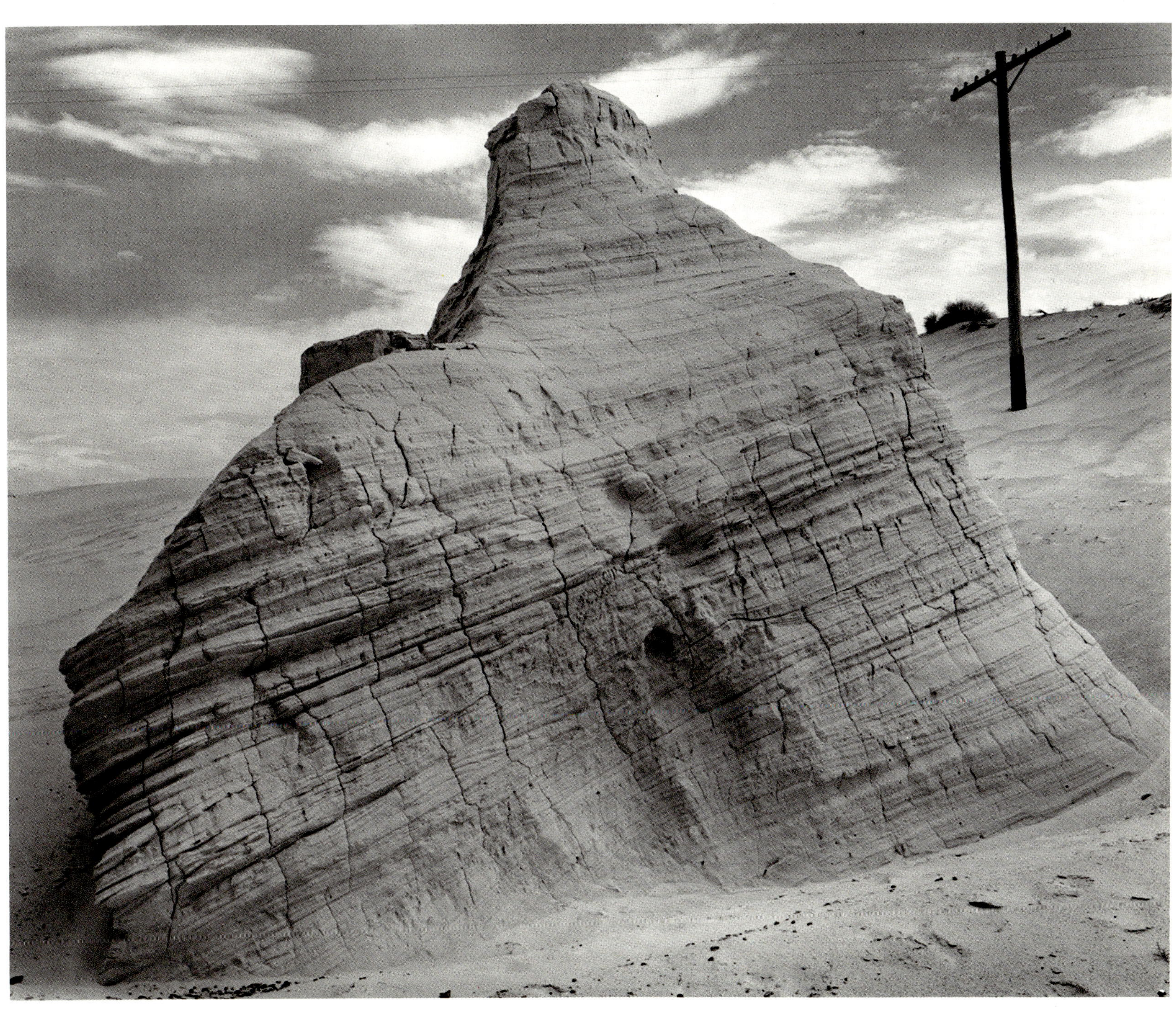

Erosion of a sand dune,
Navajo Reservation, 1979

The hogan of the Navajo is modeled after their image of the universe. The entrance faces east, the source of the sun and life, and the eight sides correspond to the points on the compass. Its domed roof copies the dome of the sky and the curve of the earth. The harmony of man, earth, and sky is embodied in these simple structures.

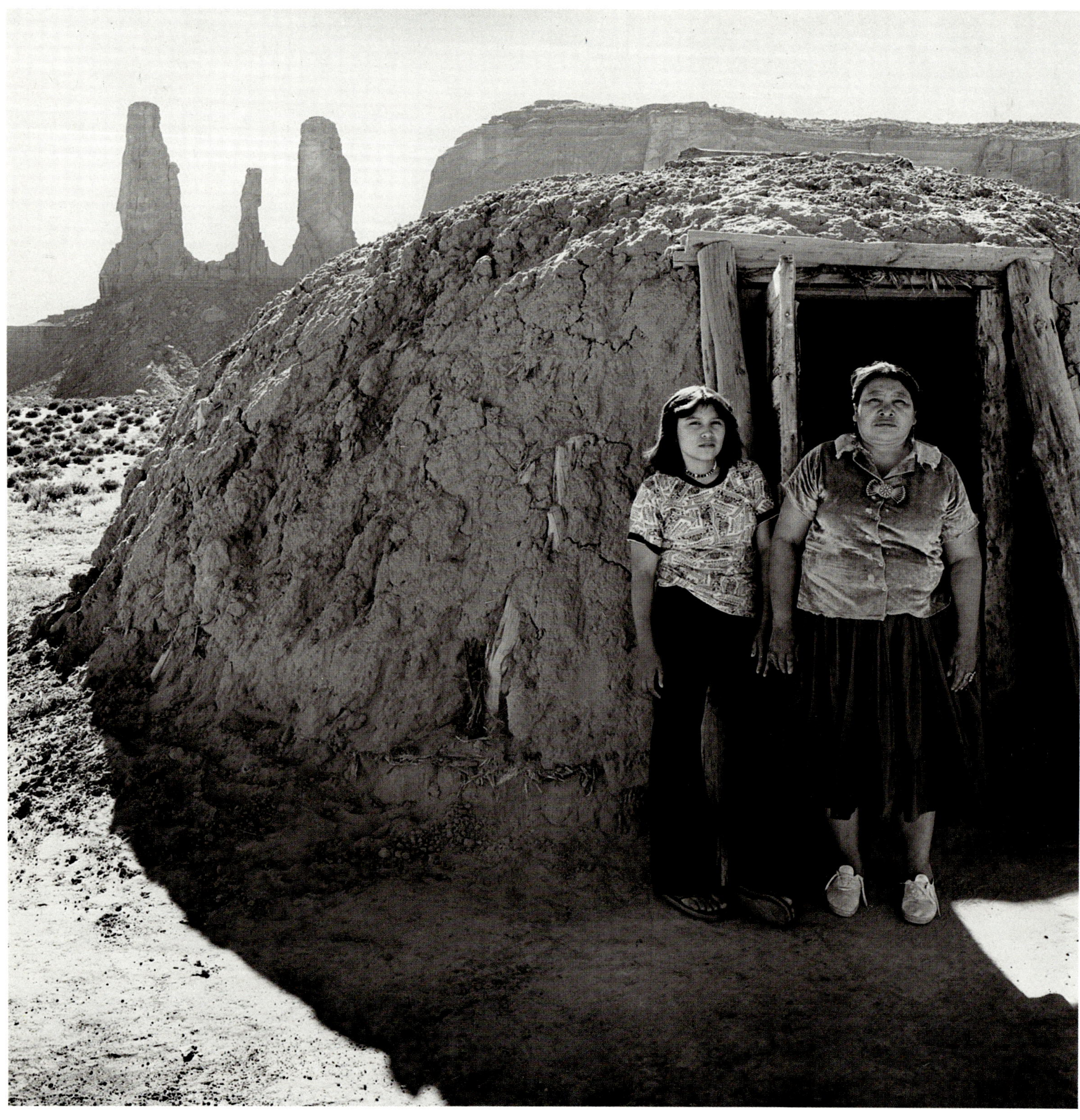

Mother and daughter in front of their hogan,
Monument Valley, 1979

Though it hasn't been obvious in recent years, much of Gorman's drawing in the mid–1970s was characterized by an anguished extension of the figure's fingers and toes. The women were beautiful and stately, but the tension in the work of this period spoke of a certain grace under pressure. It was a time of great sadness for Gorman—his mother and several other close family members and friends died during these years. Many people who knew nothing of his private life interpreted such work as an expression of the traumatic effects of change being wrought on the American Indian, or the pain felt by almost everyone in the mixed-up last quarter of the twentieth century. All interpretations are equally valid.

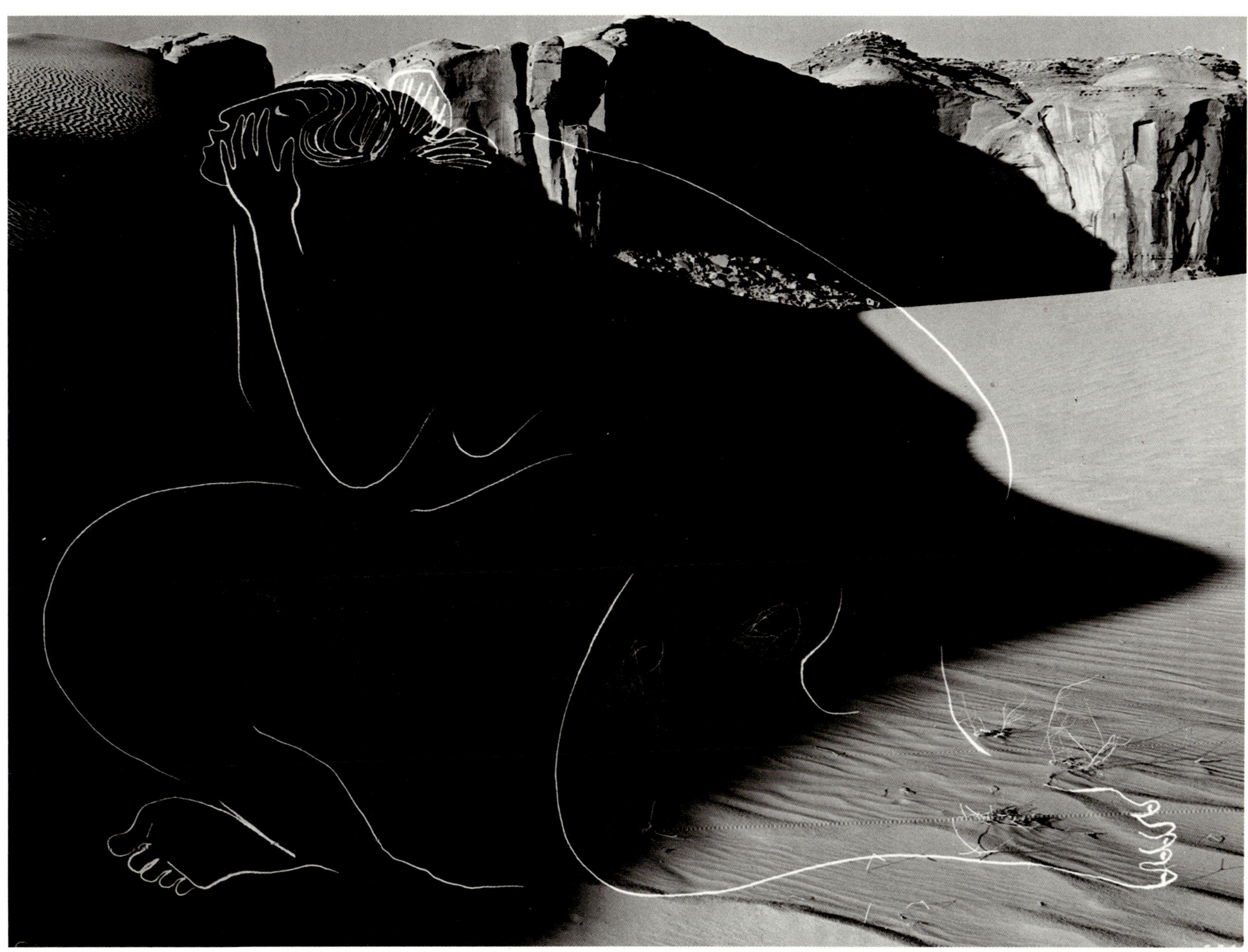

Gorman silkscreen figure and sand dunes,
Monument Valley. Silkscreen by Editions Press, 1979

"The forces of nature are an influence in my art, but I don't want to talk about it. Someone else should."—R.C.G.

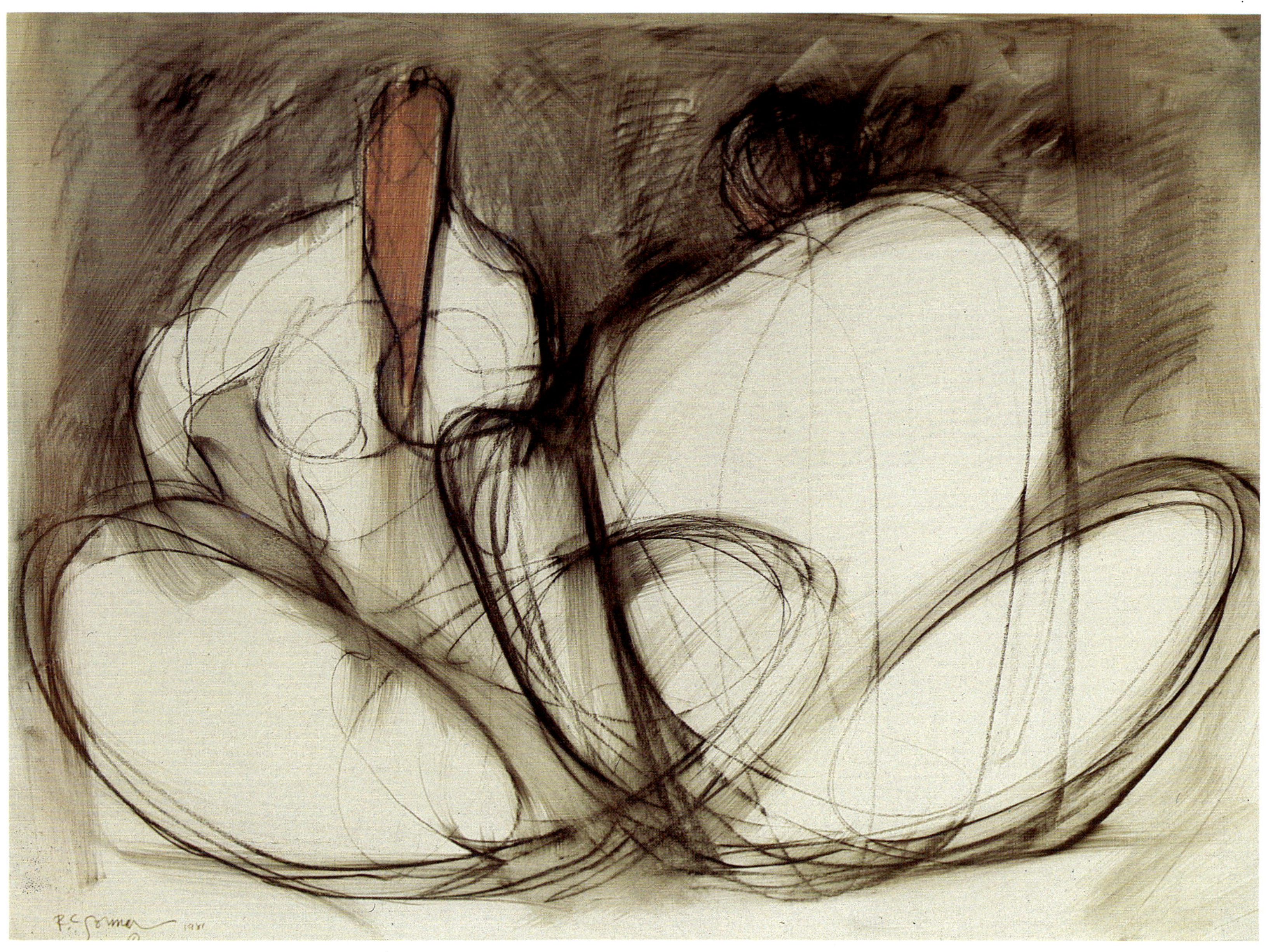

Study for Sculpture, Laughing Sisters,
charcoal and oil pastel on canvas, 1980

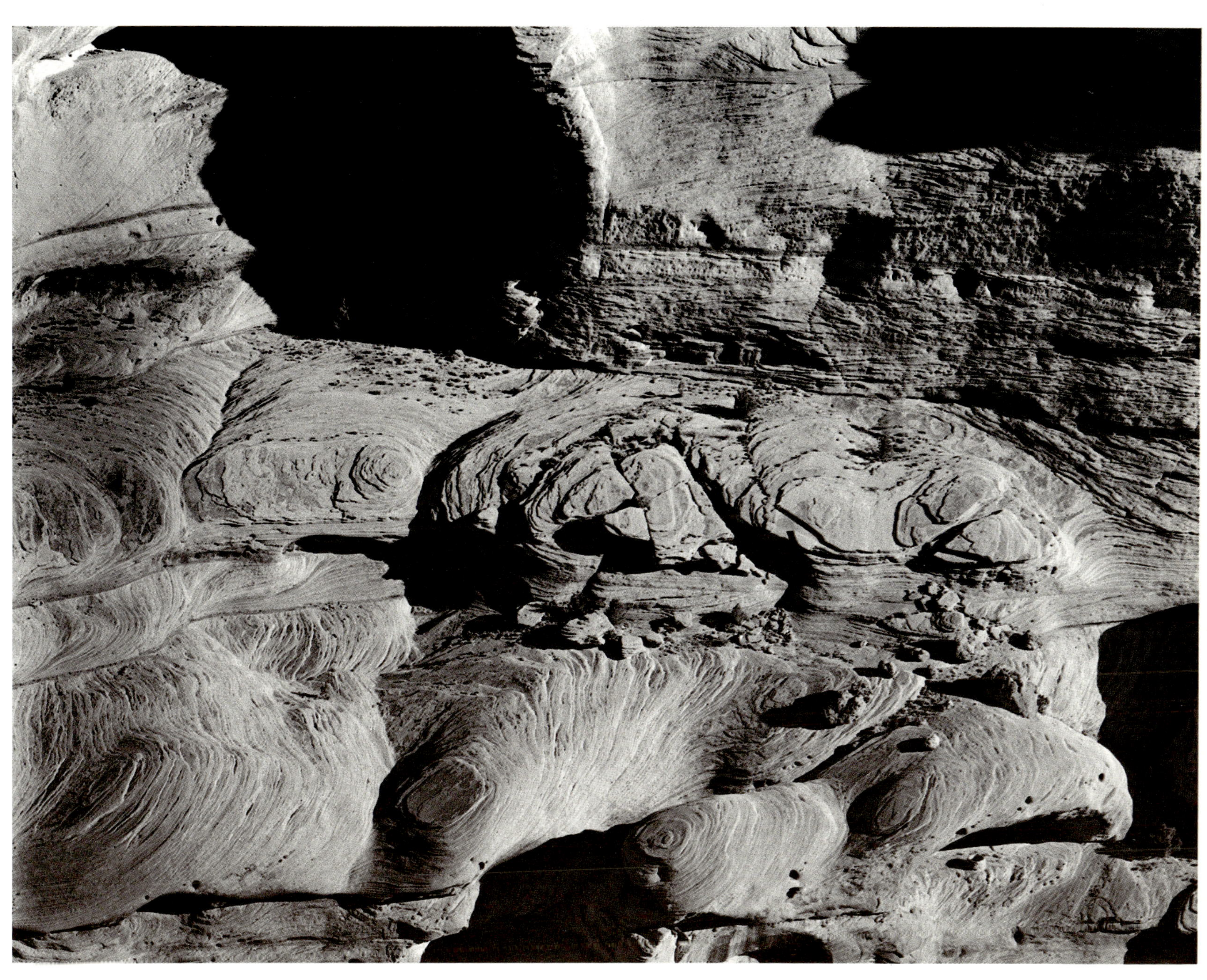

Rock swirls,
Canyon de Chelly, 1979

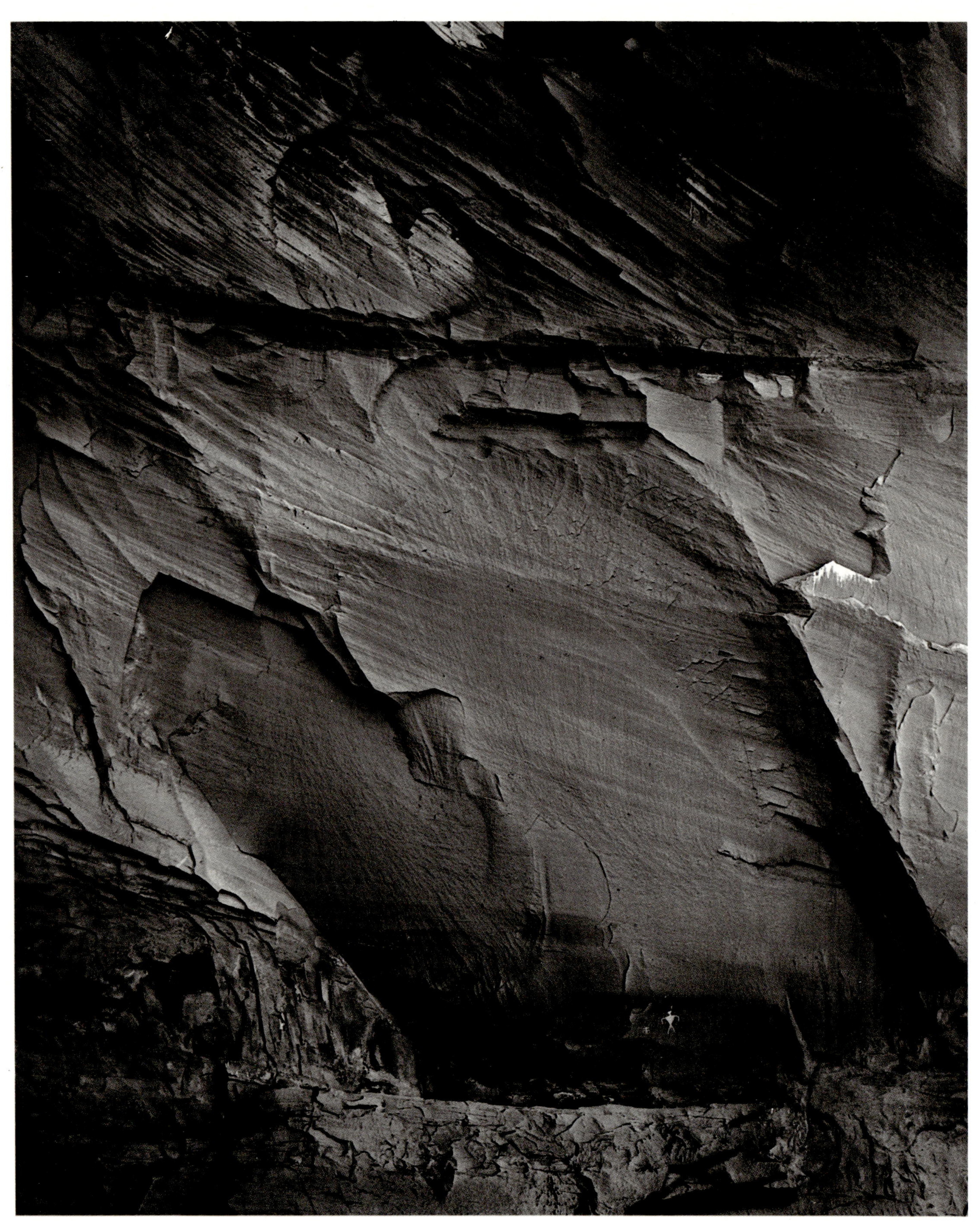

58 Rock wall,
Canyon de Chelly, 1979

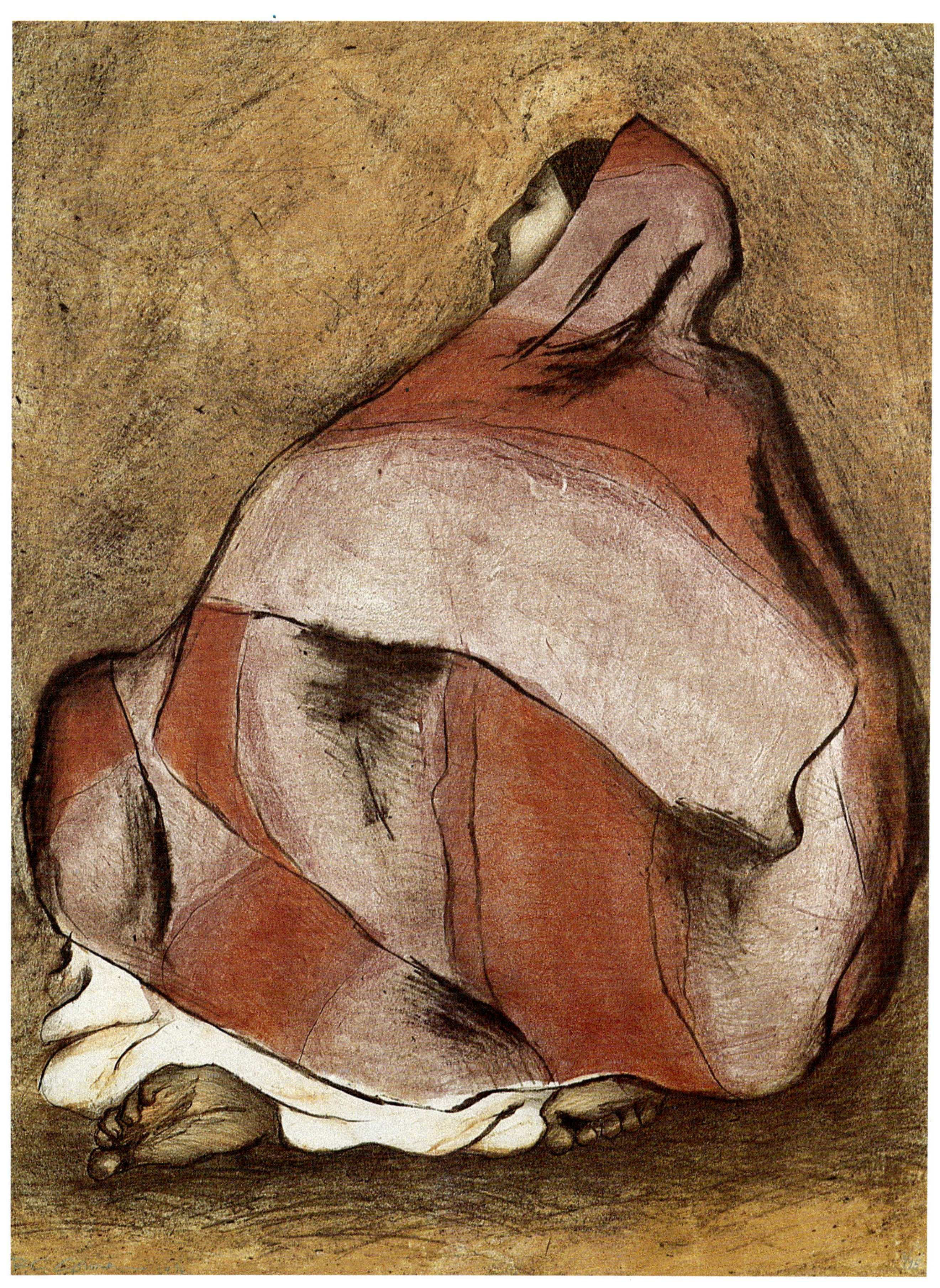

Arabesque,
lithograph, Western Graphics, 1976

"When R. C. began painting seriously, he tried to work in a photographic style, painting every eyelash. He struggled with it, then used a palette knife for a while, painted with black and white. . . . It was a process of development until he hit what he does best. Real Indian art is not made on easels, it's on rocks, as in Canyon de Chelly."—Carl Gorman

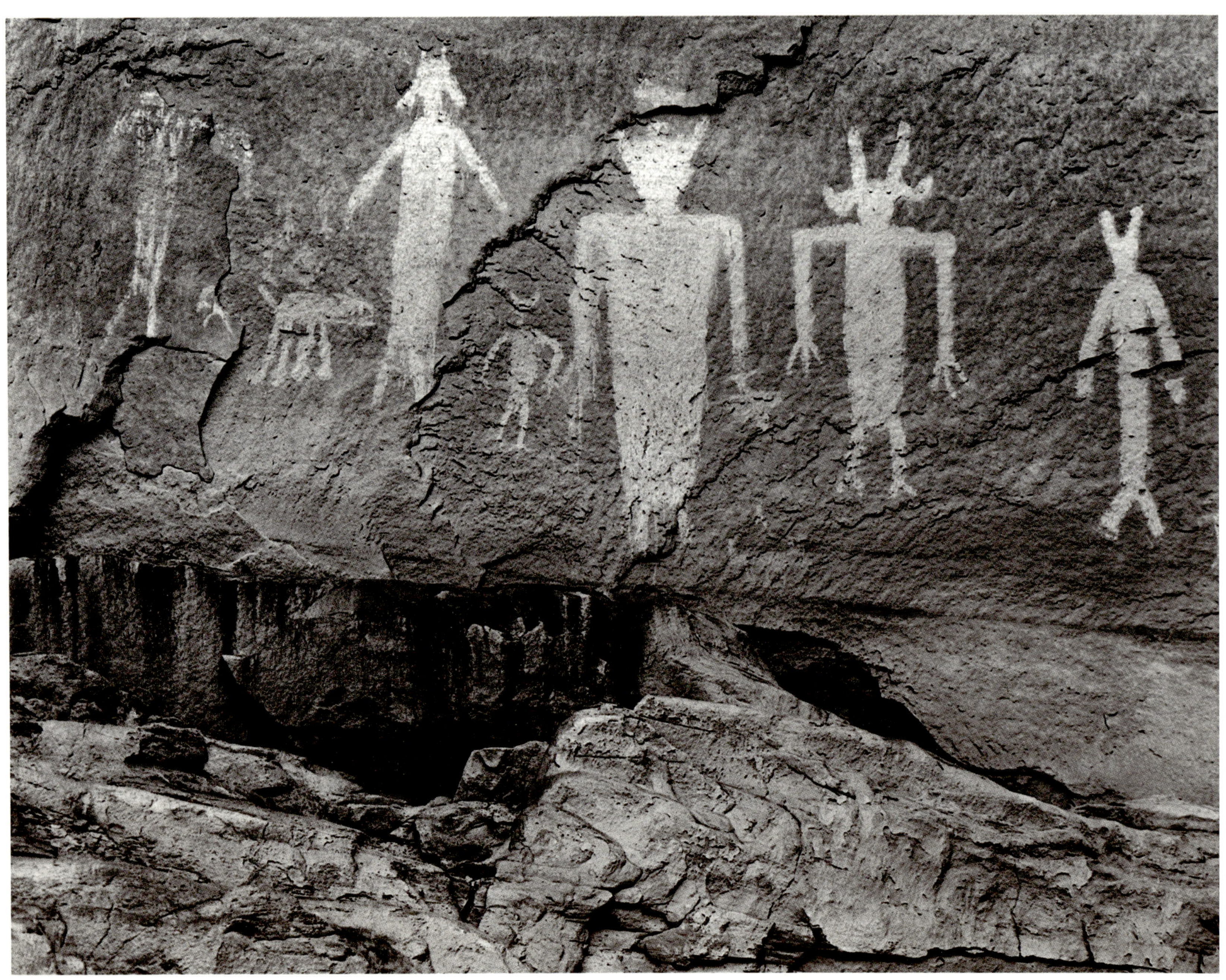

Pictographs,
Canyon de Chelly, 1979

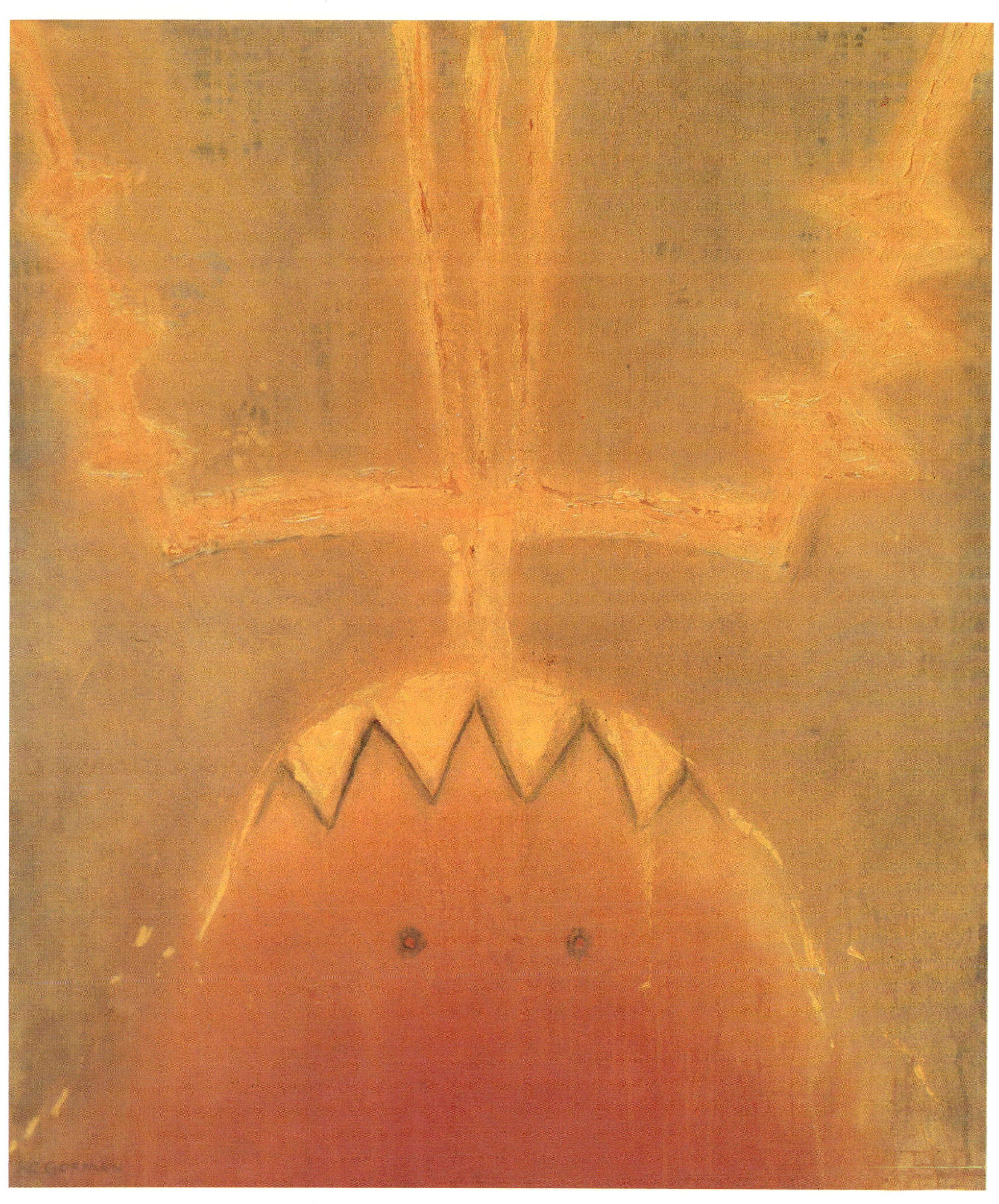

Apache Devil Dancer,
acrylic on canvas, 1977

"It's strange I should come to Taos. The Navajos are encircled by the four sacred mountains, and within those four mountains the Navajo feels, I think, protected, but on the other hand inhibited. I'm outside of that and I feel like a very independent creature who is protected by another mountain which is quite magic. But there's more than that in Taos. Let's face it, it's beautiful, and I have business here, and it's fun to be unique. I'm the only Navajo in town with a business, and I'm the only Navajo who lives in Las Colonias. Here I've built my own private pueblo."—R.C.G.

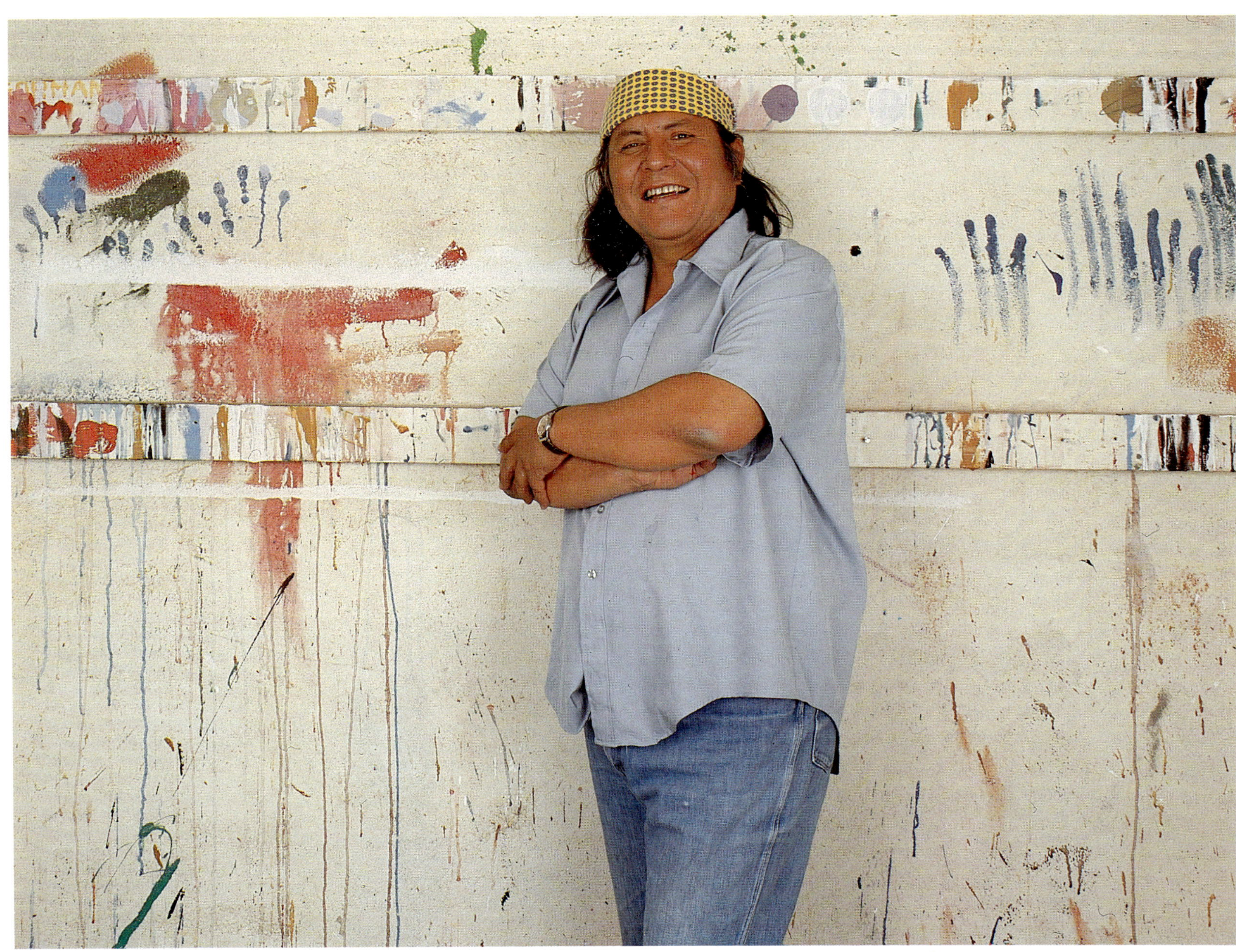

The happy artist in his Taos studio, 1981

Taos

After leaving the confines of Chinle, Gorman spent nearly twenty years roaming about. He sailed through the Pacific while in the navy, then studied art, worked, and played in San Francisco, Mexico City, and other places filled with sophisticated people before settling in Taos. Traveling so far from his roots is an important aspect of any man's quest after his own special place in the universe. As a little boy playing in the spring waters of Canyon de Chelly and herding sheep on the mesas with his strong, wise old grandmother, Gorman must have known that his destiny lay far beyond the canyon walls and the Navajo ways. His path was to be that of a warrior, not in the hunter-fighter sense, but in the broader one of man waging the battle to realize his potential in the contemporary world.

The path of the warrior's quest has always included a period of exile. In Navajo mythology, the Twin War Gods, aided by the Spider Woman, went on a long and perilous journey far from their home in search of their father, the Sun. It seems that Gorman's exile has ended, for the time being at least, in Taos. It is an art center and has a long history of harboring exiles of all sorts. But most important, it is Indian land. The strong spirit of connectedness with the earth and old ways still resides here in the mountains and kivas of the Taos Pueblo. While Gorman has little contact with the people of Taos Pueblo, the place strongly affects him and his work. He is far from the psychological restrictions of Chinle, yet still close to the essence of his home. He is free in Taos, and it is here that, personally and artistically, he has flourished.

Though Gorman had several exhibitions of his work in San Francisco in the early 1960s, it was a trip to Taos in 1964 that must mark the beginning of his meteoric rise. Here he met John Manchester, who was immediately struck by the quality of the work shown in the slides Gorman had brought with him. Manchester added Gorman to the stable of artists in his picturesque gallery on Ledoux Street, and began promoting both the painting and the personality of this engaging, exceedingly handsome, talented young Navajo painter. Several paintings that Gorman shipped from San Francisco to the Manchester Gallery sold quickly, and a one-man show was scheduled for September 1965. The show, still talked about as one of the most exciting events in Taos art history, was both a critical and personal triumph. Family from Chinle mixed with collectors from New York and Taos art lovers in the old adobe gallery that was charged by Gorman's effervescence. It was the first time the public had seen such a strong and lyrical integration of classical and American Indian sensibilities. Gorman's career was launched.

Later that year, he and his father shared an exhibition at the Heard Museum in Phoenix. He had two one-man shows in San Francisco galleries in 1966, and a solo exhibition the next year, again at the Heard. Museums began acquiring paintings, and he was featured prominently in books and magazine articles on Indian artists. Gorman is not especially introspective about his work, but in the late 1960s he was quoted as saying: "I want to catch for all time a depiction of something that is going away and won't return. These [referring specifically to the abstract paintings of rug and pottery motifs he was doing at the time] are fragments of a beauty that was momentarily caught in the process of disintegration." He had found his voice as an artist, created his signature images, and masses of people responded with open hearts and checkbooks. After a 1968 show at the Manchester Gallery, he was able to buy the gallery building and move to Taos.

The move was a propitious one, for Taos and for Gorman. He reinvigorated the town's reputation as an art colony which had waned with the passing of the artists who had first brought the town some measure of fame—the Taos school painters, including Ernest Blumenschein, Victor Higgins, Joseph Sharp, and Irving Couse. These and others had come to Taos from metropolitan centers, lured by the promise of new subject matter—the landscape and the ideal of the noble red man unsullied by the ills of industrialization. And they were attracted by the crystalline quality of the light, a freshness of natural color comparable to the crispness of Mediterranean light.

In the early 1970s the media discovered Gorman and along with him they found Taos. The handsome, talented, ex–starving-Navajo kid with the fast wit and the sharp nose for publicity was ready and waiting. He is a born actor with an instinctive talent for public relations, as skilled at painting a bigger-than-life image of himself as at rendering lyrical drawings of Navajo women. Unlike the acts of many media superstars, however, only a bit of Gorman's is hype. His posturing, humor, and gregariousness are innate personality characteristics developed at a very early age as a buffer against poverty and loneliness. He soon discovered that the world responded to his colorful mask, and the traits were reinforced. Without them, Gorman might still be tending sheep in Chinle. With them, he has the wherewithal not just to survive, but to prevail. There must be some genetic code that instills such strength, such determination and luck.

Gorman's combination of shrewdness and lightheartedness about life and himself, as seen in his self-devised advertising campaigns, is a key to his success. He craftily adapted the "What Becomes a Legend Most" theme from a fur company to help create the legend of R. C. Gorman, mugging before the camera and poking fun at himself. Gorman drives a gold Mercedes, wears Hawaiian shirts and bright print headbands, and throws huge parties for movie stars in his new palace that stands like a neon sign flashing *R. C. GORMAN* from atop the hill north of town. Bodybuilder Arnold Schwarzenegger, queen of the soaps Jean Cooper, Keith Richards of the Rolling Stones, Linda Lavin of *Alice,* poet Allen Ginsberg, and Andy Warhol are among those he enjoys hobnobbing with.

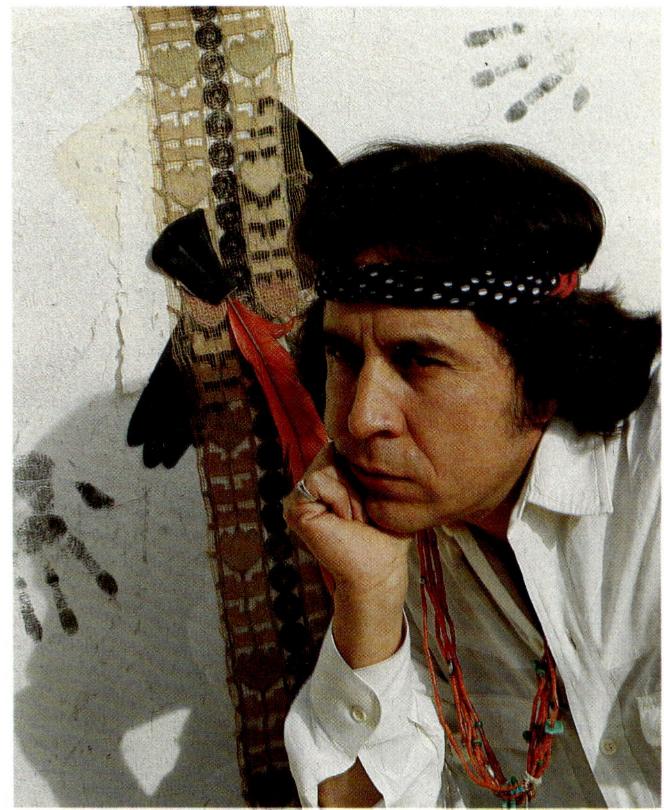

"Armond Lara is one of my favorite artists in the whole world. One reason is that he's half Navajo, and the Navajo part certainly shows through. Maybe he's not a painter at all—maybe he's a magician."—R.C.G.

Armond Lara,
Taos, 1981

The public image aside, he is a genuine patron of young New Mexico artists, Indian and Anglo alike. He owns several of Gary Mauro's lyrical stitched muslin murals of animal and human figures. One of them, which measures eleven by twenty feet, hangs above the swimming pool in his home. Along another wall of the pool room is a triptych by Bill Gersh, a struggling, fierce Taos painter who has a local reputation as one of the best, most uncompromising artists in the region. The work was actually sold to him by his friend and temperamental twin, Elizabeth Taylor, at the opening in Taos of the Taylor Gallery, owned by Elizabeth's brother Howard and his wife. Gorman also has a wide collection of work by Indian artists, including Fritz Scholder, Earl Biss, Kevin Red Star, Randy White, and Armond Lara. While he claims to be apolitical and resists being drawn into issues of American Indian rights, he is quick to foster the careers of Indian artists.

Gorman's generosity is most pronounced in his aid to reservation-bound relatives. To expand their horizons, Gorman has treated numerous cousins and nieces to higher education, trips abroad, and visits to Taos.

Gorman says: "I've gotten everything I have without being greedy. Some

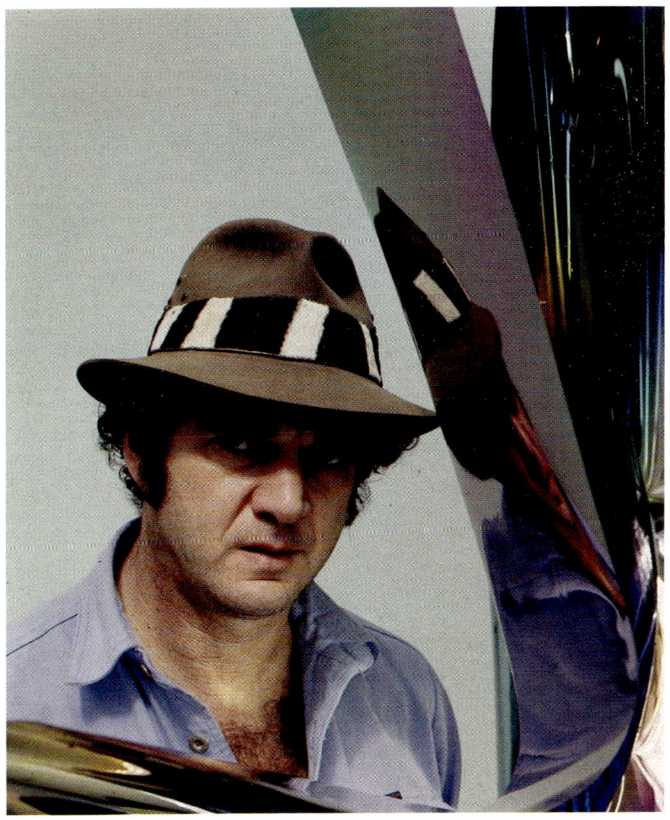

"Larry Bell is another of my favorite artists. Every artist I've collected, I've collected because, one, I love their work, and two, because I can't do what they do. I love to be surrounded by artists who to me are great. We talk about famous artists as being great— Dali, Rodin —but these artists are just as great. I know them personally. I like my own work as much as theirs, but there is an envy in what I collect."
—R.C.G.

Larry Bell,
Taos, 1981

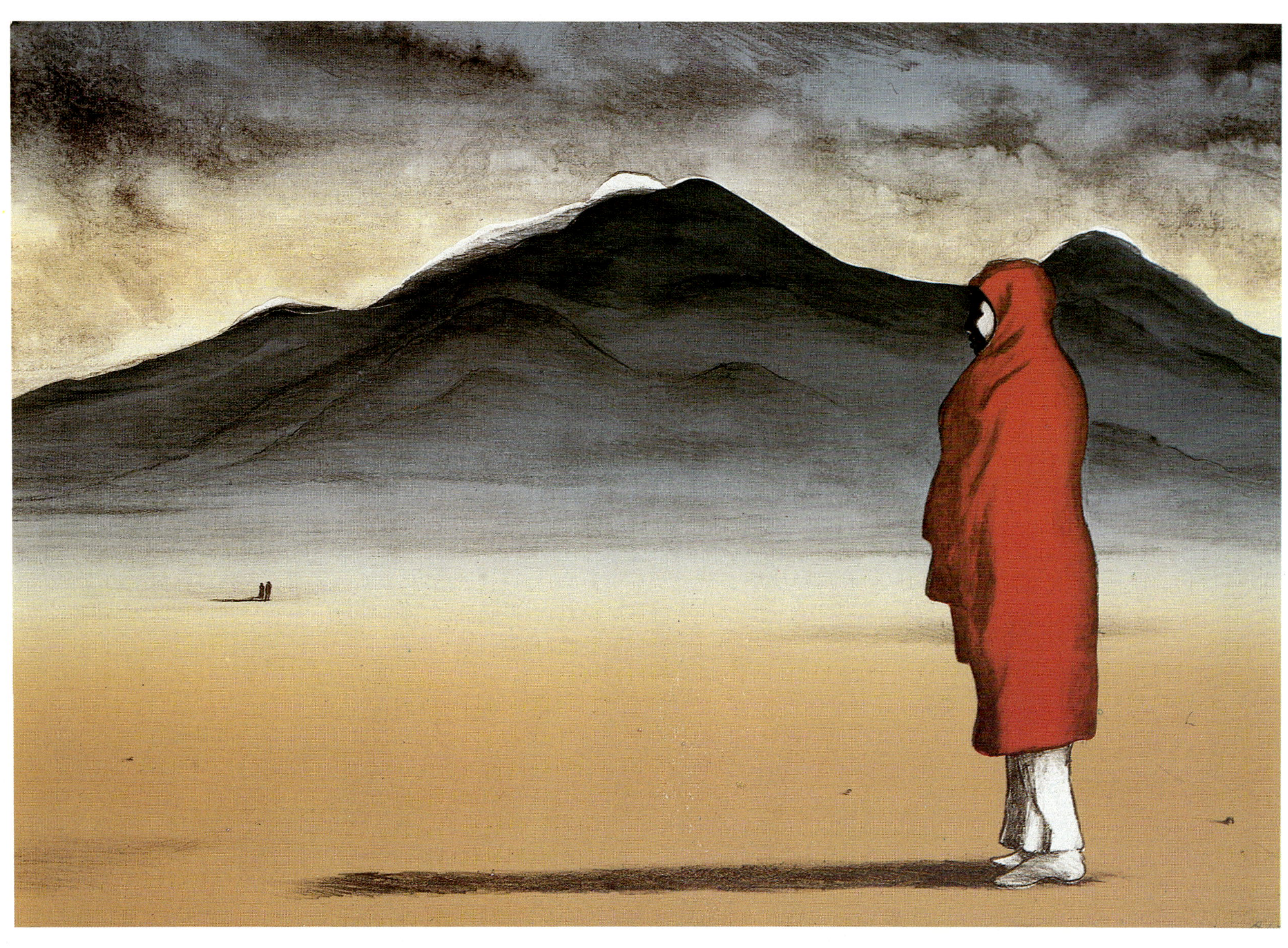

Expectation (Enigma Suite),
lithograph, Hand Graphics, Ltd., 1976

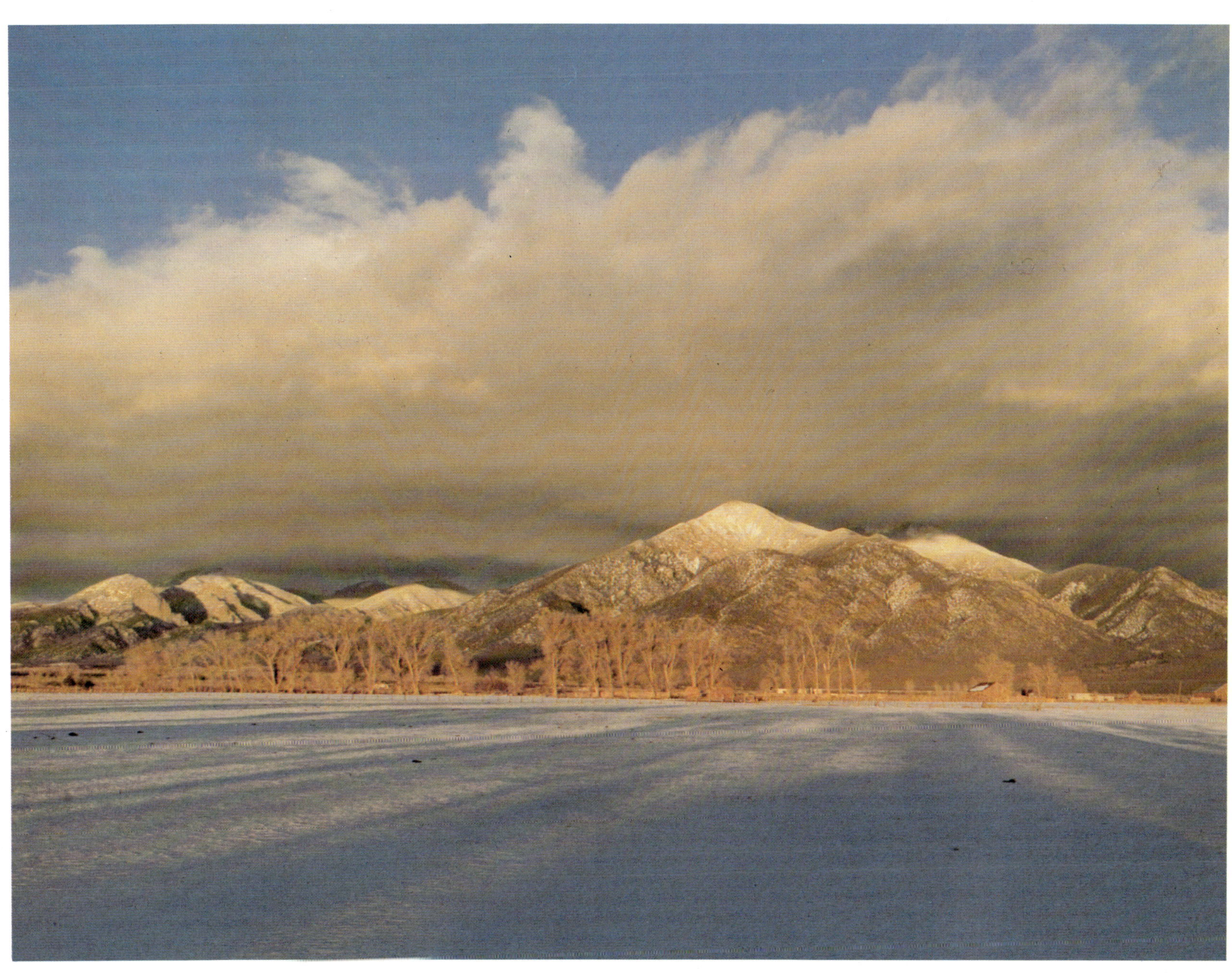

Taos Mountain,
Taos, 1982

"I started working with Gorman and his ceramics in 1978. He's very trusting. Our whole agreement is verbal, but I've never felt more secure about a business situation. He may not even know it, but he is a very good businessman. Gorman has a genuine mystique about him. With those quick flashes of personality, he can be as spontaneous as his drawing."—Greg Grycner, publisher of Gorman's ceramic editions

"R. C. is very intuitive. Sometimes I'll be thinking about something but, for some reason or other, I won't talk about it. Gorman will hit on it exactly. And maybe that explains some of his success at public relations. He just knows what people want or need."—Ellie Hamilton

"There's some kind of magic in Taos. I wouldn't have little Munchkins working for me [Gorman used to call Hamilton and Grycner his Munchkins] if I didn't believe in magic. I wouldn't have a cat that talks —Lola—if I didn't believe in magic. The other cat, Maria, I just know practices magic." — R.C.G.

Ellie Hamilton was killed October 7, 1982, in a mountain-climbing accident.

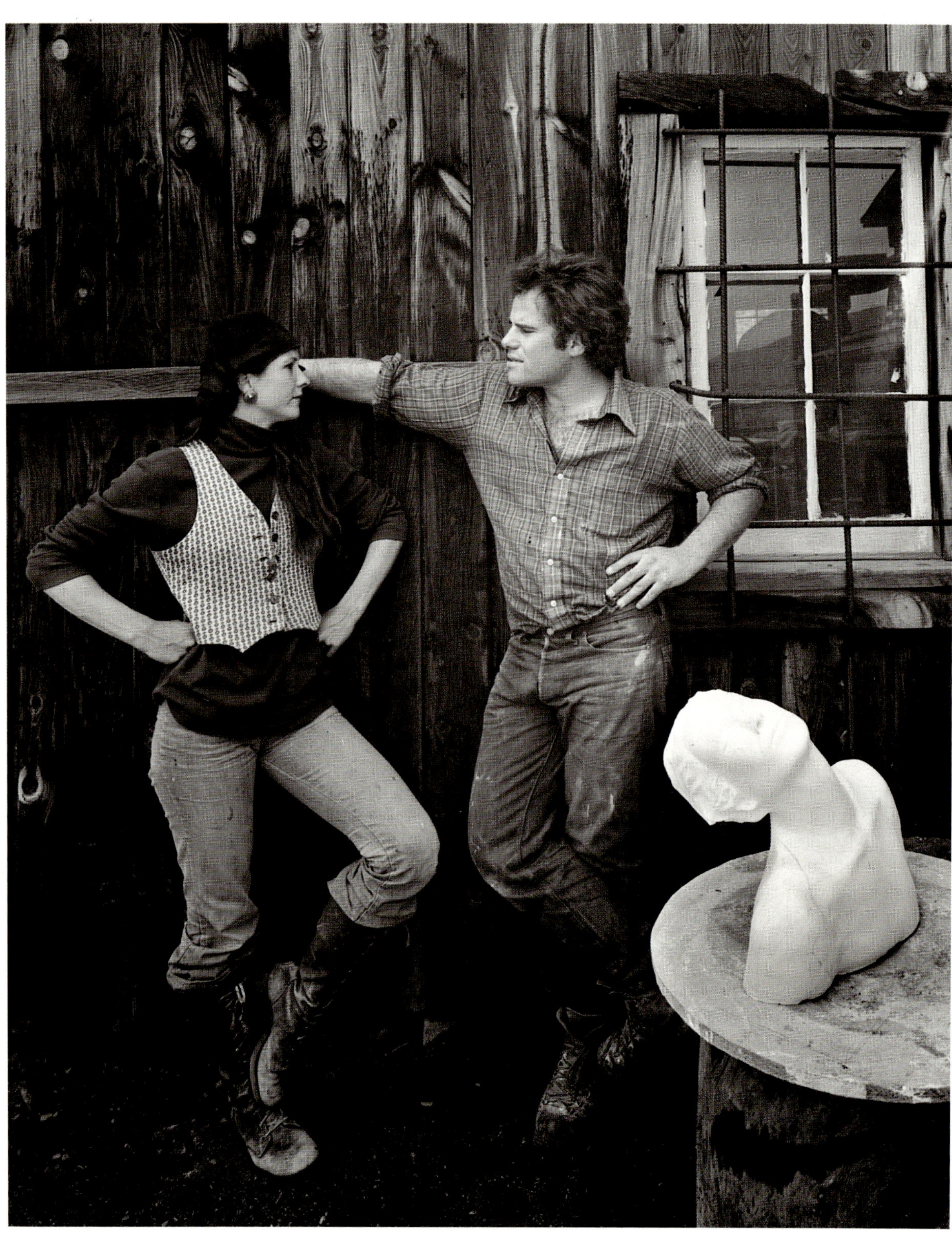

Gorman's friends Ellie Hamilton and Greg Grycner, Taos, 1981

"Curtis stretches all my canvas, hauls my work around, hangs it. He's so serious, his sense of humor wry. He thinks I'm not serious enough, and he tries to encourage me in reference to my art. In the ten or eleven years I've known him, he's taken my art as seriously as anyone can take it. Other people who work for me are in awe of it in a different way, because they can't do it. But Curtis is an artist. He's started painting, and strangely enough, I haven't influenced his work. Miró has, and we've seen many of Miró's things on our travels, and I own a couple of them. So maybe in that way I have influenced him after all."—R.C.G.

"Many good artists can't promote themselves, they haven't the ego Gorman has. He thinks he's wonderful, and he tells everyone so. They see his work, and realize he is."
—Curtis Grubbs

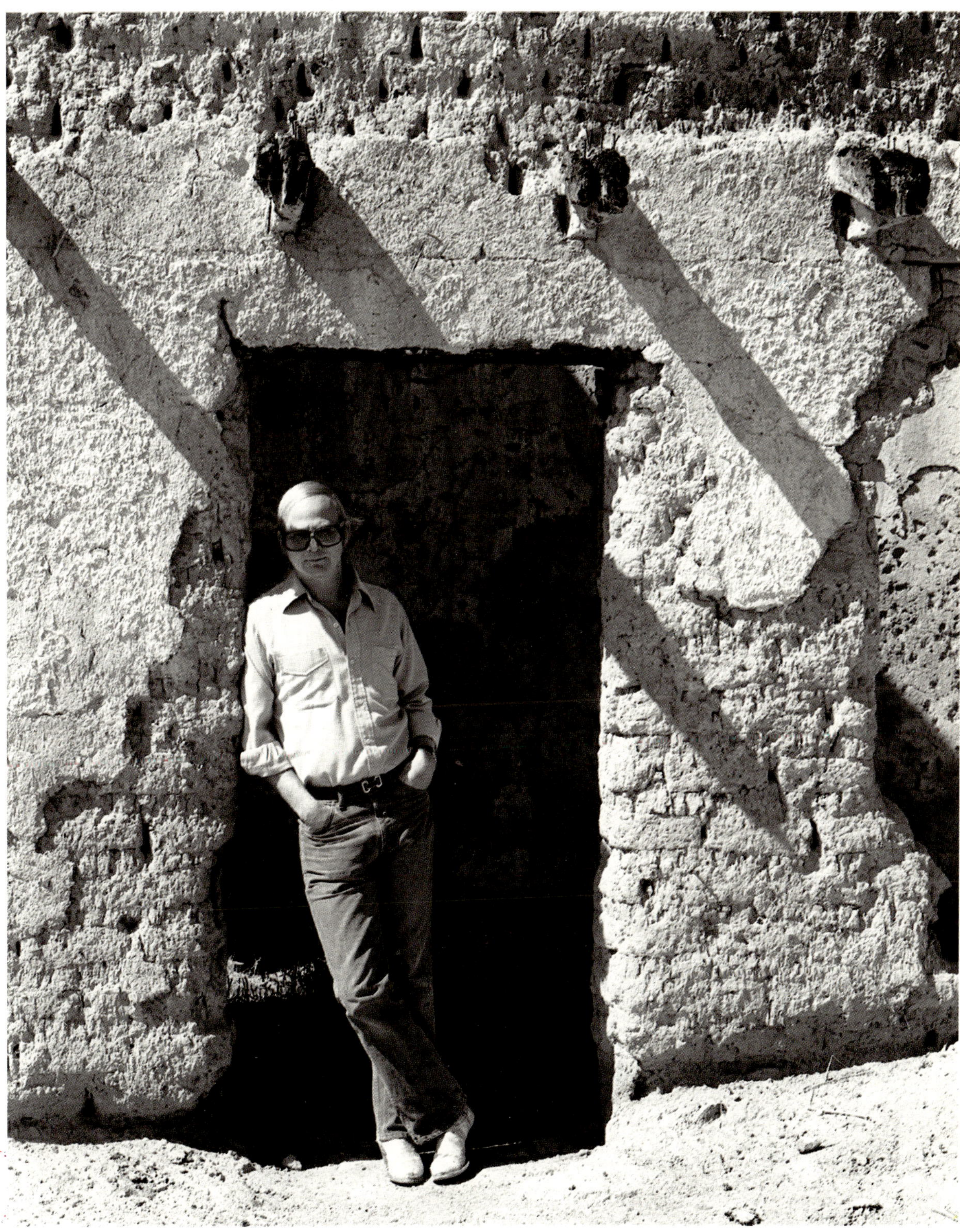

Curtis Grubbs,
Taos, 1981

people who have struggled to get to the top have shuffled people aside to get there. But they ended just like the rest of us—they died."

Gorman's output is prodigious, though he is seldom to be found drawing or painting more than two hours a day. He produces lithographs at a half-dozen presses scattered between Barcelona, Taos, and Tokyo, makes sculptures with Editions Press in San Francisco, and designs ceramic plates, vessels, and tiles that are manufactured and marketed in Taos by his assistant, Greg Grycner.

An indicator of both his popularity and zest for promotion, his book *Nudes and Foods: Gorman Goes Gourmet* sold 20,000 copies in the first three months after its release. Gorman freely admits that such efforts are designed to serve publicity rather than artistic purposes, and as vehicles for Gorman to have, and share, a good time. The book's photographer, Robert Willis, was a friend, the recipes came from local artists and business friends, and other friends posed for the drawings.

The driving force behind the amount of work Gorman produces is his desire to reach as many people as he can, perhaps as a hedge against mortality. "I'd rather have my work in a lot of hands," he told me, "than hoard it myself. So many people who are critical of my work can't push their own work. Children are being born every minute of the day, and they are the ones who will be collecting me in the future. I'm a working man. I get up at five-thirty every morning . . ."

Taos is a dusty, funky little town, tucked away at the foot of the mountains, on the road to nowhere in particular. Yet a romantic aura has risen up about the Taos Valley that continues to attract artists, rugged individualists, and seekers of peace and metaphysical truth. There is much talk about the *power* of the place, about being *held* by the landscape, as if the arroyos were the tentacles of some giant benevolent octopus.

Opinions as to the nature of the people there vary considerably. Robinson Jeffers, a frequent visitor to Taos during the 1930s, described them as "pilgrims from civilization, anxiously seeking beauty, religion, poetry; pilgrims from the vacuum." Vladimir Nabokov, who spent the summer of 1954 near Taos on a butterfly-hunting

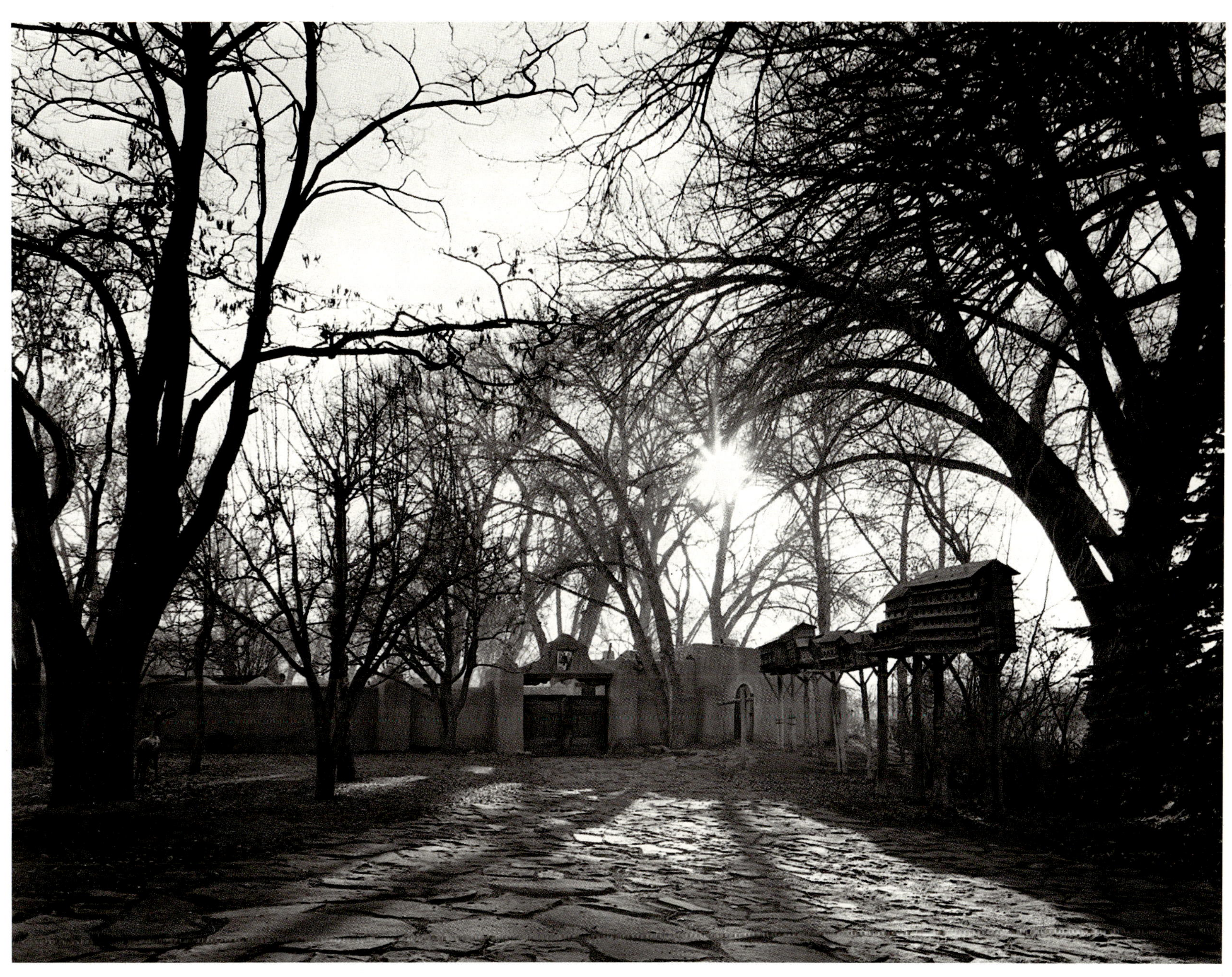

Winter sun at the Mabel Dodge Luhan house,
Taos, 1982

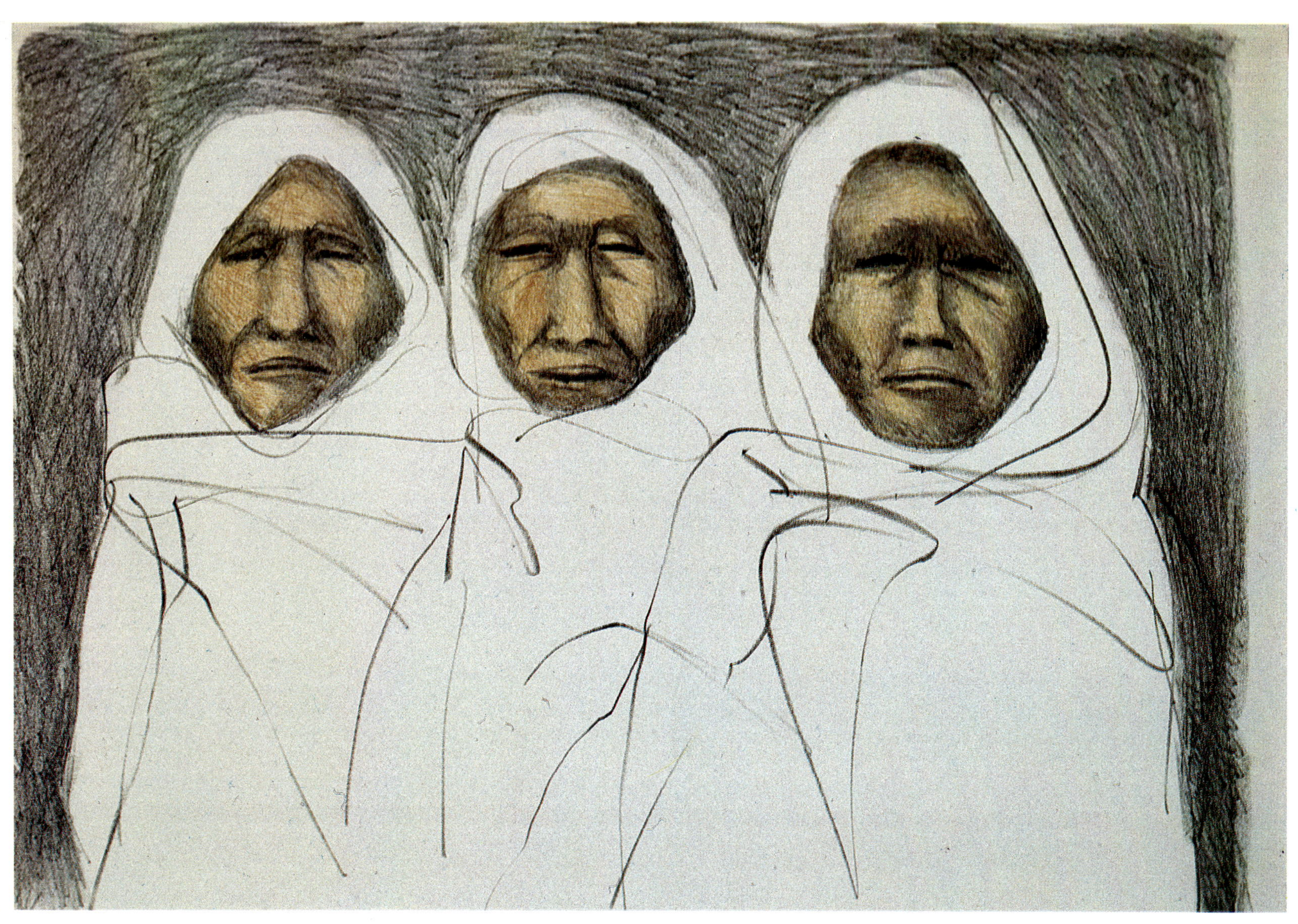

Taos Men,
lithograph, José Sánchez,
Mexico City, 1970

"Most white Americans are coyotes. You don't know where you come from. You can't relate to your roots, because you haven't any. You are all individuals, but related to what? Within our own particular tribes, we Indians are not so individualistic as you, but our tribes are certainly individual. The Navajos would never be like the Taos Pueblo people, or the Taos Pueblo would never, among Indians, want to be confused with Santa Domingo or any other pueblo. They're very different. I may seem like anybody else when I'm here in Taos, but at home, in Chinle, I do as the Navajos do."—R.C.G.

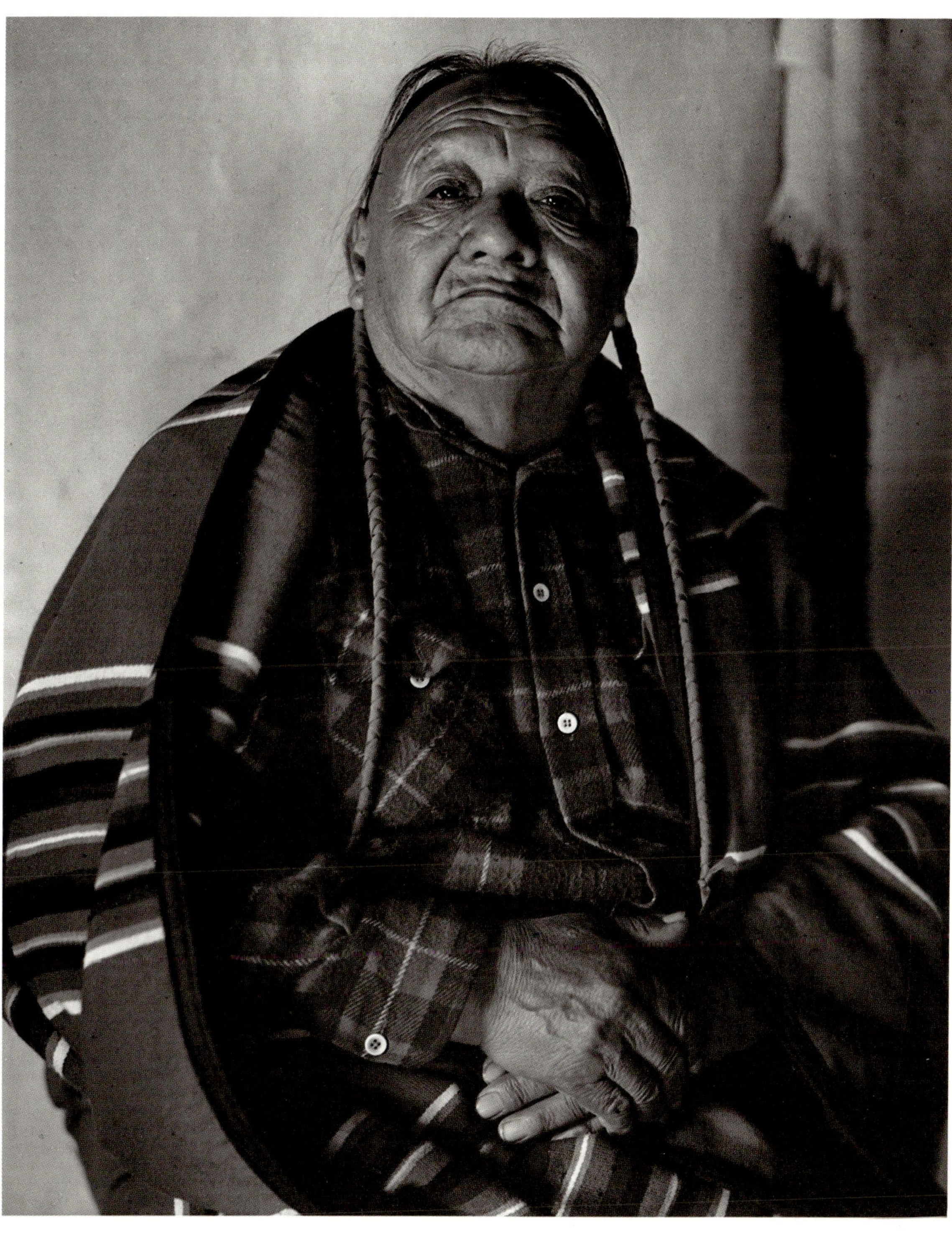

Albino Montoya,
Taos,Pueblo, 1980

expedition, expressed a somewhat different view in a letter to Edmund Wilson: "We are near a superb canyon where I go for my hunting, and twelve miles from Taos, which is a dismal hole full of third-rate painters and faded pansies. The house cost only $250 for the whole summer, and an orchard was thrown in. Unfortunately our Spanish neighbors take all the fruit and a colorful smell of drains pervades what is euphemistically called the patio."

Both these opinions, and undoubtedly others, are valid and serve to point up the complicated web of paradoxes that makes Taos such an intriguing, intense microcosm of the human situation. The intensity is evident when one approaches the valley from Santa Fe to the south, tops the pass at Pilar, and is confronted by the gripping beauty of the valley spread out below. The Sangre de Cristo Mountains (the name, Blood of Christ, intense in itself, was given to the mountains nearly four centuries ago by the Conquistadores) form a ring around three sides of a sloping plain that is cut by the deep, angry rip of the Rio Grande gorge. The mountains are covered with piñon pine, and, at higher elevations, spruce, fir, and aspen. The valley plain, once lush with grass, was overgrazed by sheep seventy-five years ago and is now covered by sagebrush. In the summer the weather is warm and dry, but the high desert winters are often cruelly cold. Spring is a season that usually bypasses Taos. Octobers are spectacular.

D. H. Lawrence in his essay *New Mexico* admitted to having his first feeling of a "living religion" at Taos Pueblo, and praised the landscape with his characteristic passion: "In the magnificent fierce morning of New Mexico one sprang awake, a new part of the soul woke up suddenly, and the old world gave way to the new."

Taos Pueblo Indians, descendants of the Anasazi, were the first recorded people to settle in the valley, forced some eight hundred years ago by drought or famine to migrate from the Mesa Verde land of southwestern Colorado. They are a placid people who coexisted relatively peacefully for centuries with the equally insular but hot-blooded Spanish who entered the valley with Coronado's expedition in search of Quivira, a mythical city of gold, in 1540.

Cut off from the nearest center of Spanish authority—Durango, Mexico—by more than fifteen hundred miles of desert, the Spanish settlers gradually created a unique culture in north-central New Mexico, elements of which have survived to this day. They developed a style of architecture incorporating Moorish adobe brick techniques with the Pueblo Indian practice of constructing by building up layers of mud mixed with straw. Though primitive, functional, and dusty, the native architecture has a charm and a sculptural quality that fit naturally with the landscape. The feminine curves of adobe buttresses, such as those supporting the massive walls of the St. Francis of Assisi Church in Ranchos de Taos, echo the soft flanks of the mountains behind. The play of light and shadow on the warm, reflective surface of hand-plastered adobe, and the Earth-Mother swells of her curves, have made the Ranchos church one of the most often painted and photographed buildings in the world. Gorman himself has made it the subject of several paintings and lithographs.

New Mexico has retained much of its wild, lawless flavor, and is the perfect place for men like Gorman who have a need for freedom from social and artistic restrictions. As Gorman comments: "Rome was decadent, but it didn't crumble in one night. Let's hope we're in the same boat. I imagine Egypt had its Richard Nixons, Joe McCarthys, and R. C. Gormans. But, you know, Christian white ladies are overcareful. They're always trying to convert you to their ways. They're afraid of chili, blood sausage, mutton stew, afraid to drink with you, much less go to bed with you."

The Pueblo, the Ranchos church, the mountains, the mesas, are all still here, and mystics still regard Taos as one of the world's centers of spiritual power. Gorman himself regards Taos Mountain with such reverence. He built his palatial home on a ridge so that the mountain would never be out of his sight. The mountain serves many as a humbling personal reminder of how petty are the ultimate differences between Indian and Anglo, man and bird, bird and rock. That is the essence of the religion of Taos Pueblo, which lies at the mountain's feet: "Acknowledge the wonder." And that perhaps is the belief that holds the idea of Taos together, that for hundreds of years has kept Taos from self-destructing.

The paradoxes and tensions of Taos run parallel to those in Gorman's own life and work. His Chinle roots are as humble and romantic as Taos's own.

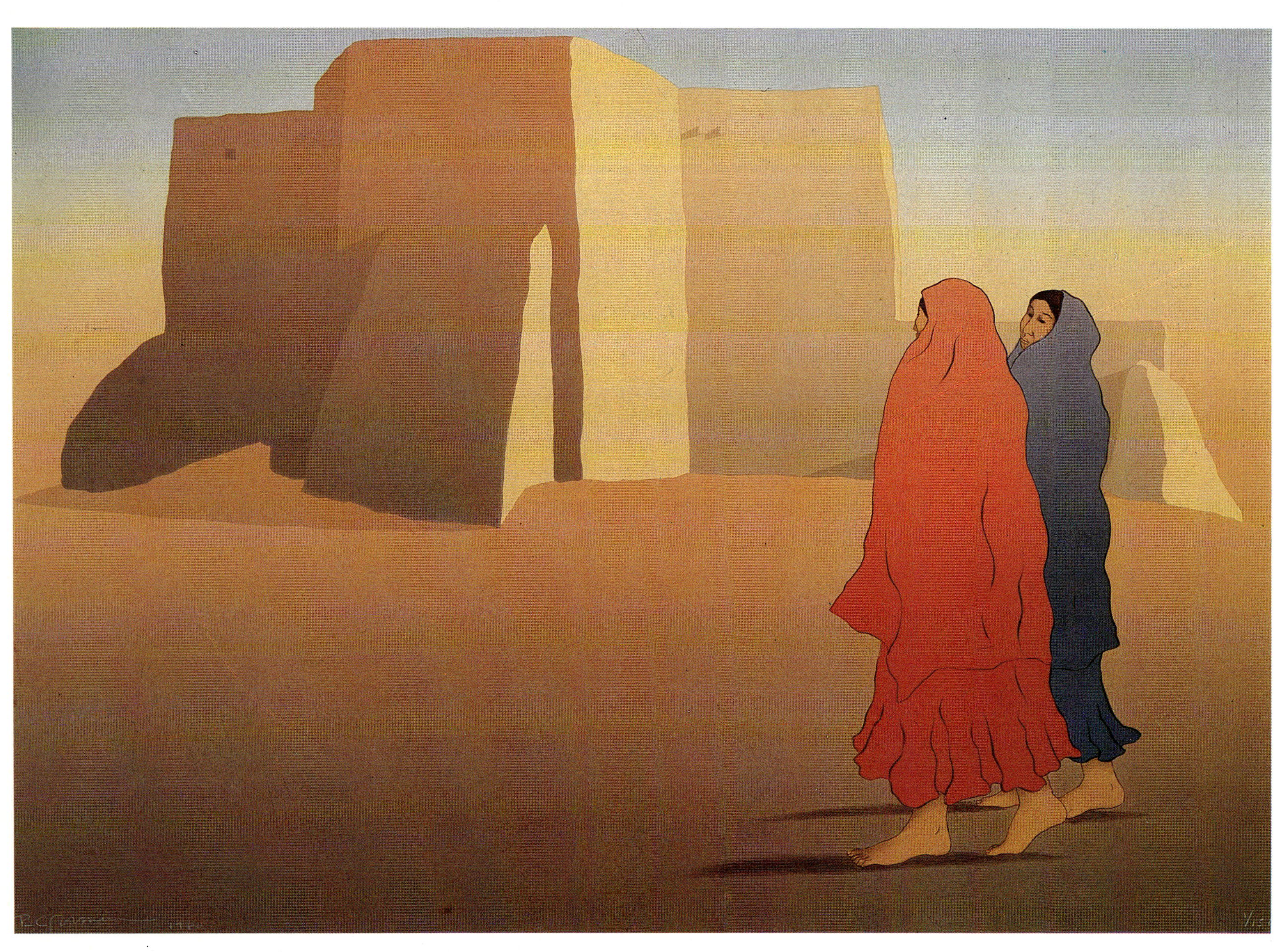

Women from Ranchos,
lithograph, Houston Fine Arts Press, 1980

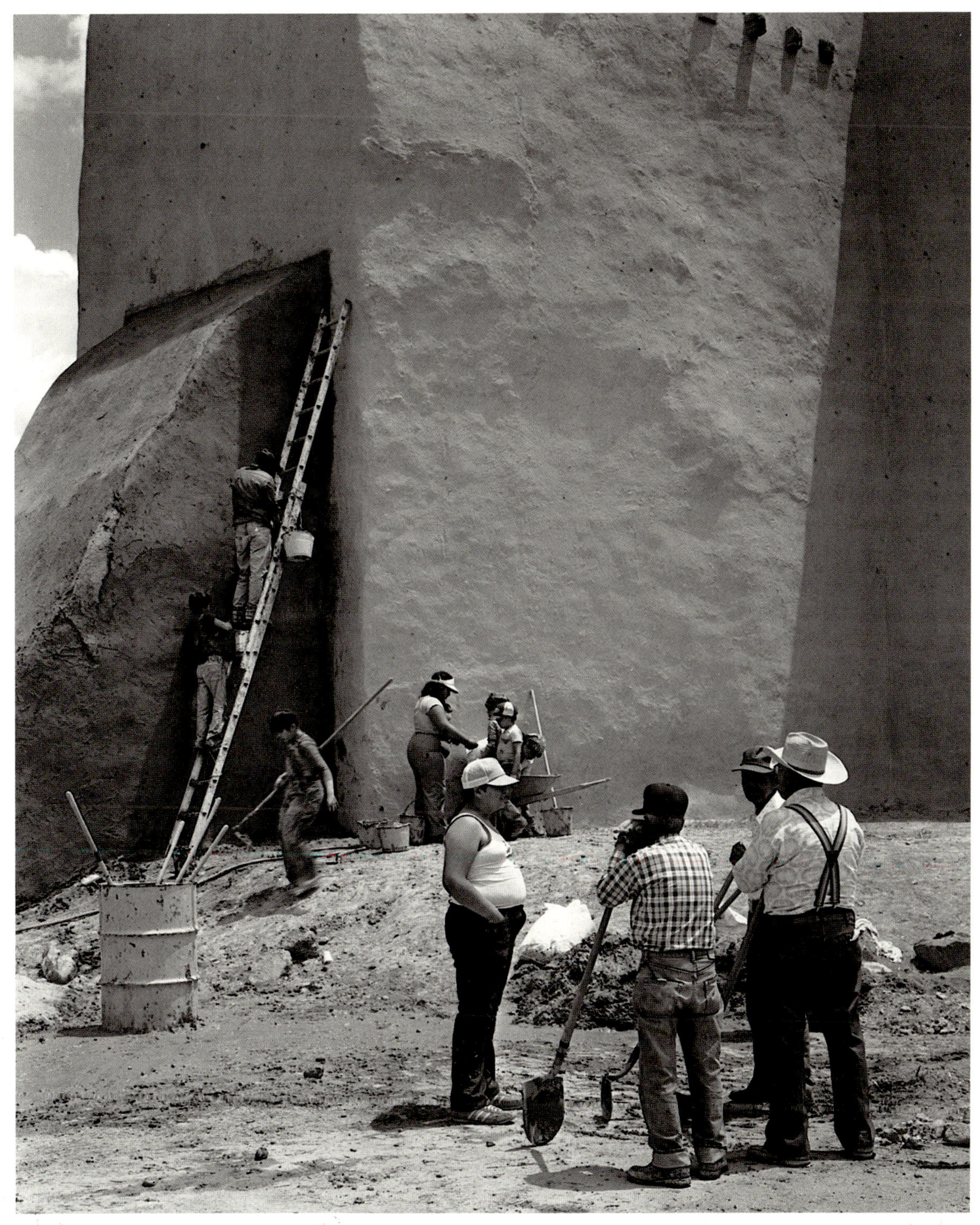

Replastering of St. Francis of Assisi Church,
Ranchos de Taos, 1981

"Art seems to flow from Gorman, as if it has some magic life of its own. Regardless of how often I observe his creative wizardry, I find myself always fascinated with each new piece. Gorman seems to draw his artistic energy from so many sources, each available at the moment of his need. His models, conversation with friends, the shapes and moods of his environment, all translate immediately into his art.

"I remember having lunch on Gorman's patio on a beautiful summer day. We were with Al Wong, the famous dancer and instructor, who was in Taos for a month-long Tai Chi workshop. Al, Curtis Grubbs, Gorman, and I discussed art, and Al explained the various calligraphy strokes in the Tai Chi idiom. Air, flowers, stones, water: all have strokes and techniques of their own. Gorman suddenly rose, walked into his studio, and stood in front of a large 4-by-6-foot black canvas, brought by Curtis just before lunch. Al went to his car and returned with a 300-year-old Chinese flute, and he played it as he walked slowly through the house. The Oriental flute music echoed softly through the space. Gorman turned to Curtis. 'Oh, I don't think I can do this. It's been seven years since I did a big oil!' Suddenly, he dipped a large brush in white paint and in one continuous stroke painted two large seated women. It happened so quickly, so effortlessly, I forgot to push my shutter. All of us were stunned. It was so beautiful, so Oriental, and it materialized right before our eyes. Al threw his arms around Gorman. Gorman, embarrassed, muttered, 'Oh, it's not done yet!' He looked my way. I got my photograph."—Chuck Henningsen

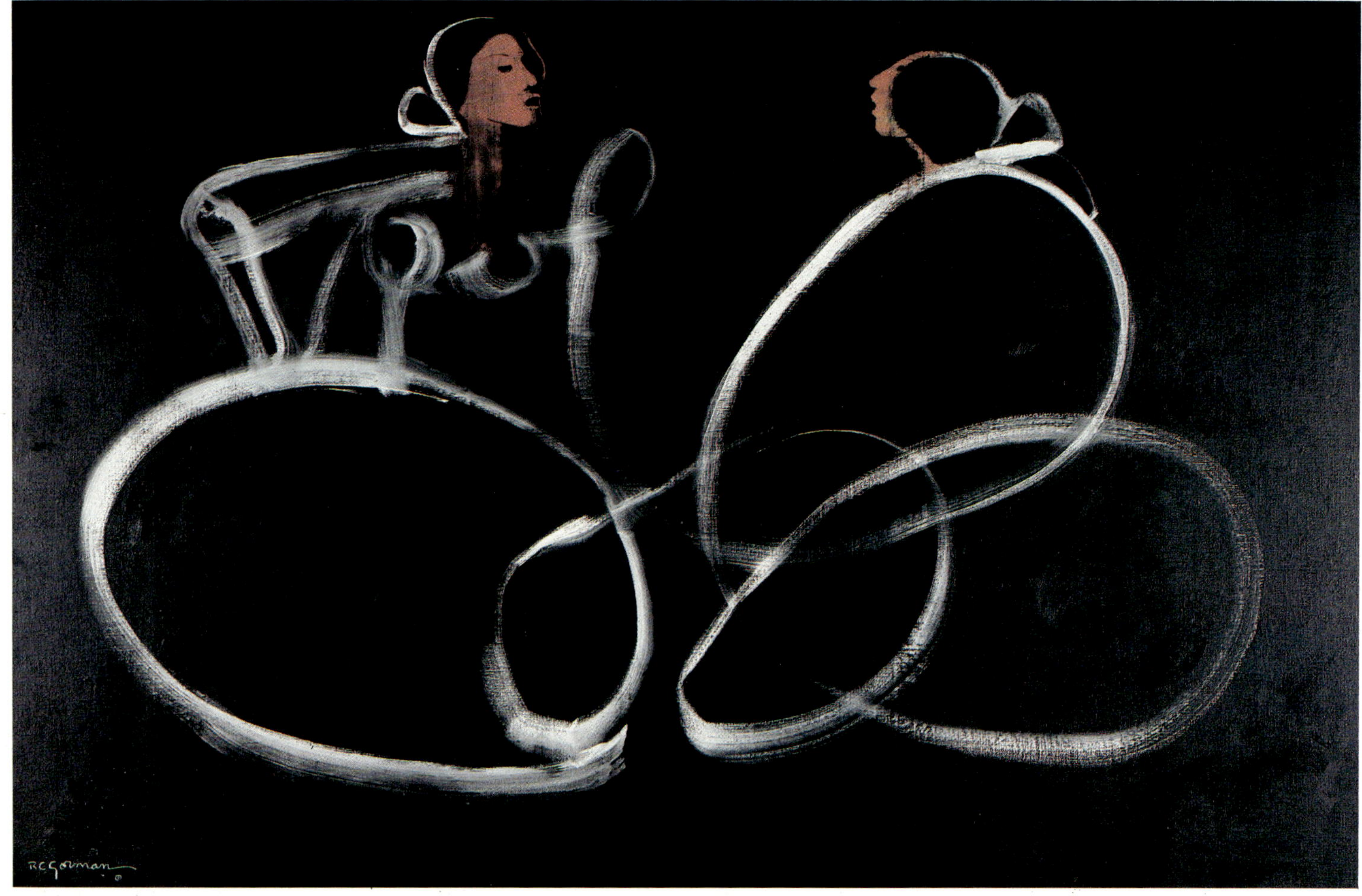

Two Women,
oil on canvas, 1981

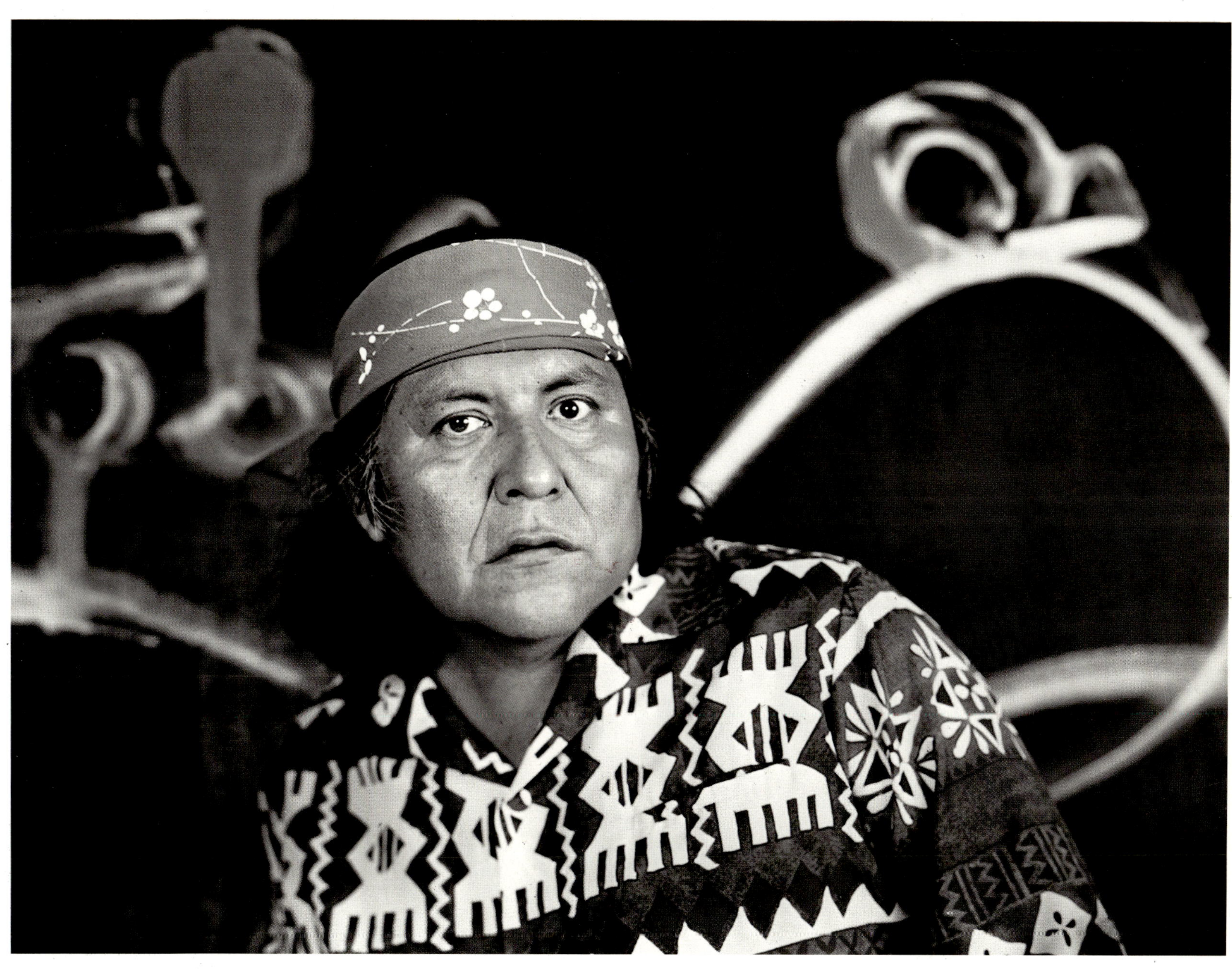

Gorman,
moments after completing **Two Women**,
Taos, 1981

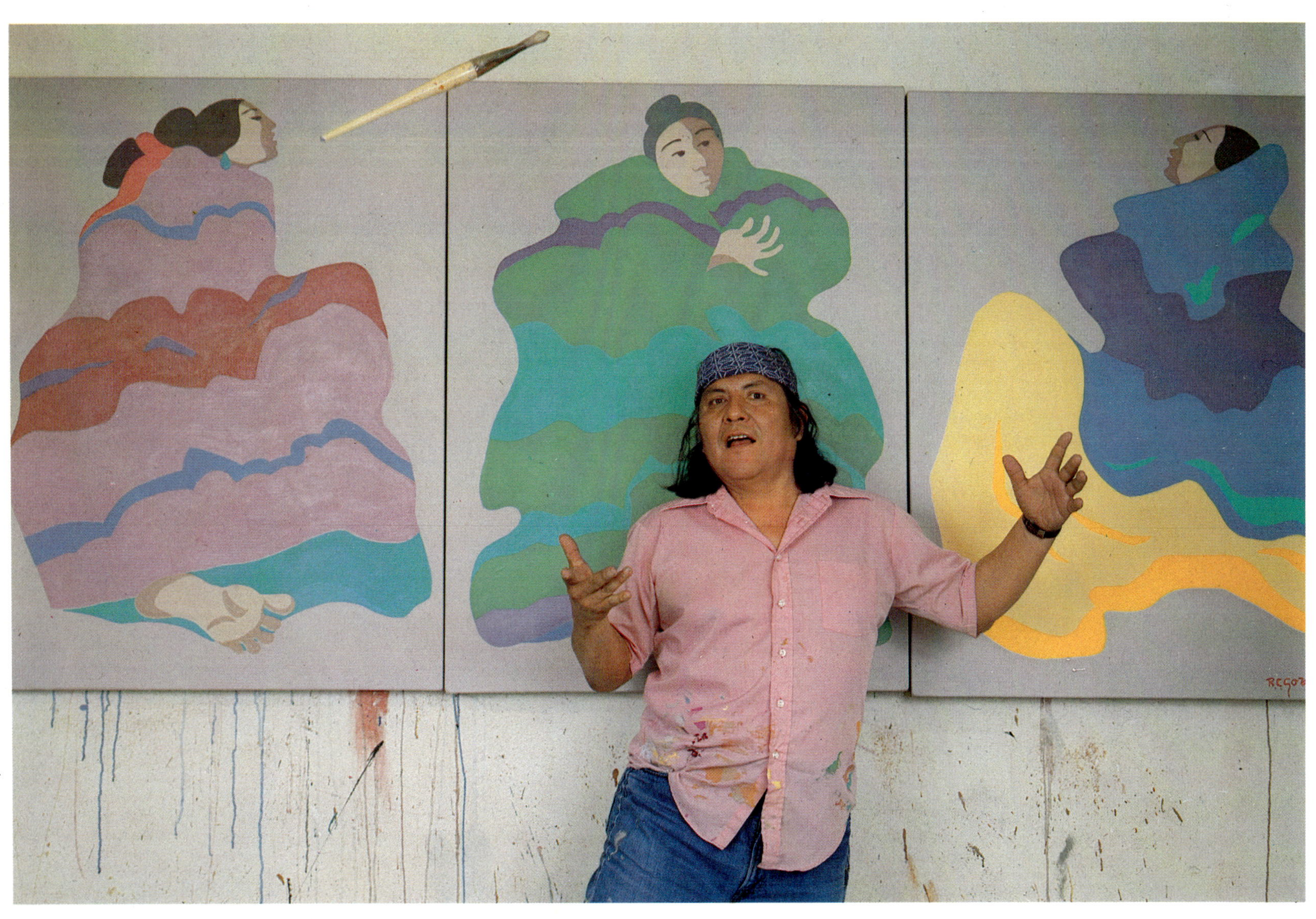

Gorman celebrating completion of triptych, **Storyteller**,
Taos, 1981

Gorman works fluidly and spontaneously. He always draws from live models, who arrive at his studio early in the morning. Poses and props are decided upon, and then he begins to work, accompanied by a steady stream of chatter and clowning. There is little conscious thought involved in his creative process. His art appears to be the product of his hands rather than his head. There is the sense that the physical activity of painting or sculpting is connected to a muscle memory of ages of women kneading bread or weaving rugs, or men pounding stamped designs into silver jewelry. Gorman's is an earthy art, and its subject is often the hands and feet of his models. It has a basic majesty and dignity not unlike the sculpture of Rodin, in which the power of the human figure is symbolized in massive hands and feet, our tools for movement, expression, and accomplishment.

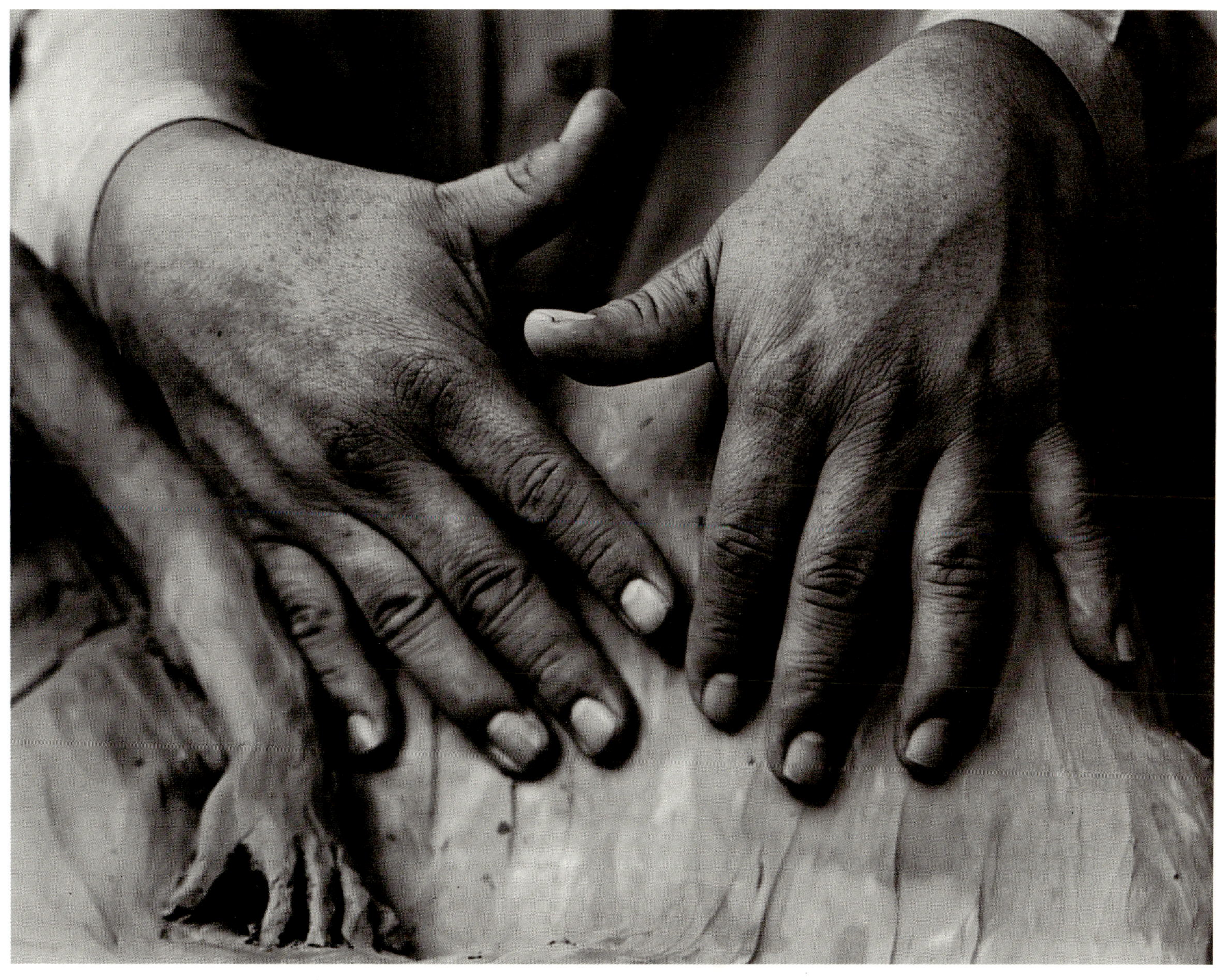

Gorman's hands sculpting clay,
San Francisco, California, 1980

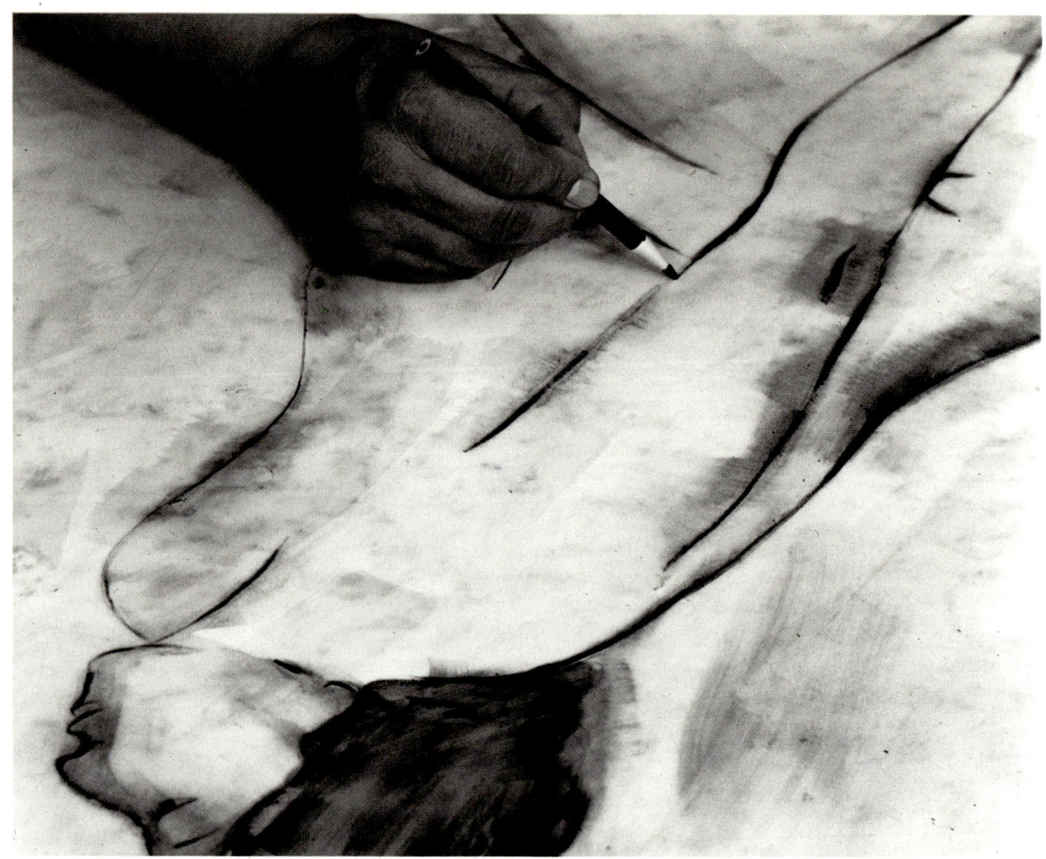

Gorman drawing
on lithography stone,
Taos, 1981

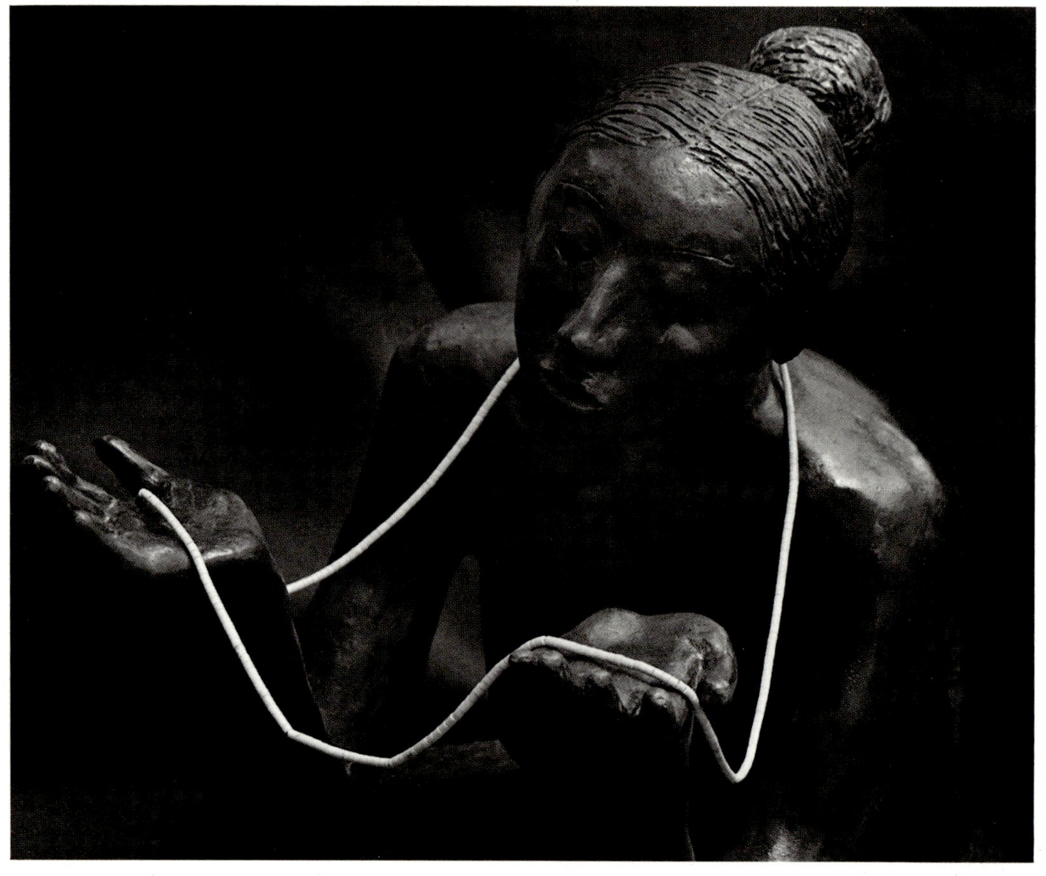

Cocheta,
bronze casting,
Editions Press, 1980

"Gorman's best drawings are often those that come the quickest and most spontaneously. He has said that for him art should be like a prayer he says every morning."—Curtis Grubbs

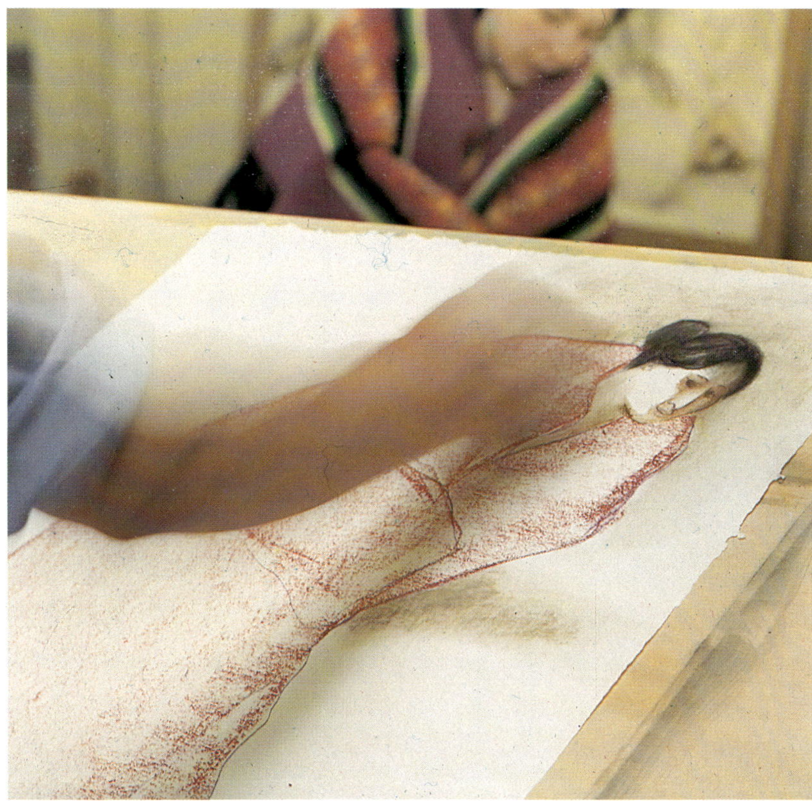

Gorman at work,
San Francisco, 1980

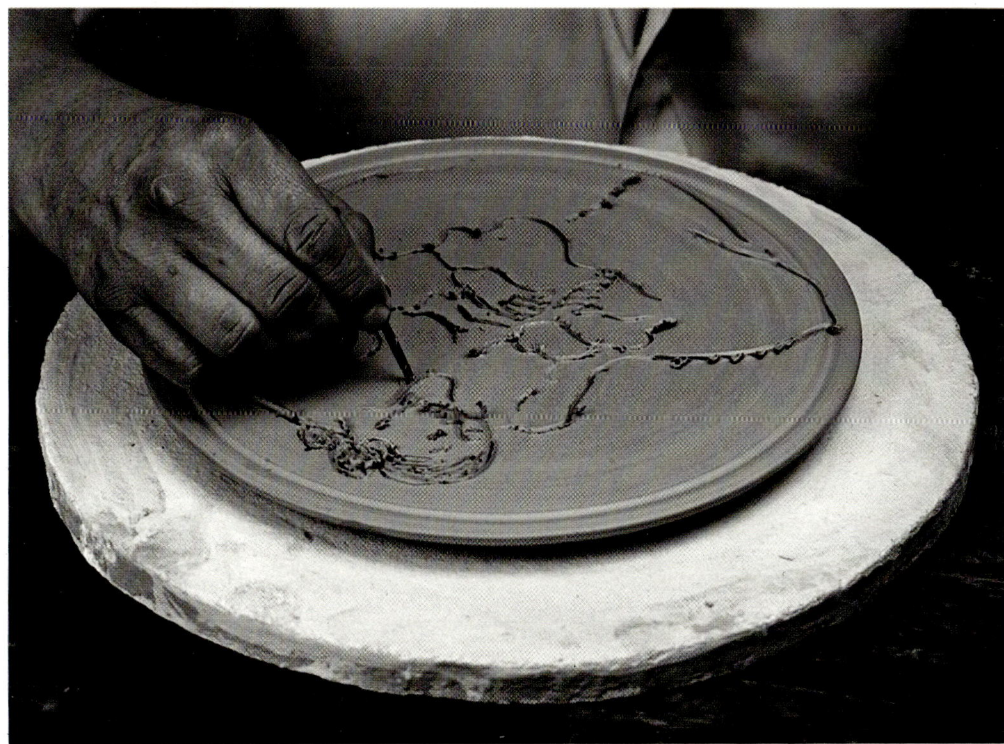

Gorman drawing on ceramic plate,
Taos, 1981

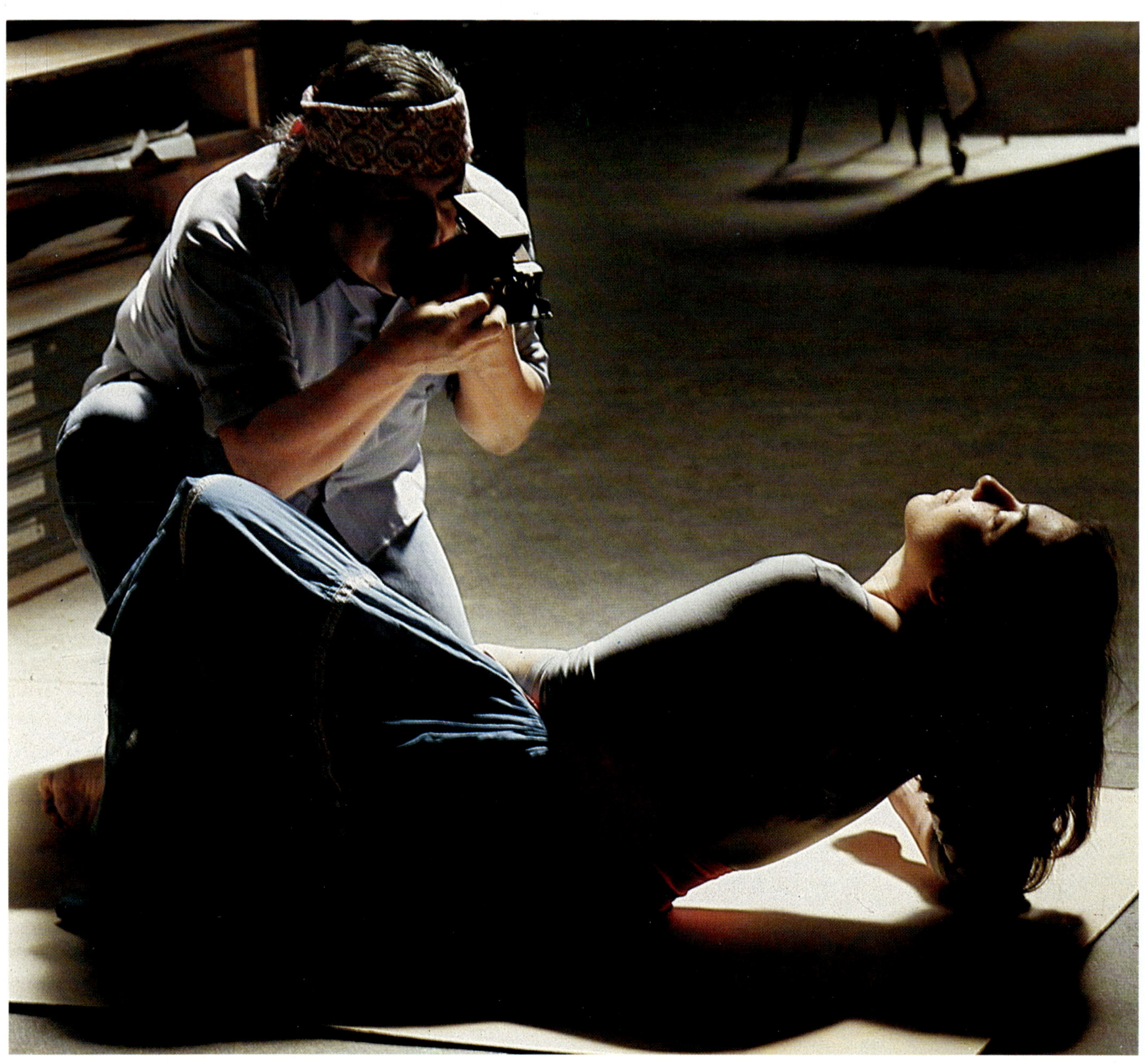

Gorman photographing model Evie Lincoln,
San Francisco, 1980

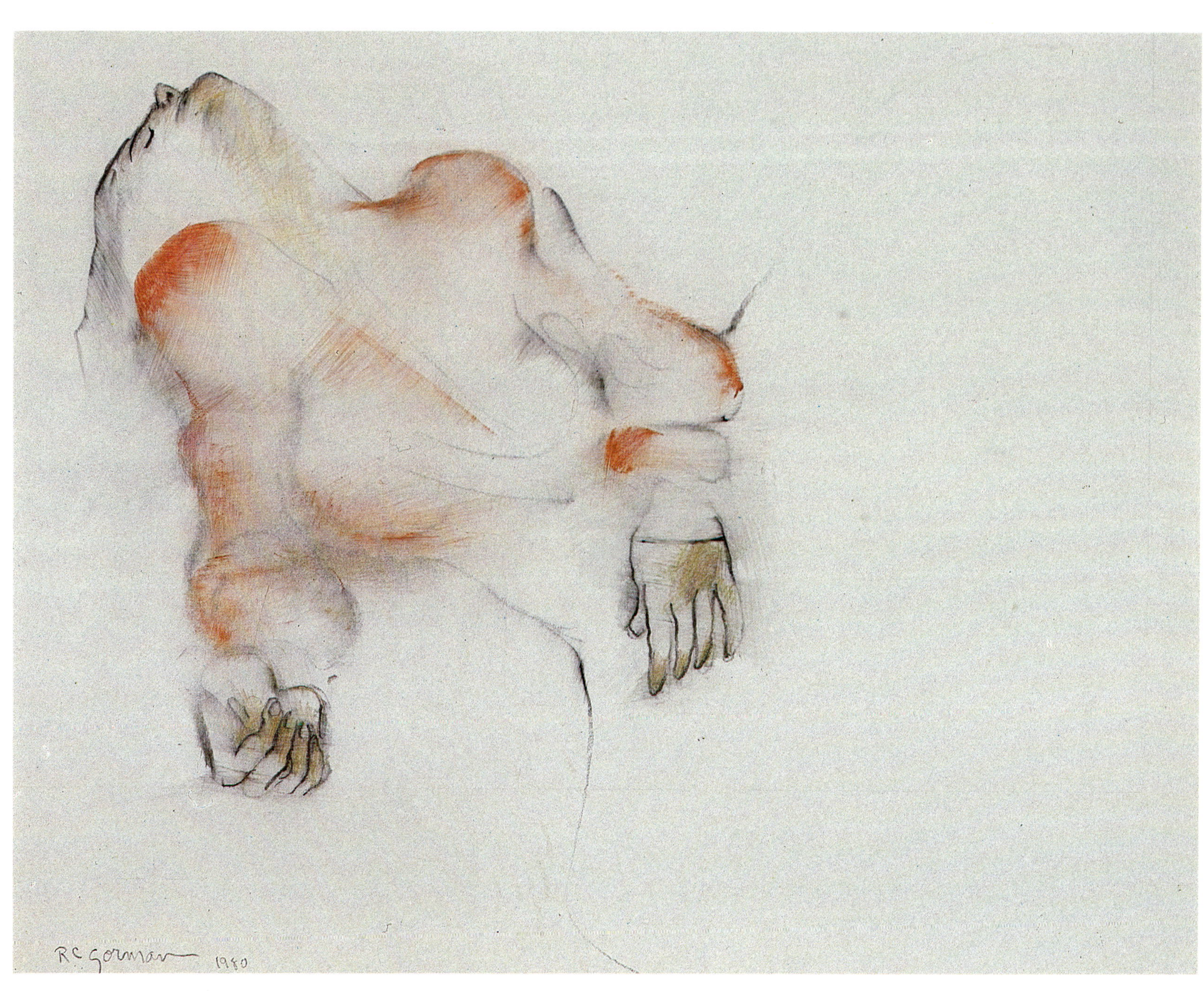

Study for Sculpture, Rosa;
oil pastel drawing, 1980

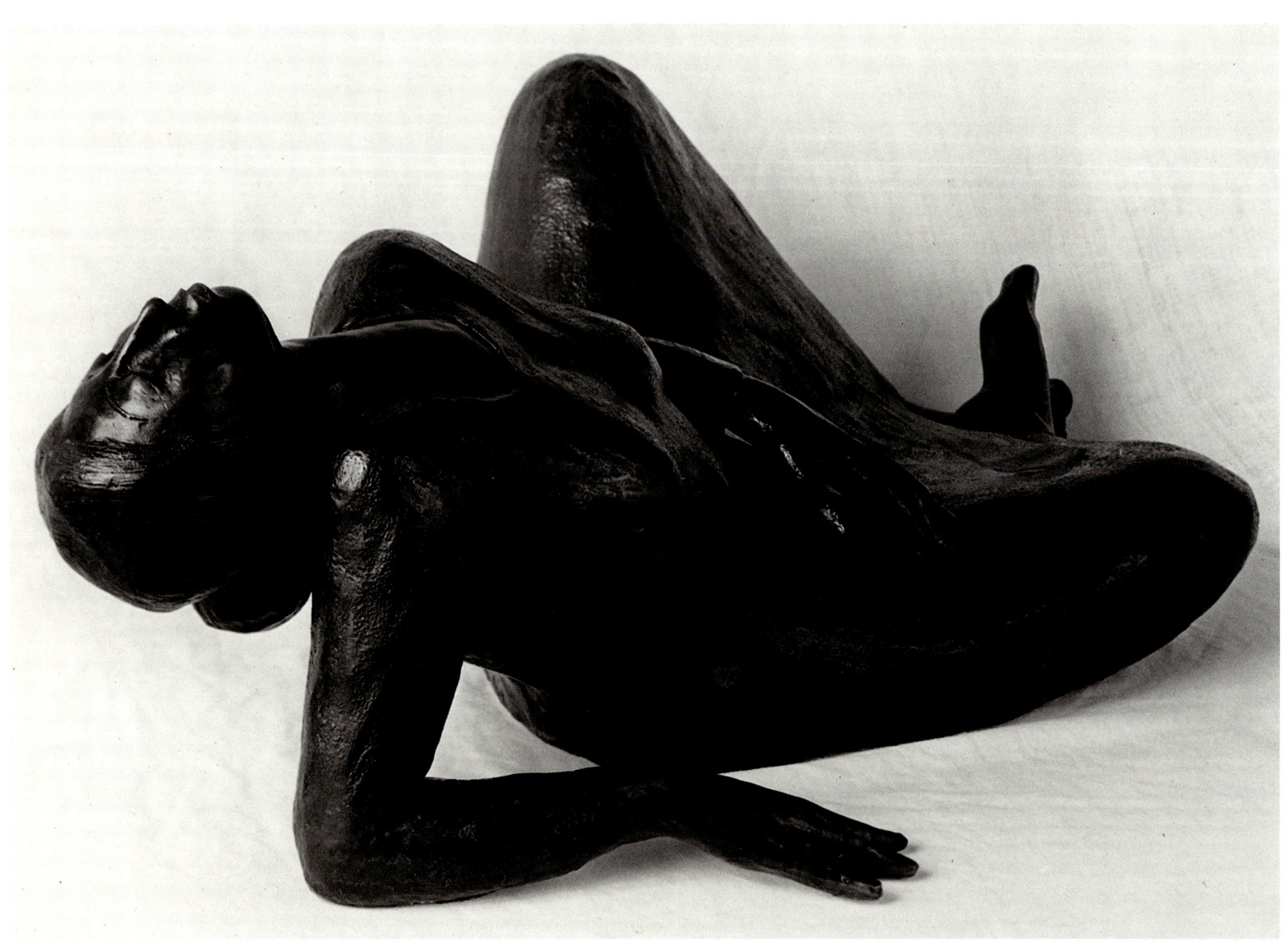

Rosa,
bronze casting, Editions Press, 1980

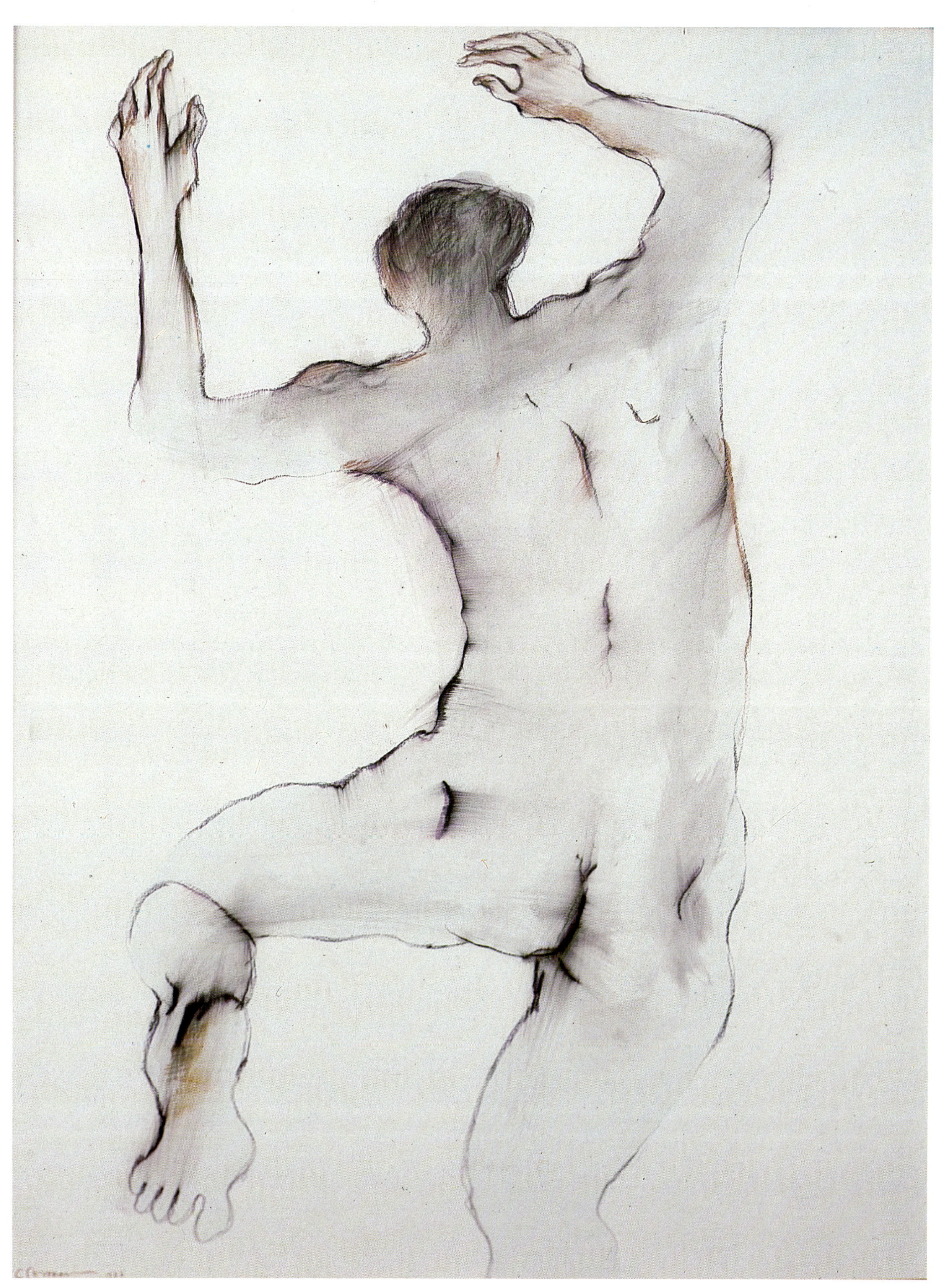

Male nude,
oil pastel drawing, 1982, Gallery Mack, New York

"This is a working body. Even though she's faced away, I know she's kneading bread or cutting meat for dinner."—R.C.G.

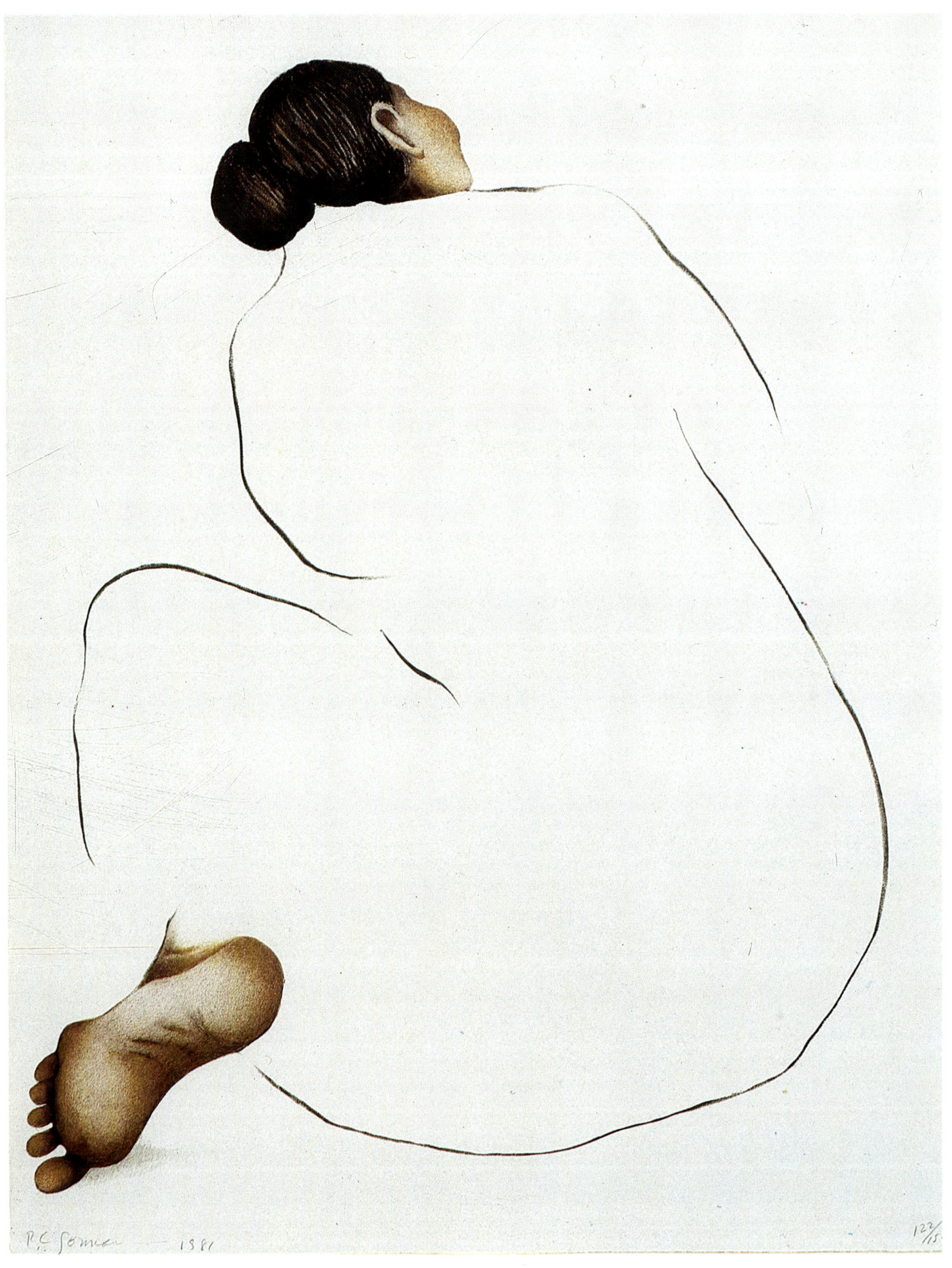

Kali,
lithograph, Origins Press, 1981

"I don't have a thing about shoes, so maybe it's feet. Shoes don't motivate me. Bare feet do. What does an actor on stage work with? His hands and feet. That determines how solid he is on stage."—R.C.G.

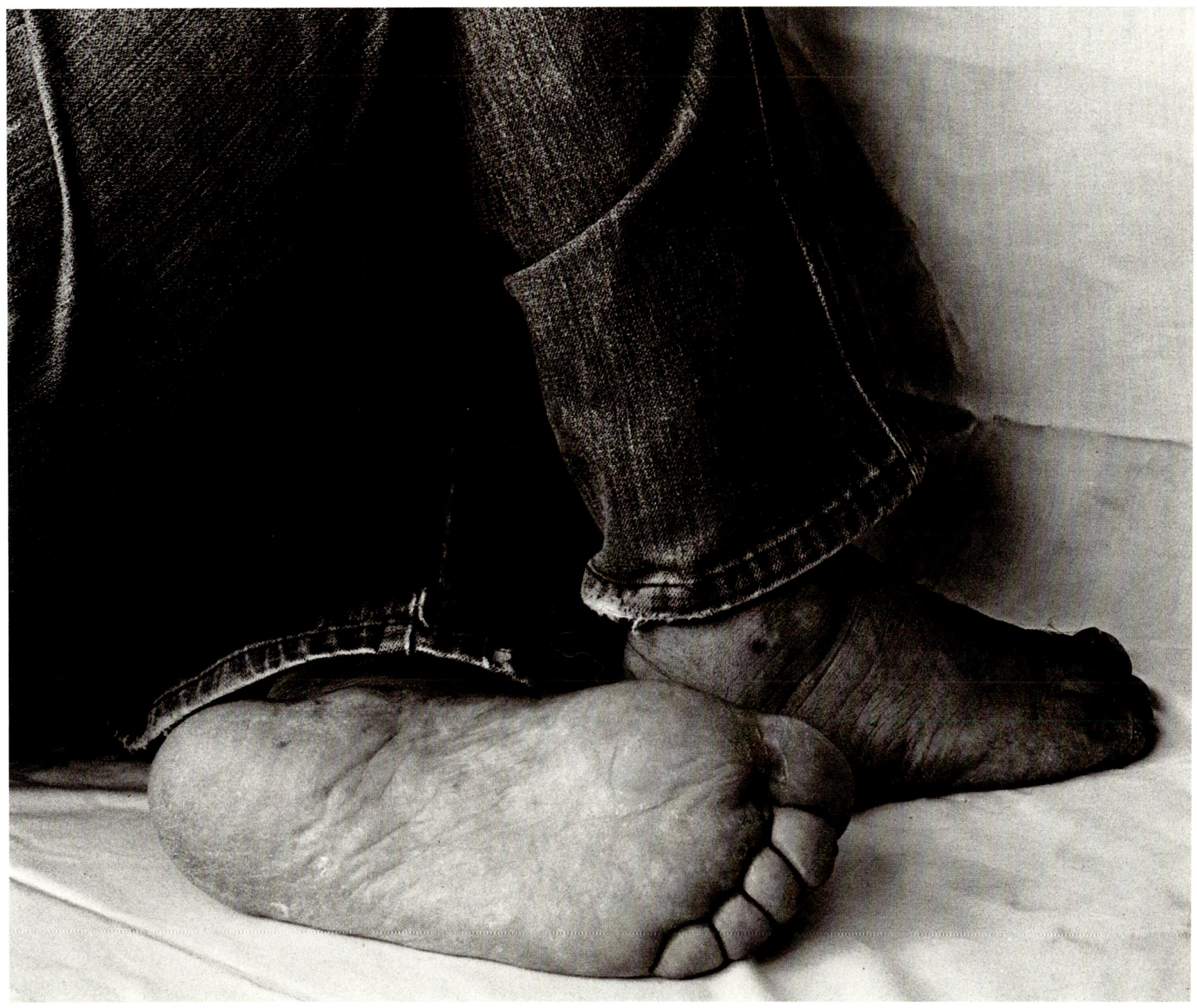

Gorman's feet,
Taos, 1980

"During the several years I photographed Gorman, I was constantly struck by the amount of laughter that always seems to prevail in his house and surroundings. Celebrities and laborers alike troop through his world, and Gorman constantly holds court amidst joking and giggling. Gorman's penchant for fun and chatter is also evident while he draws or paints, and I felt frustrated trying to capture the experience by pointing my camera over his shoulder. Finally I hit on an idea; I set up a Plexiglas easel and snapped away as the art, the emotion, and humor poured out."—Chuck Henningsen

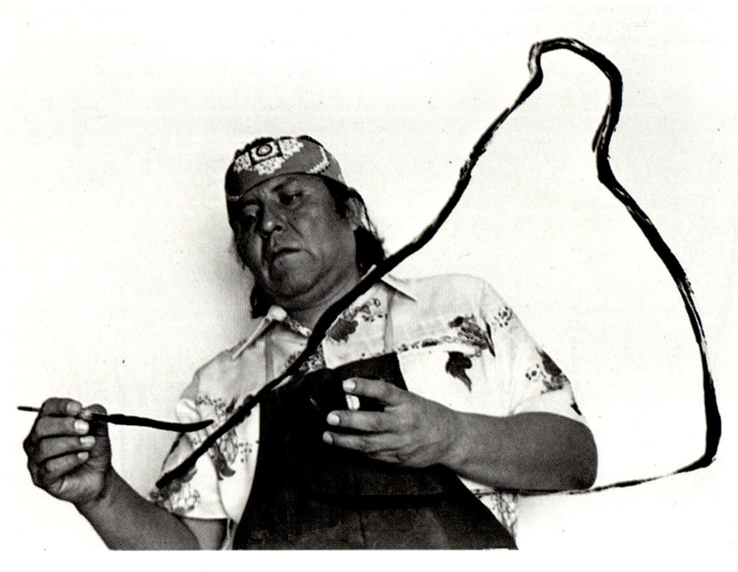

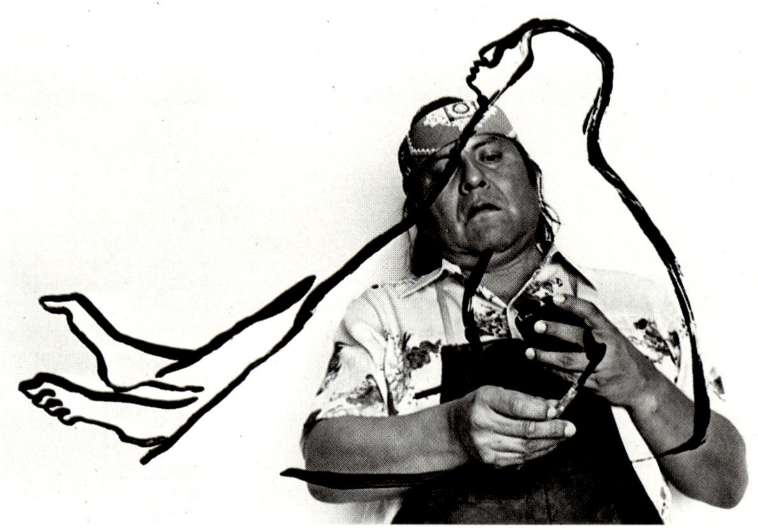

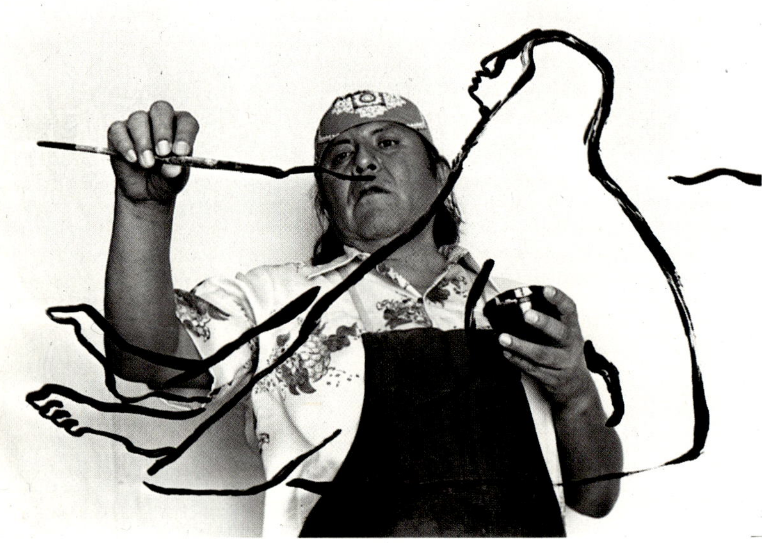

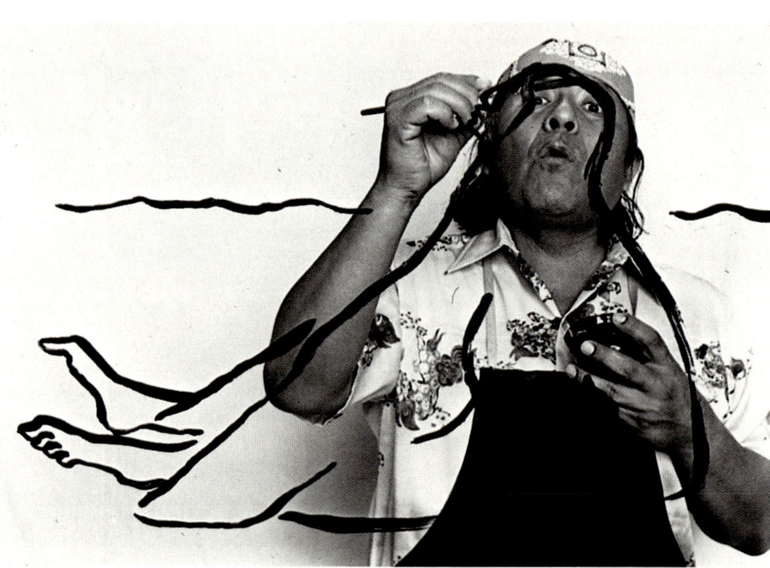

Gorman executes see-through painting,
San Francisco, 1980

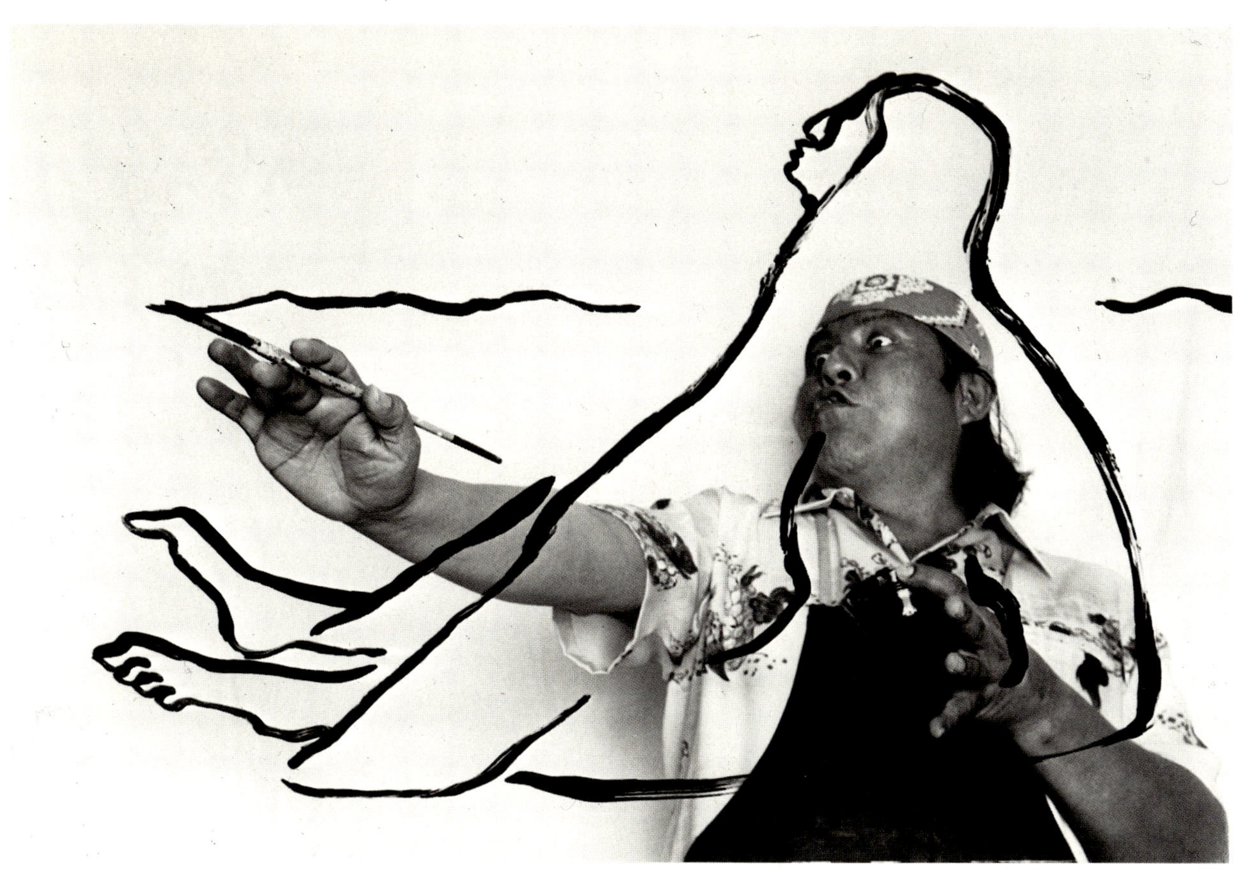

Gorman enjoys
the last line,
San Francisco, 1980

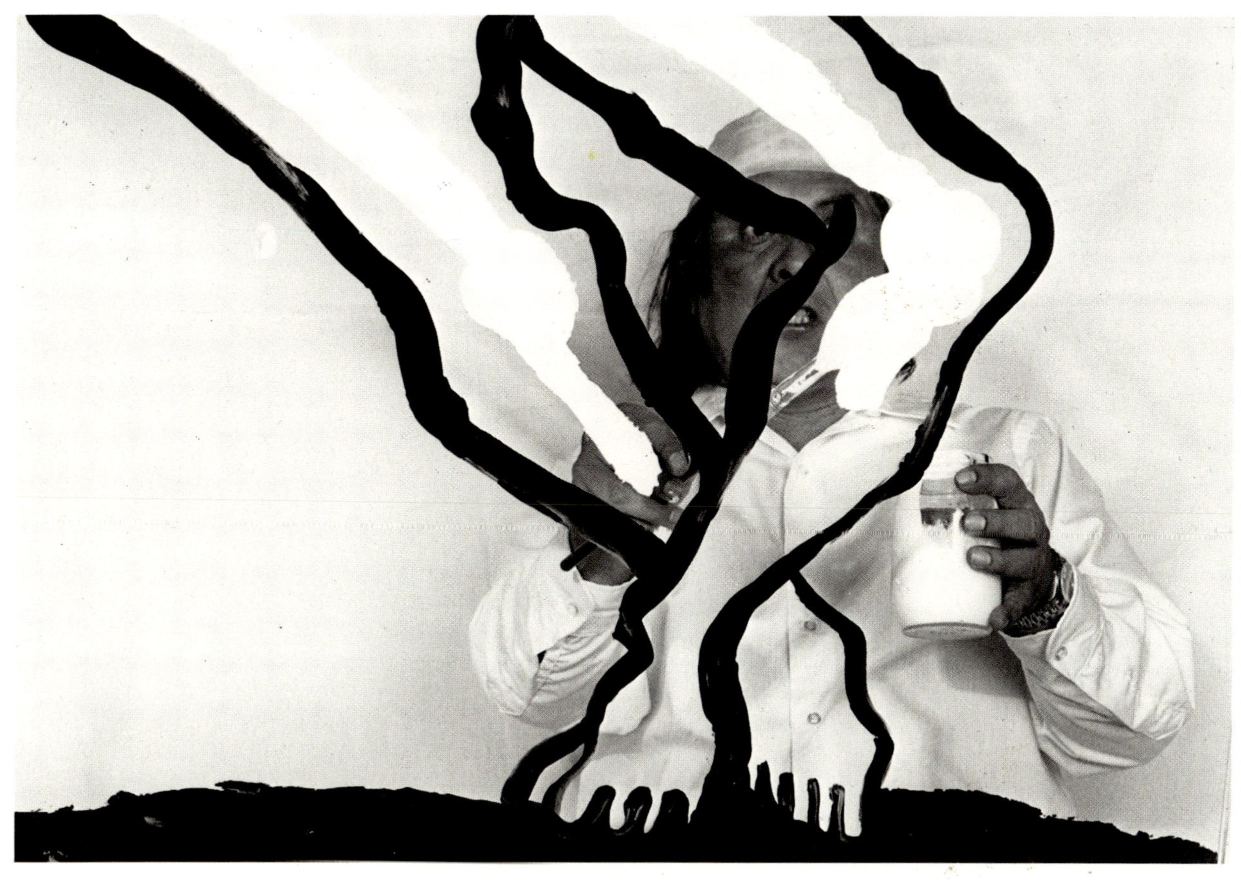

Gorman paints
Michael's Feet
on Plexiglas,
Taos, 1980

With the exception of his niece Miriam, Gorman's models are seldom Indian. He searches instead for characteristics of every woman.

"I look for physical things in a model, like bone structure and grace. The model sets the mood for the piece, so she should be cheerful and strong. Also, she needs the ability to project, like Elizabeth Taylor, who can project such heat! Or Maria Benitez, the world-famous flamenco dancer from Taos. She's electric. I wish I were like that. I've met presidents and princesses, counts, one duke—deposed—and none of them had her electricity."—R.C.G.

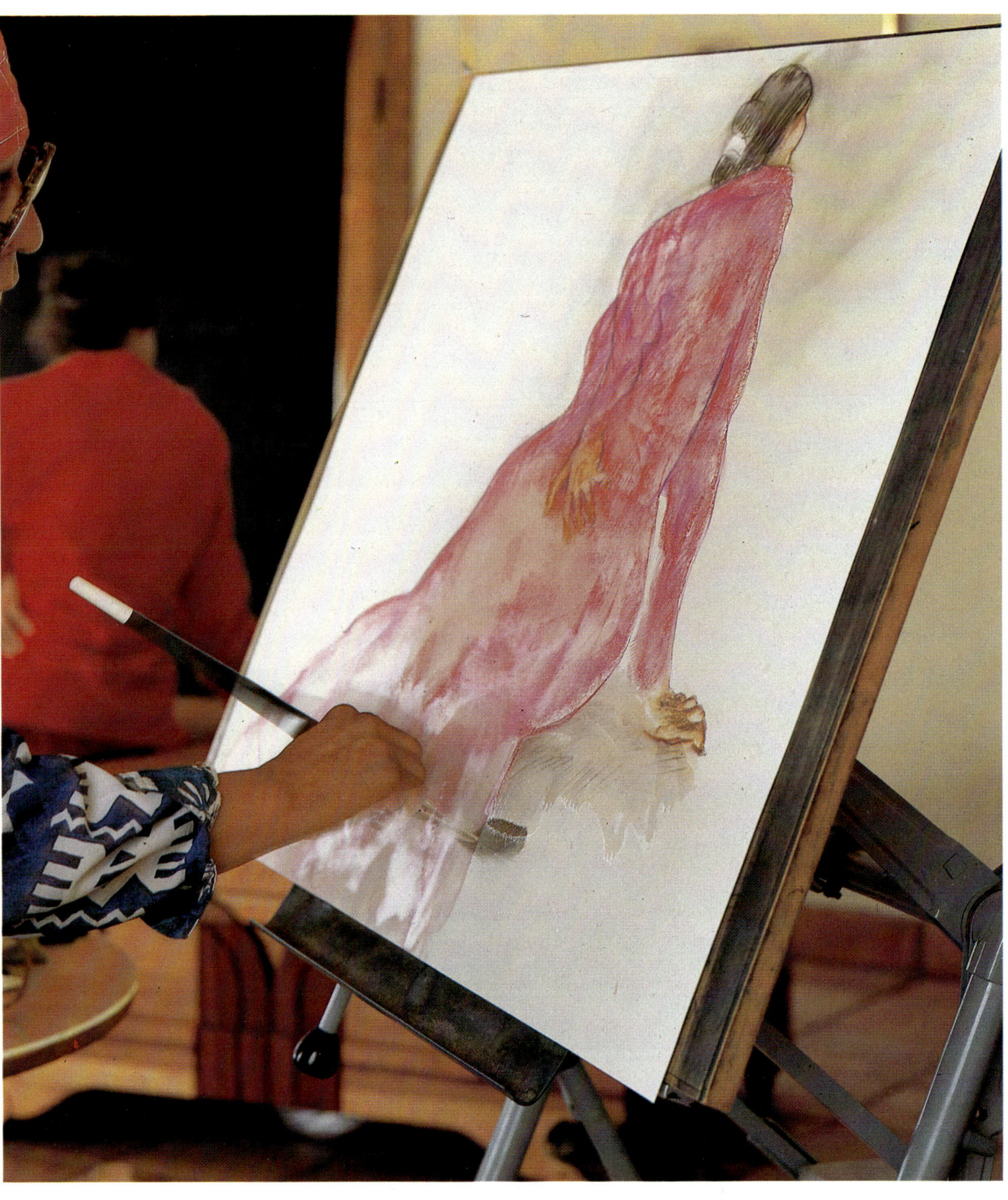

Gorman painting model Laila Bynoe in Taos studio, 1981

"Laila Bynoe was slim and unmarried when we first started working together. She's now had four or five kids. She's changed, but she's better than ever."
—R.C.G.

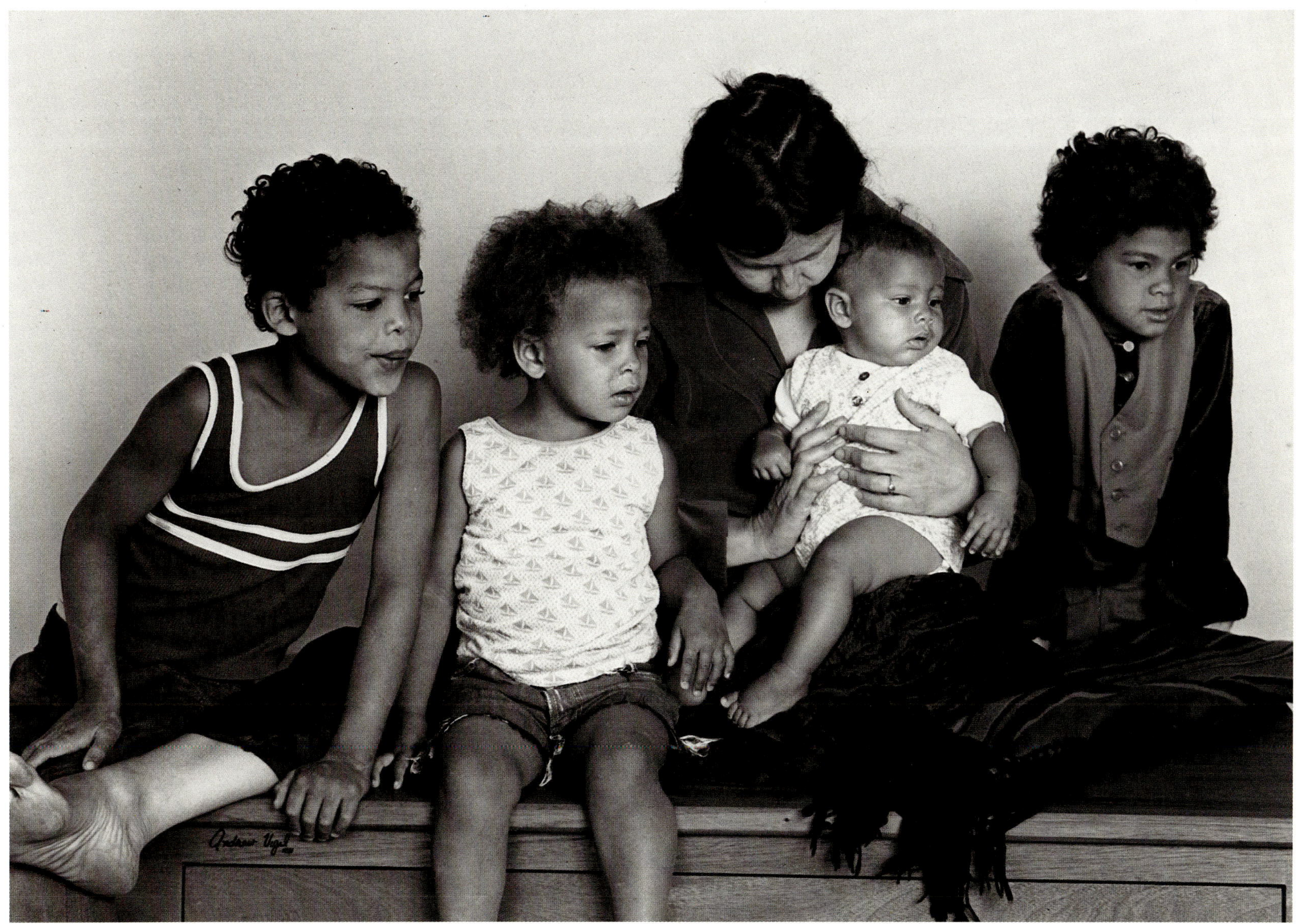

Laila Bynoe and her children,
Taos, 1981

"The older I get, the more relatives I accumulate. Miriam happens to float by at just the right time."—R.C.G.

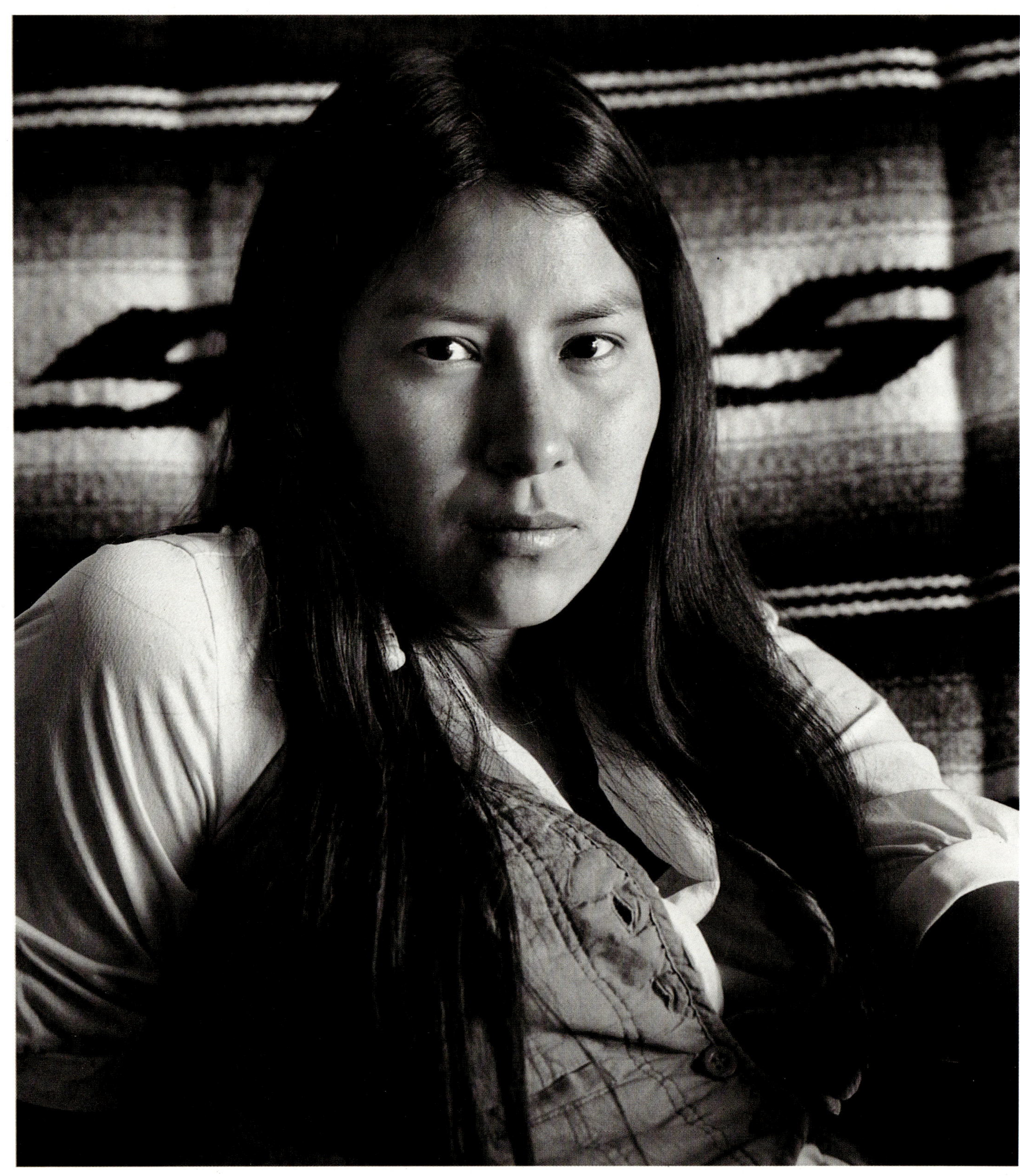

Miriam Gorman,
Taos, 1980

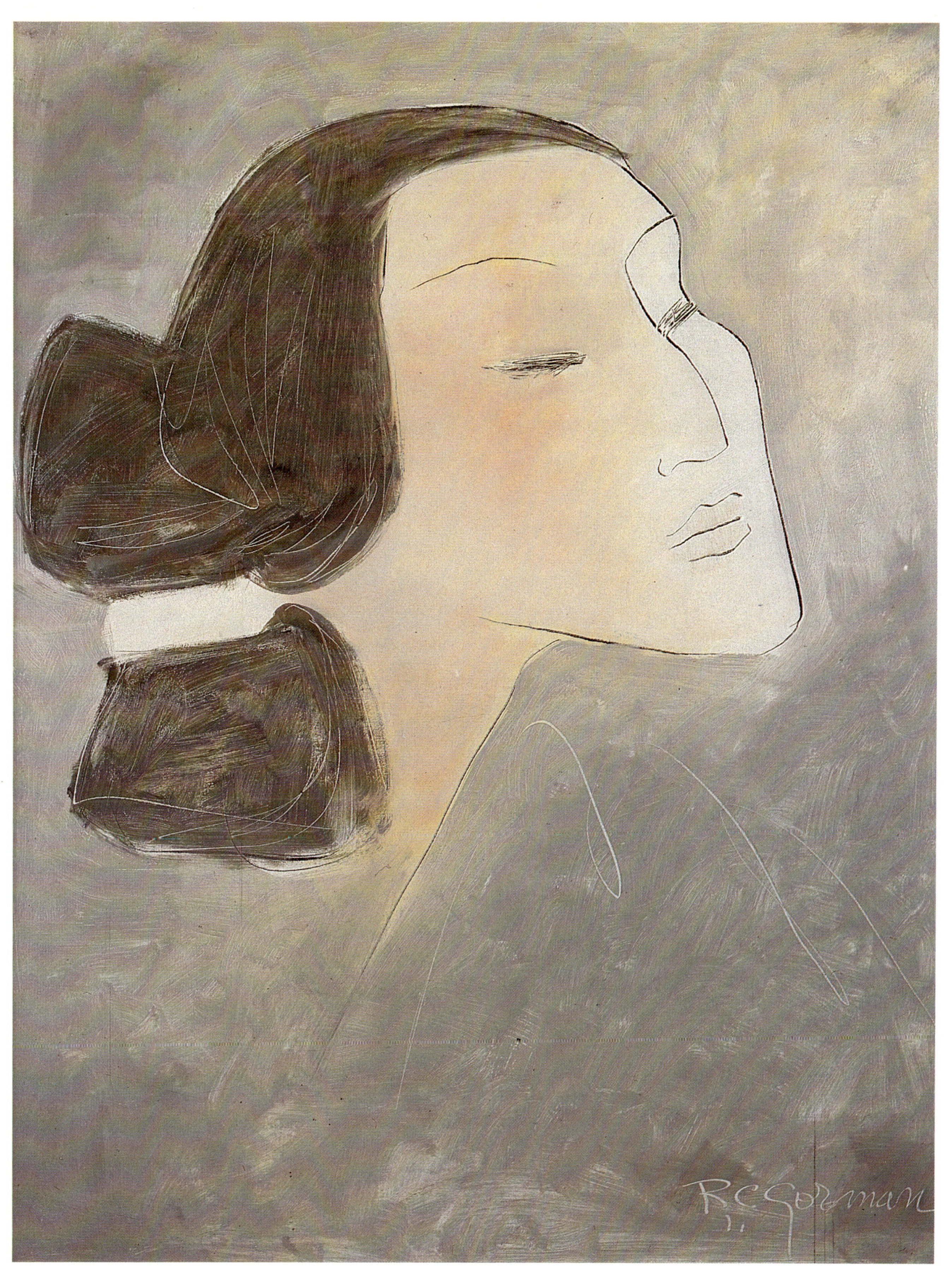

Miriam,
oil, 1981, Collection of Mr. and Mrs. Herman Deutsch,
Long Island, New York

"The most beautiful thing about this woman is her nose."—R.C.G.

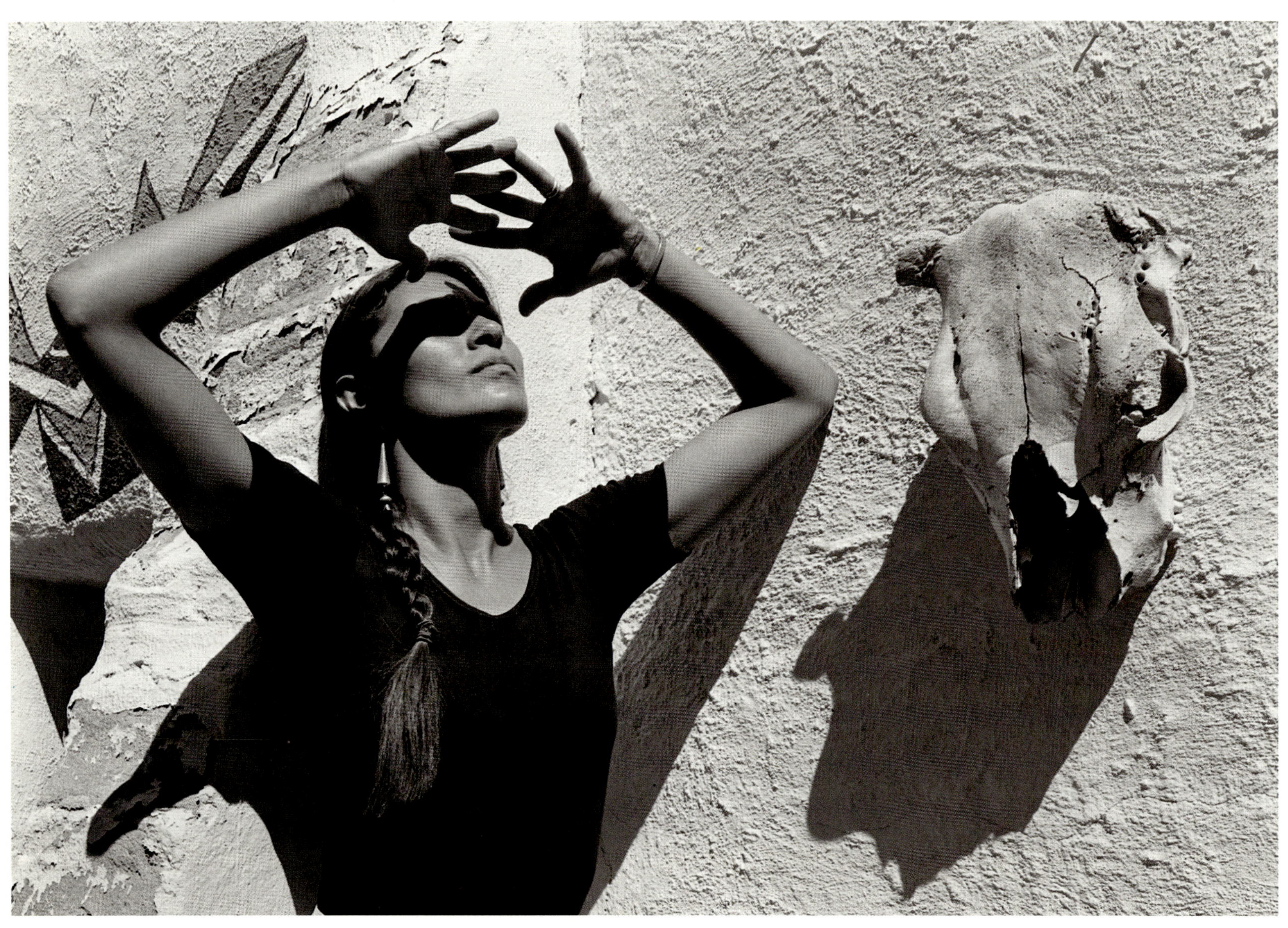

Sandra Davies, Gorman model,
at Navajo Gallery, Taos, 1980

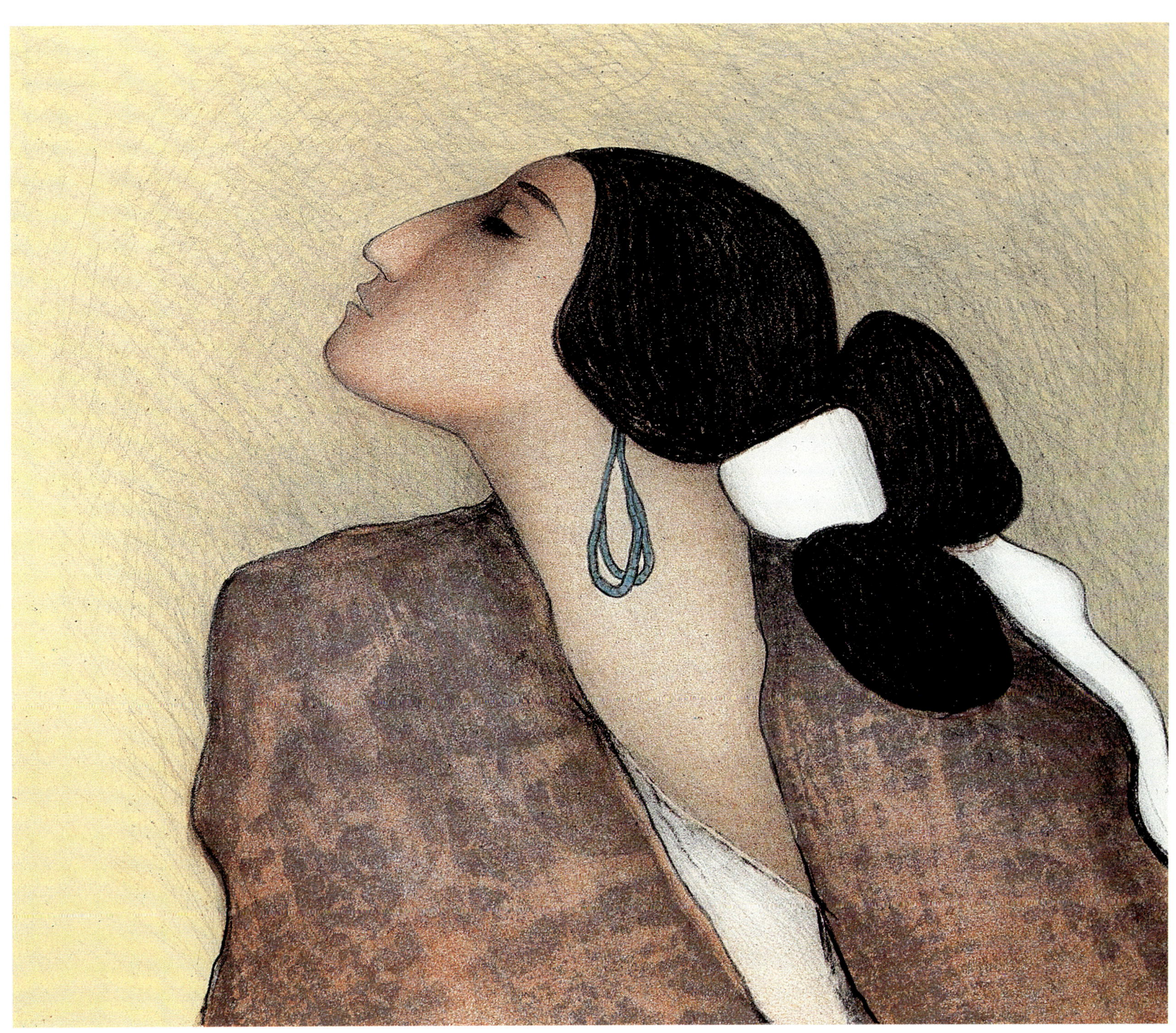

Danya,
lithograph, Western Graphics, 1980

"John and Stella are obviously proud Indians, and I respond to that. I am quite aware that I am an Indian, and I must make people respect that. By the same token, I never feel different from anyone else except when I stand in front of the mirror in the morning and get my shock treatment for the day."—R.C.G.

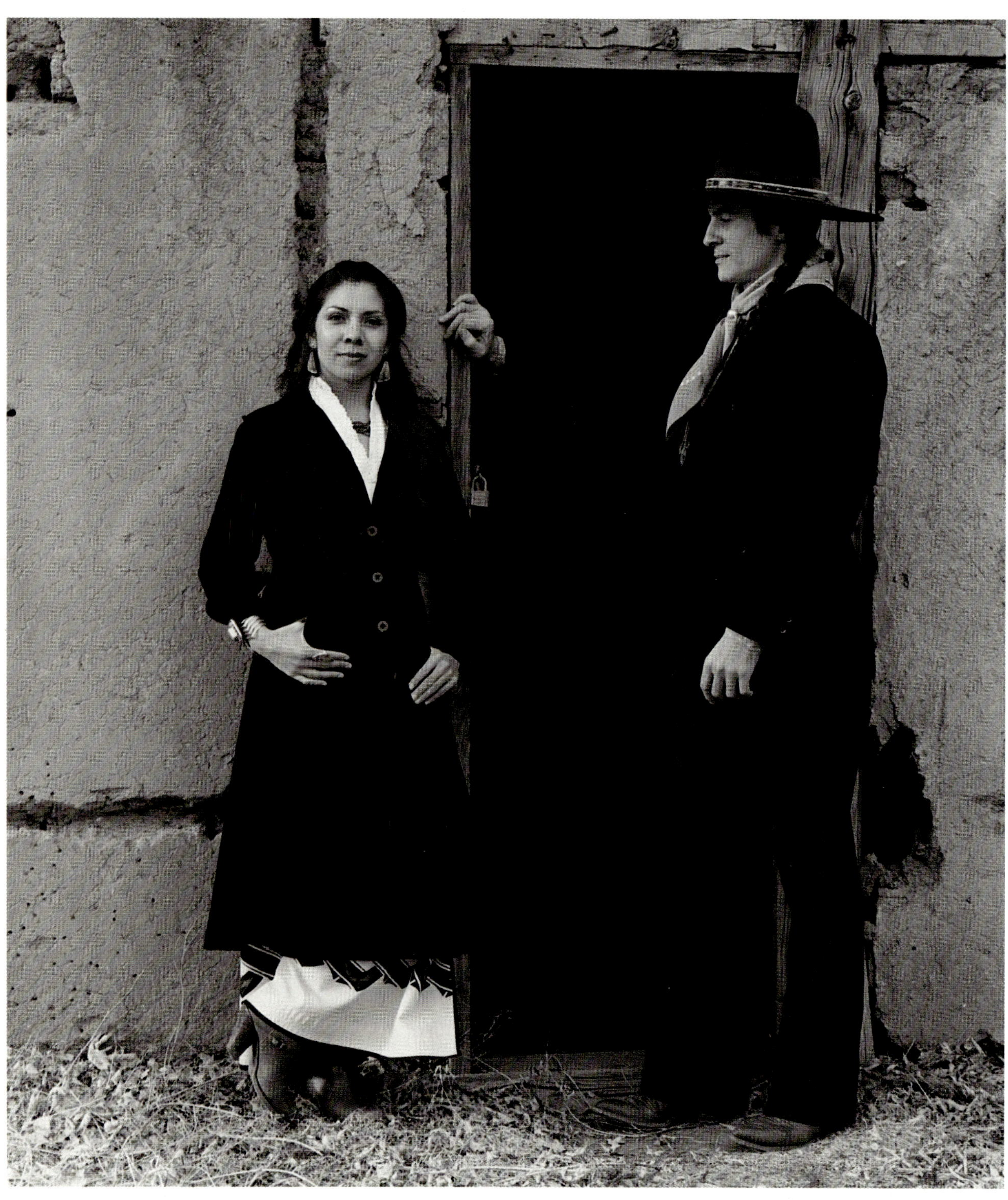

John and Stella Eagleday,
Taos, 1981

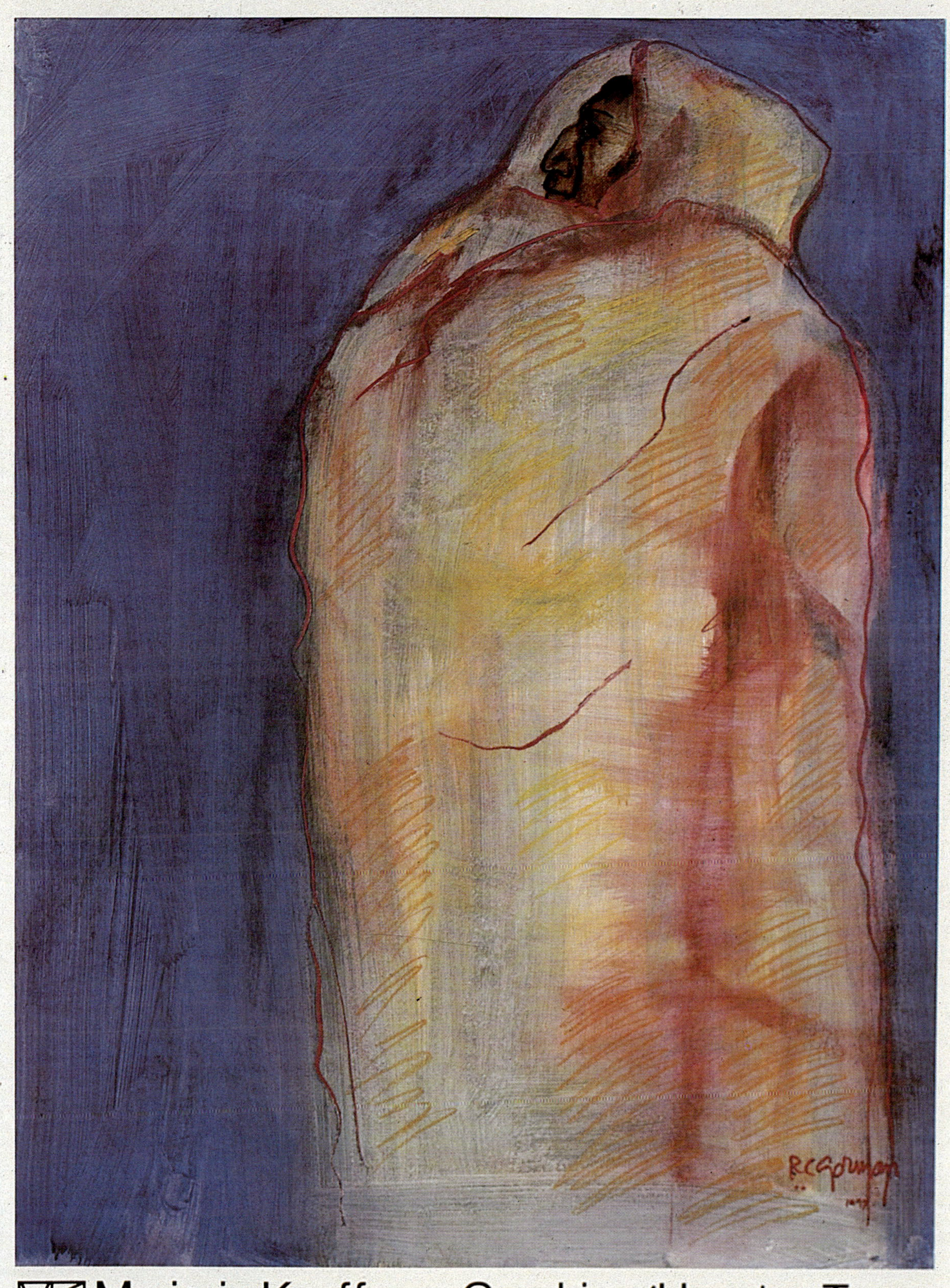

Taos Man,
poster, Marjorie Kauffman Graphics,
Houston, 1977

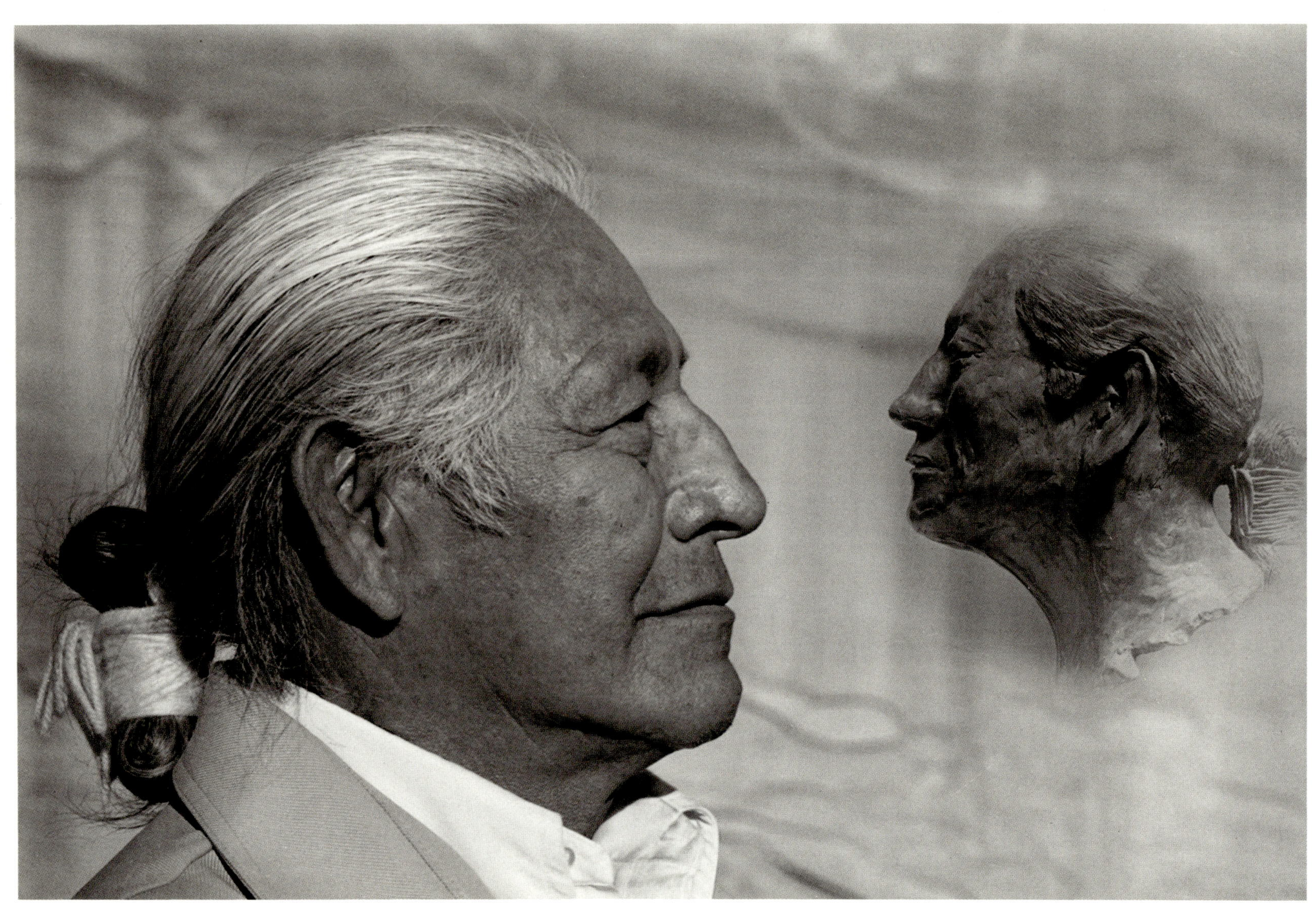

Carl Gorman with **Code Talker**,
bronze casting by R. C. Gorman (Editions Press), Taos

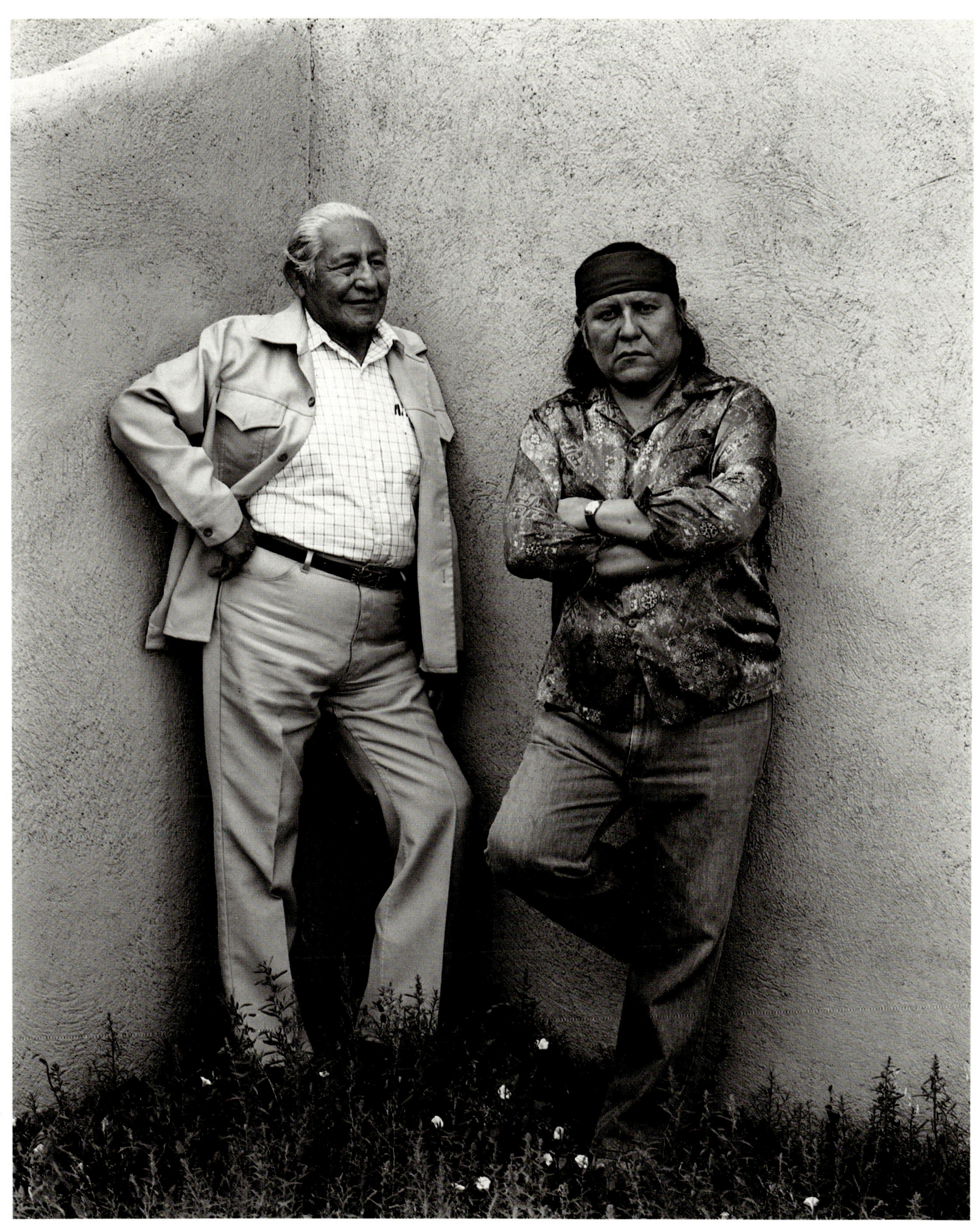

Carl and R. C. Gorman, father and son,
Taos, 1981

"This looks like a movie set. I gave a party for Bob Young, the architect who designed my studio. Sonny had wanted to come here and dance, so he brought his great troupe. Ginger is not the Hollywood princess type. She's real."—R.C.G.

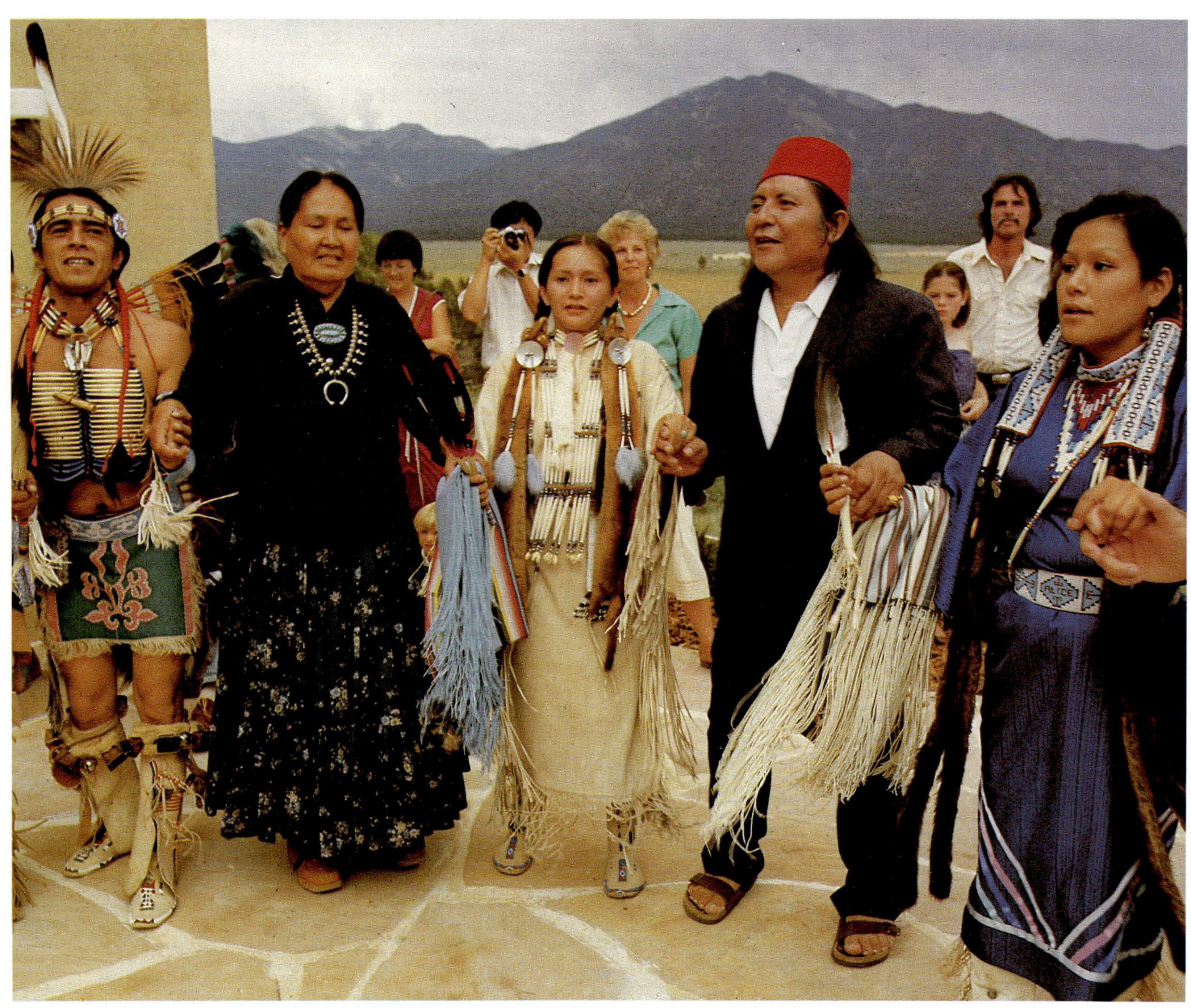

Sonny Spruce, Aunt Mary, Ginger Archuleta, R. C. Gorman, and Taos Mountain Shadow Dancers, Taos, 1981

"Like all the Navajos, I have a great reverence for that mountain and consequently for the people of Taos Pueblo. They're much quieter than Navajos, they take themselves more seriously. Maybe it's a protection against the tourists that flock around them and invade their privacy day in and day out. But they're a beautiful tribe. They love ceremony and color, and they include religion in everything they do. The Christmas Eve dance at the Pueblo is one of the greatest shows on earth."—R.C.G.

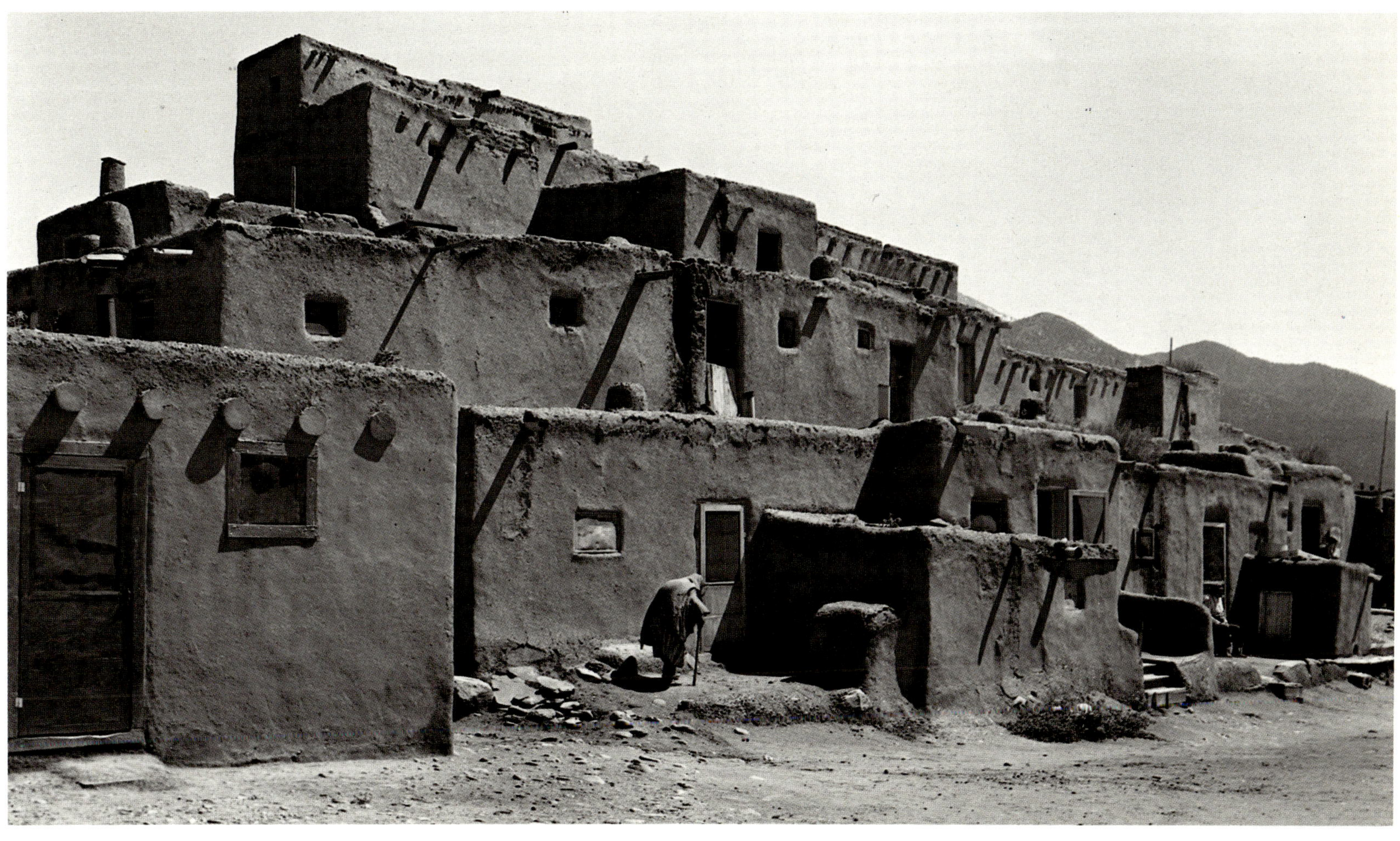

Taos Pueblo,
Taos, 1980

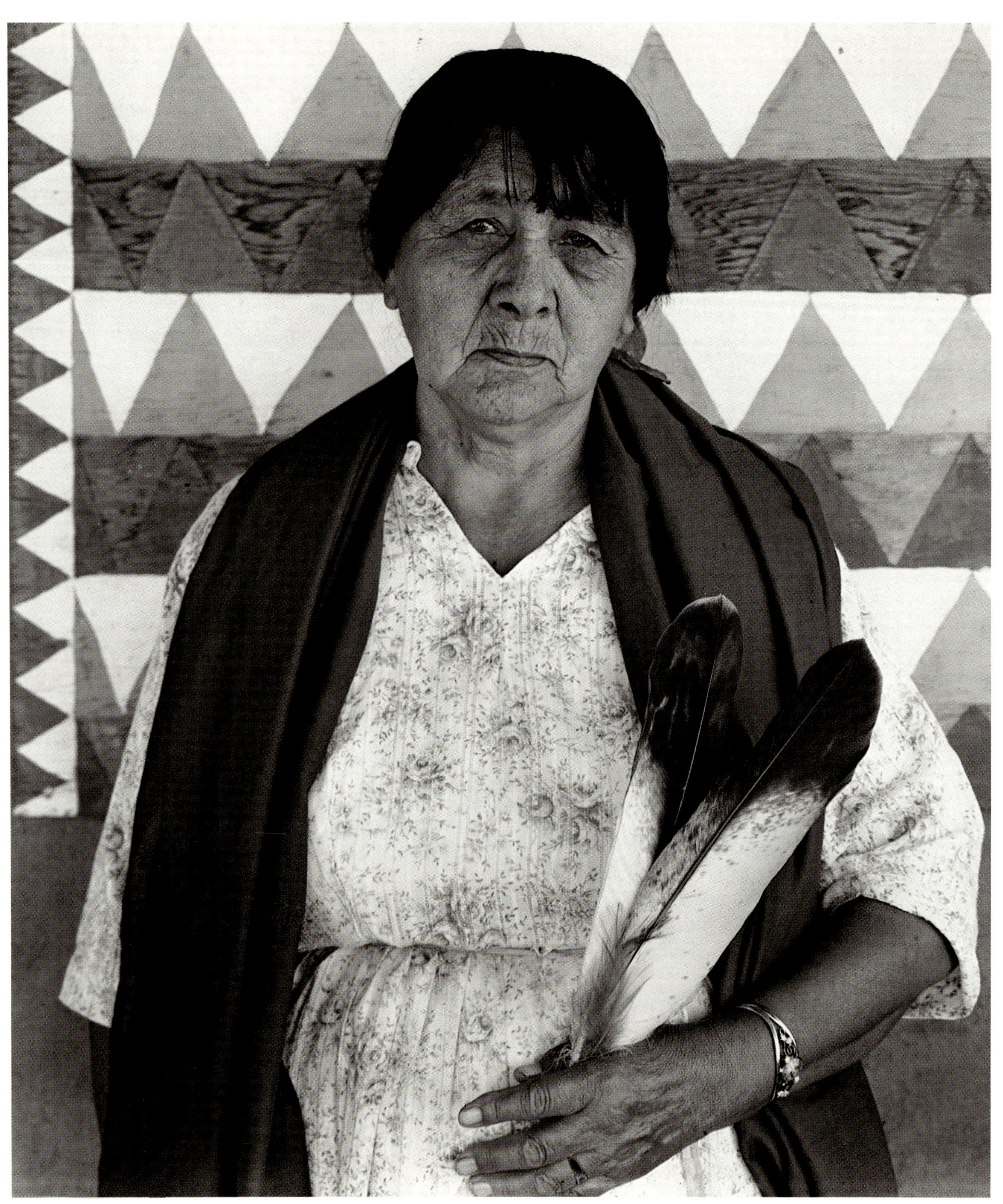

106 Eaglefeather Woman,
Taos Pueblo, Taos, 1980

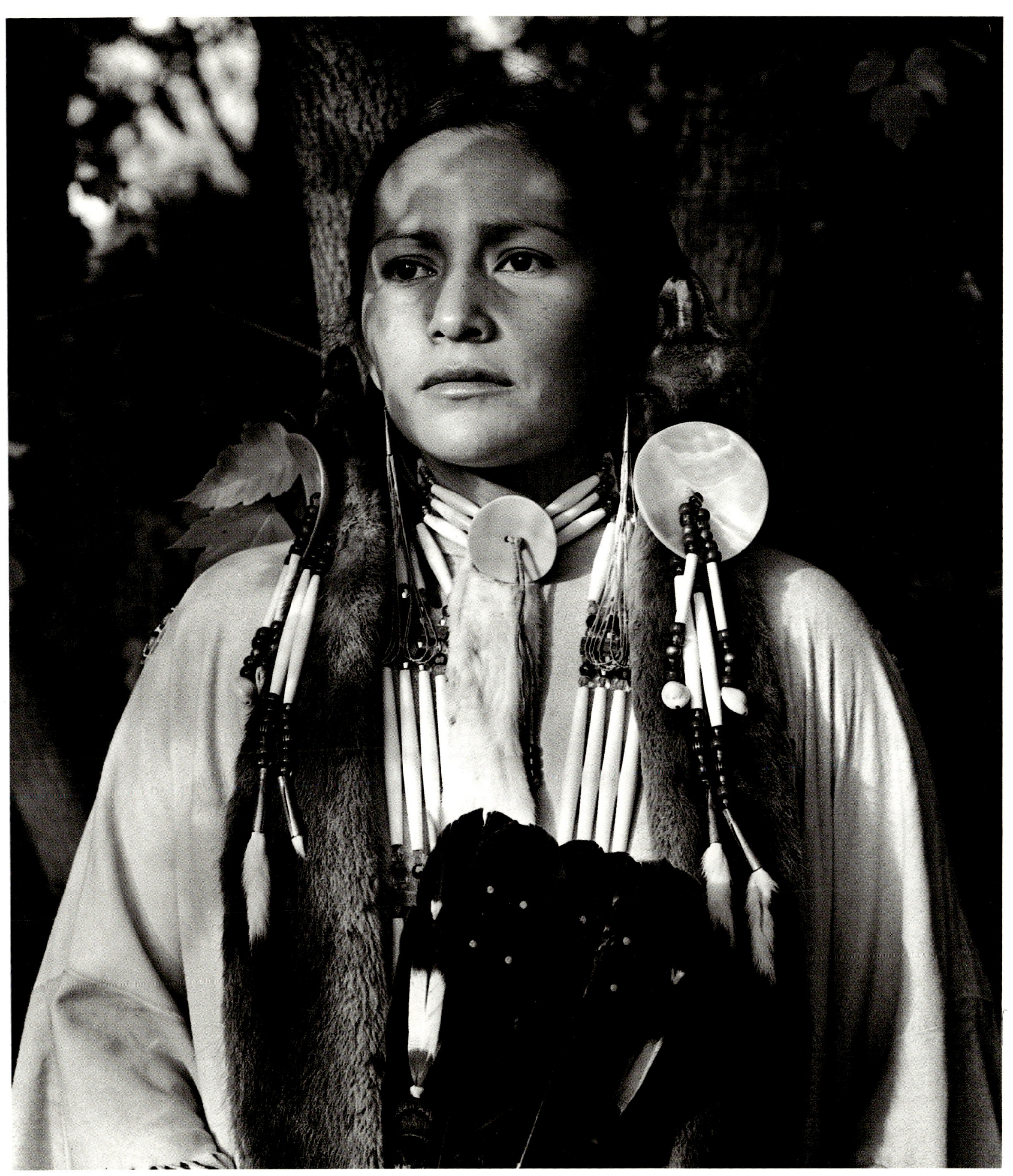

Ginger Archuleta in dance costume,
Taos Pueblo, 1981

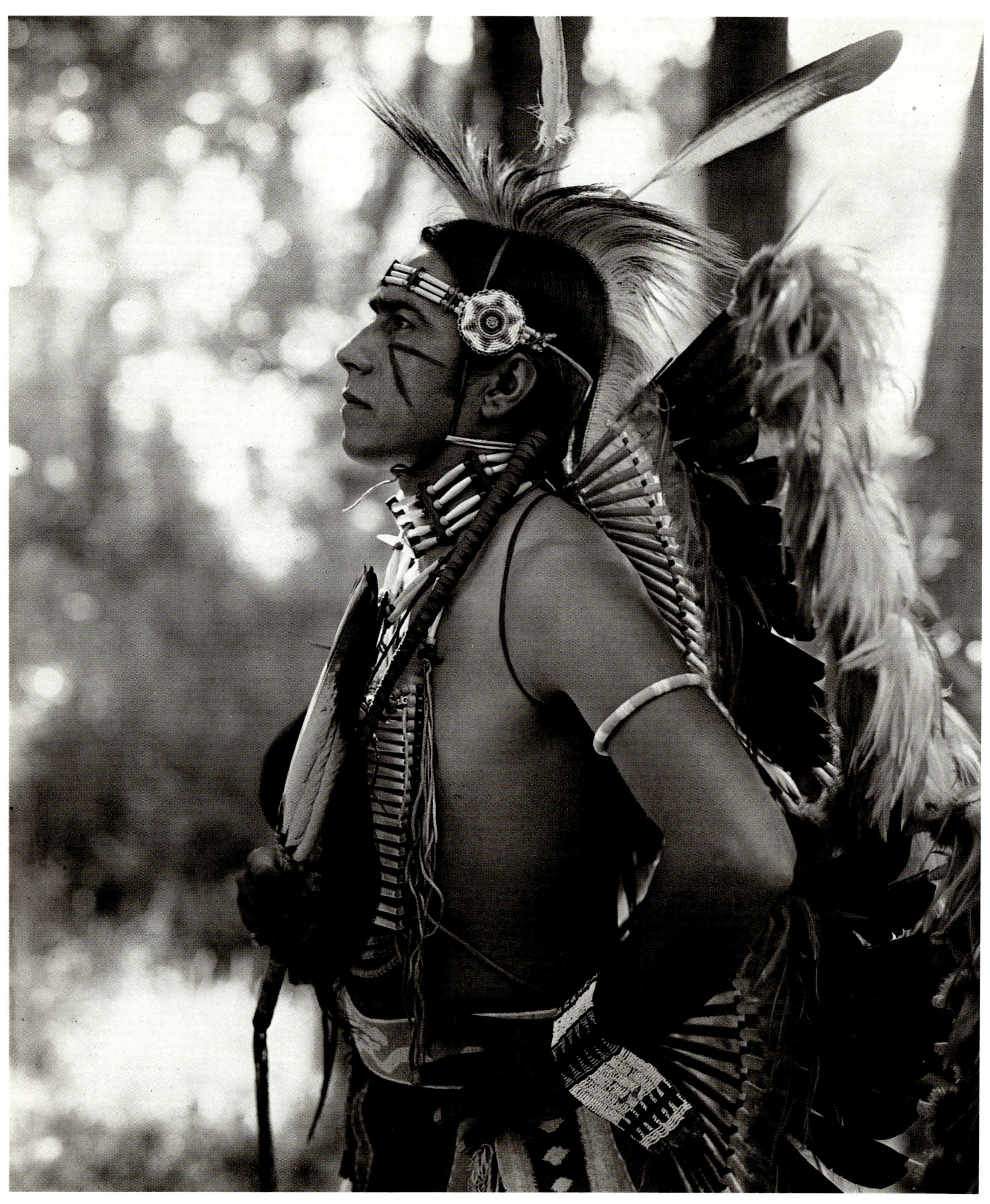

108 Sonny Spruce,
Taos Pueblo, 1980

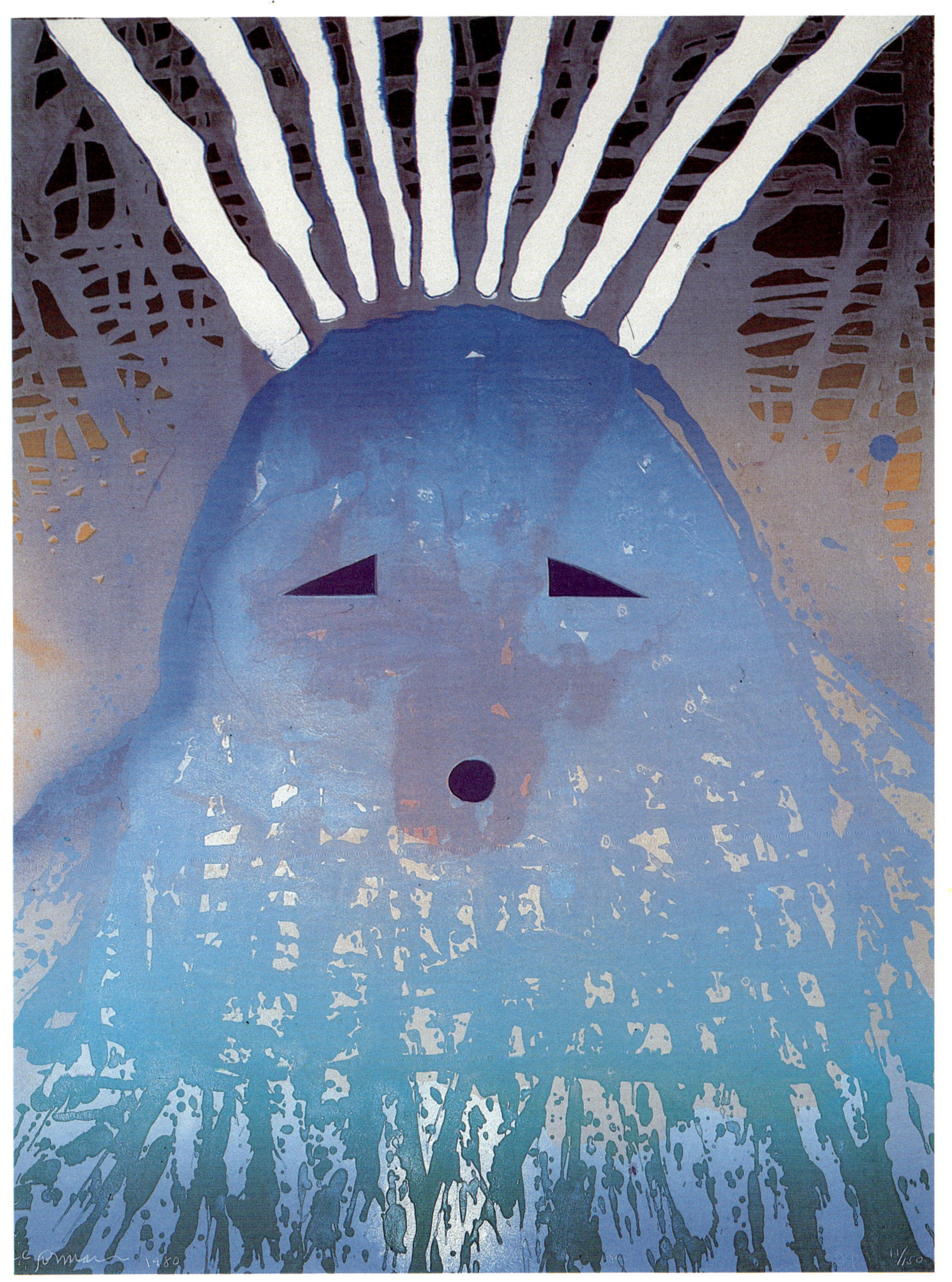

Born of Water,
lithograph, Origins Press, 1980

"The society at Taos Pueblo is very conservative. There are very strict rules that have kept the religious life together. There is an old Taos language, a man's language that the women don't even understand. Many of the songs are in that language, and the old men keep the words in their heads. If they die without teaching them to apprentices, then the songs and the lore die too.

"The religion is about being in balance, about not separating yourself from everything around you, from other people and nature. It's a feeling religion. There is spirit in everything, in rocks, in trees, in animals."—Sonny Spruce

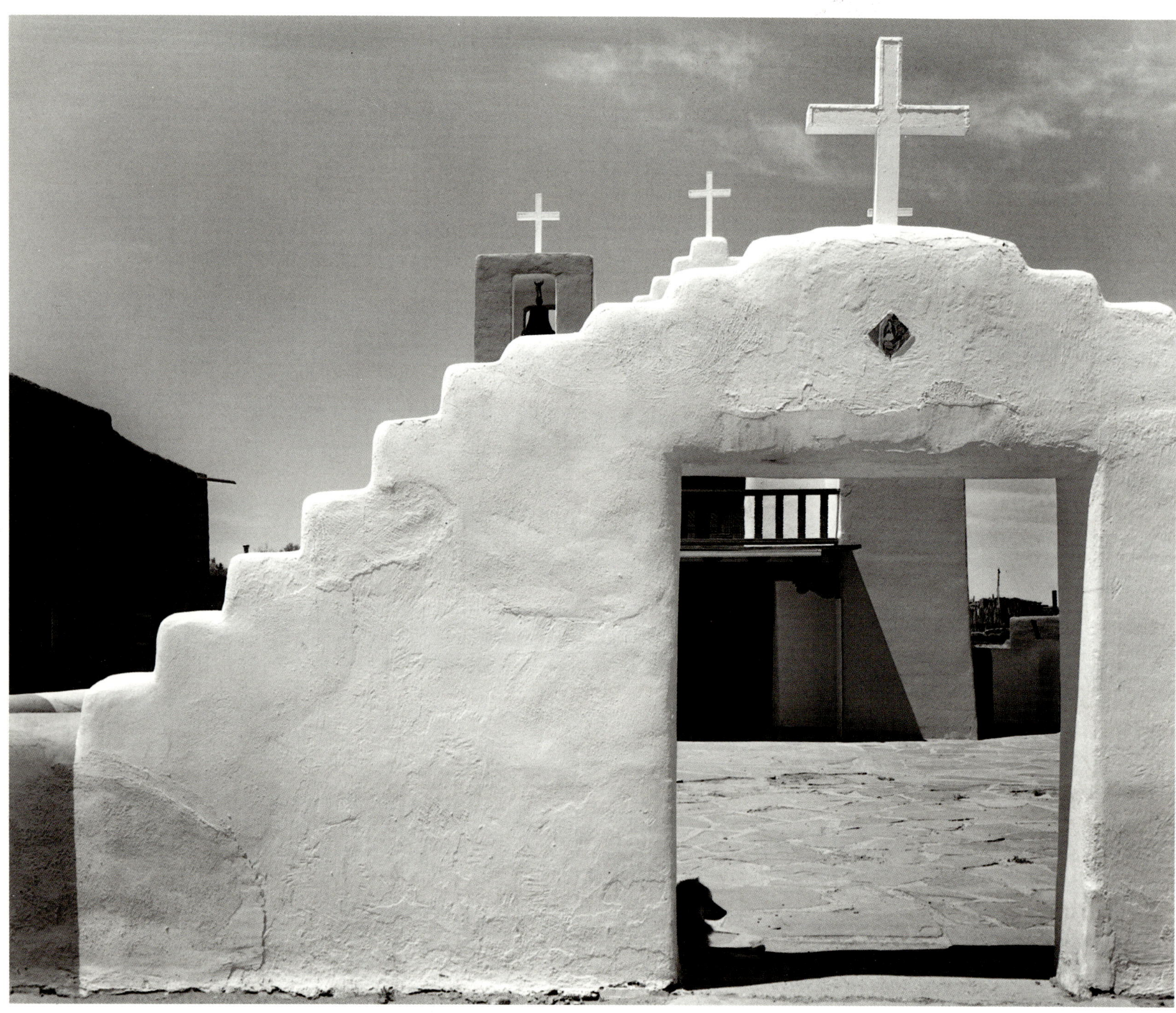

Taos Pueblo Church,
1980

"I've learned a lot from Gorman, about confidence mainly. Just talking to him makes me feel more confident about myself and my own work. Sometimes I think Gorman works like a great composer—he hears the beautiful music in his head and then writes it down."—Jim Wagner

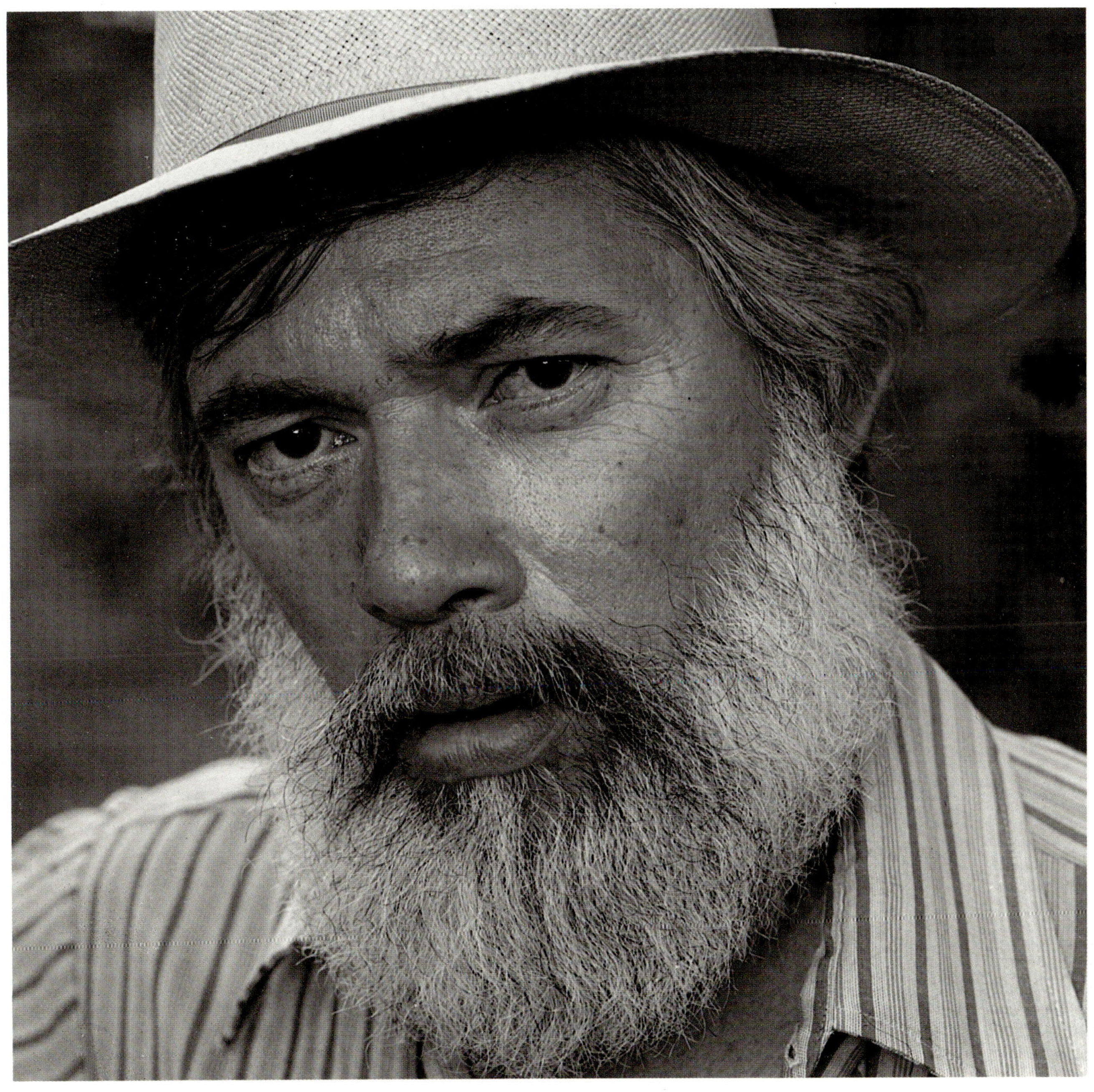

Artist Jim Wagner, Taos, 1980

"Navajos have always worn headbands because we have low hairlines. Without them, the hair is always in our face. Also, it keeps the brain warm. It's used for a napkin, a scarf. After it's used, it winds up on the head, or you can wear it in the back pocket. A red one signifies danger.

"If someone was reaching out in the dark and they felt the headband, they'd know it was me. It's odd the way people react to it. I was staying in a famous Chicago hotel once, the Ritz-Carlton. I'd been there a week, impeccably dressed in suits, neckties, silk shirts, plus the headband. One night, coming back to the hotel from a party, the doorman stopped me and said, 'Are you staying in this hotel?' I said, 'Yes,' and he said, 'Show me your keys.' I did. 'Well,' he said, 'you'll have to take off that headband.' I brushed by him and went to my room and then checked out and went to the Drake, where they had a more civilized dress code. Ever since, the Drake has been my absolutely favorite hotel."—R.C.G.

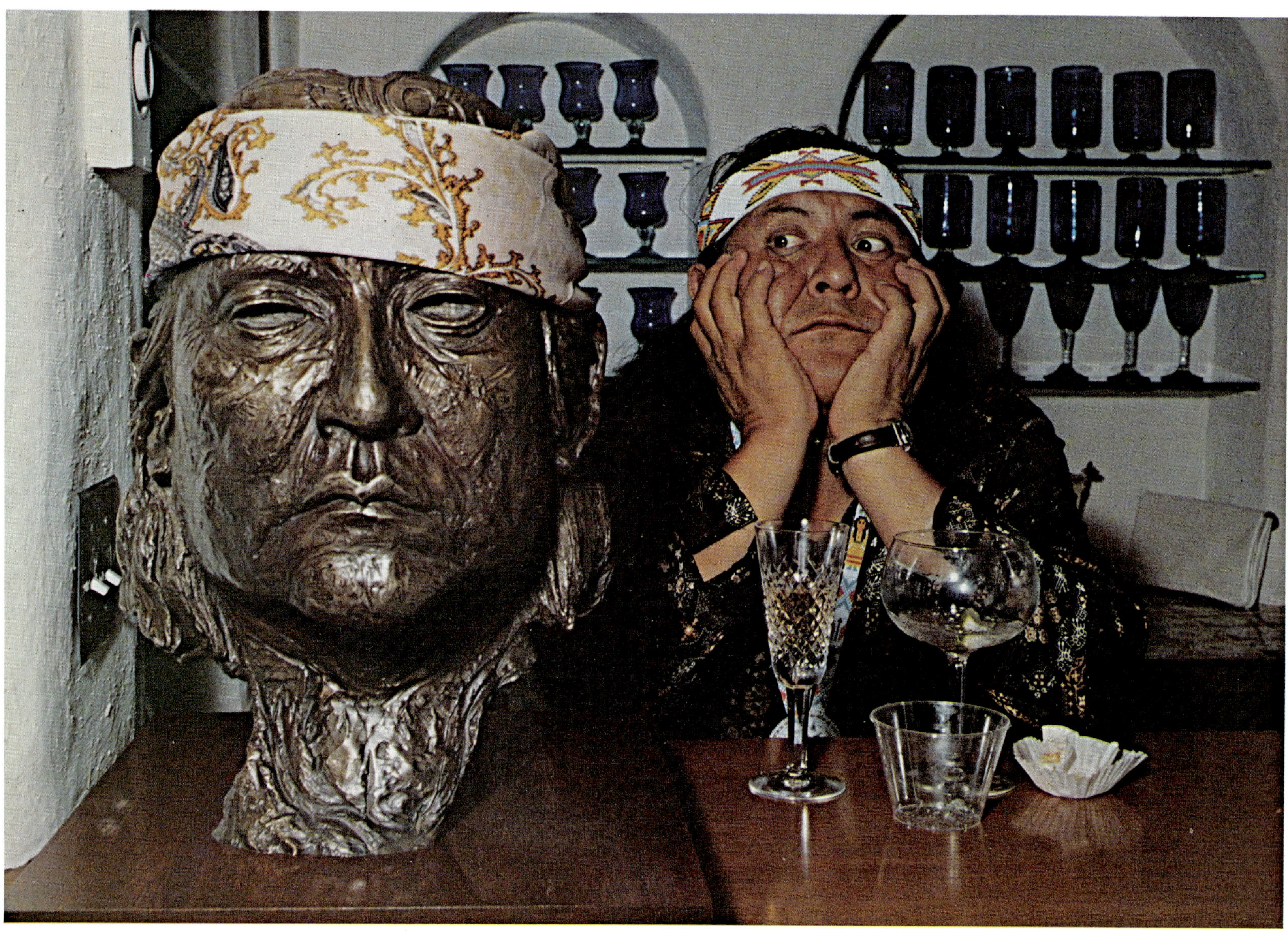

Gorman sits with bronze bust by Ellie Hamilton (Southwest Bronze), Taos

"A good party requires the right combination of people. It needs key, controversial people who have humor and beauty and aren't afraid to say what they think. Elizabeth Taylor is a great party woman. She encourages people to have a good time. Of course, I have my own collection of demented, fun people in Taos. . . . I have so many of them."—R.C.G.

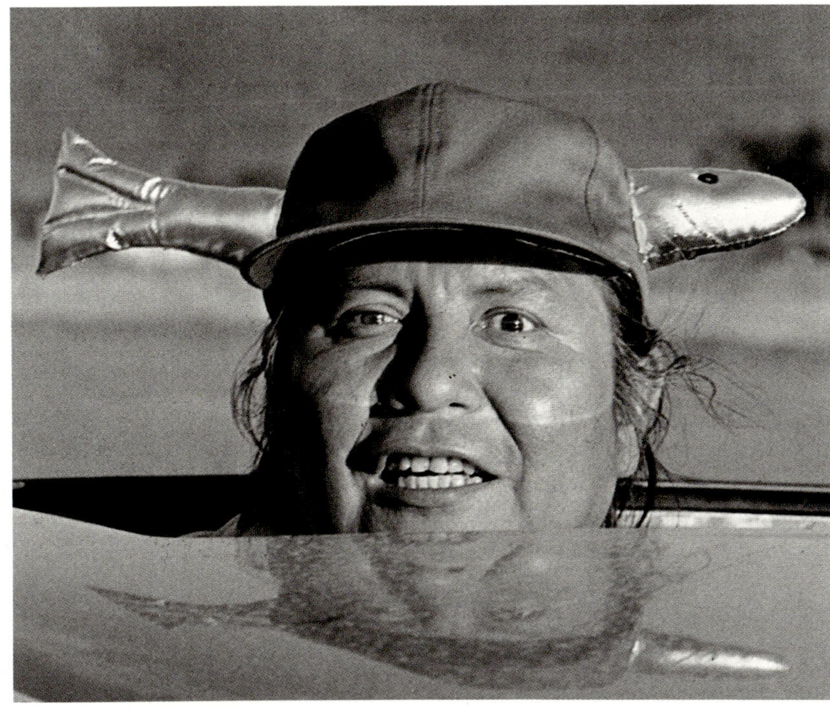

Gorman in his favorite fish hat, Taos, 1980

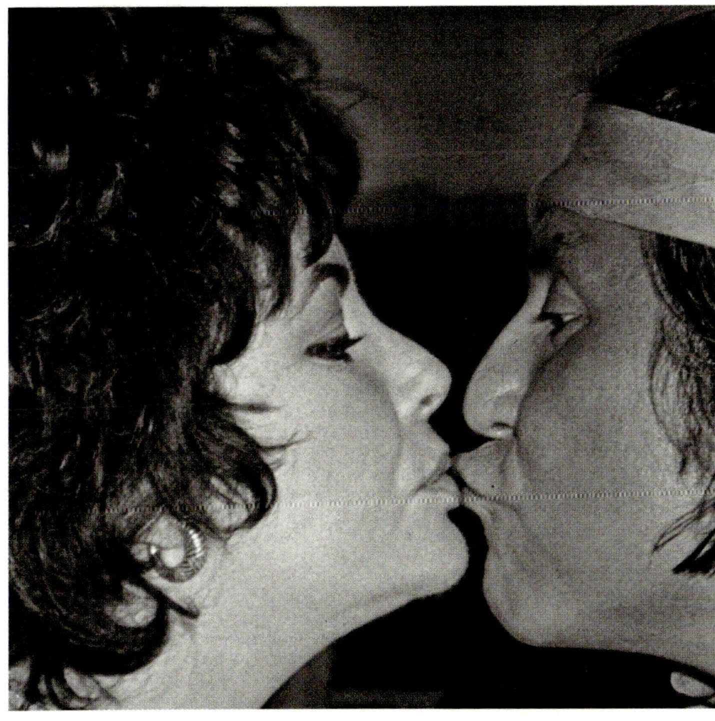

Elizabeth Taylor and friend, Taos, 1980

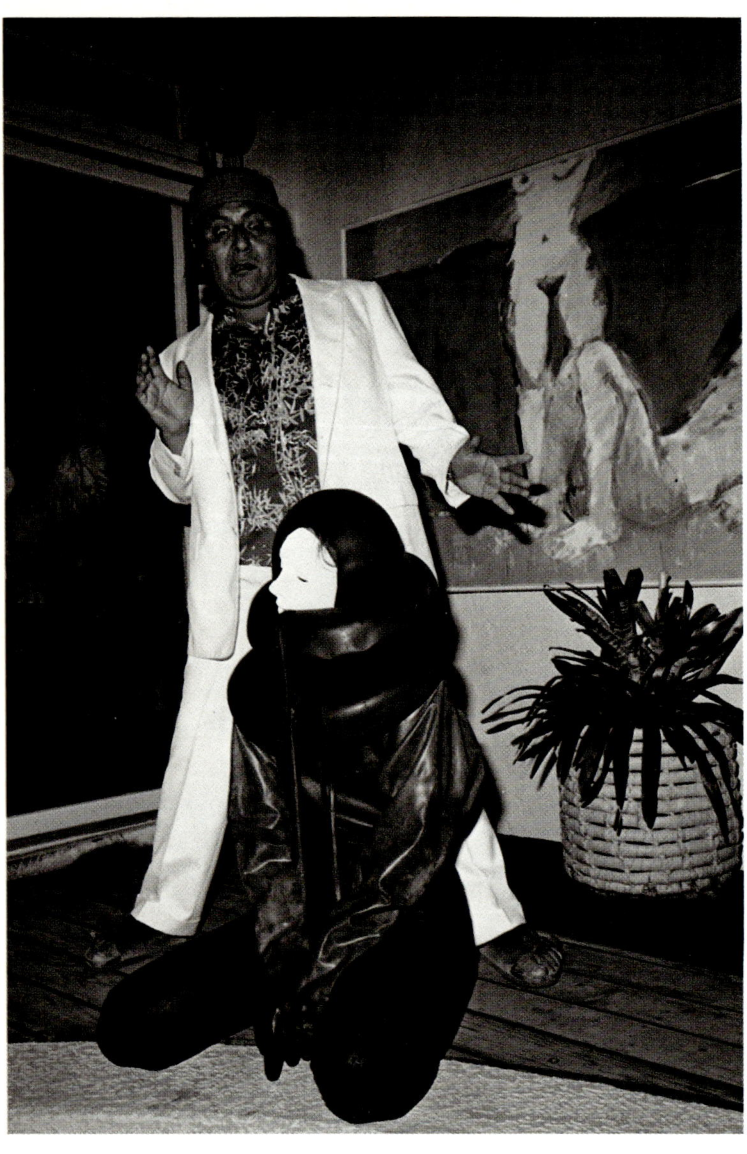

Gorman meets the Rubber Lady,
Taos, 1980

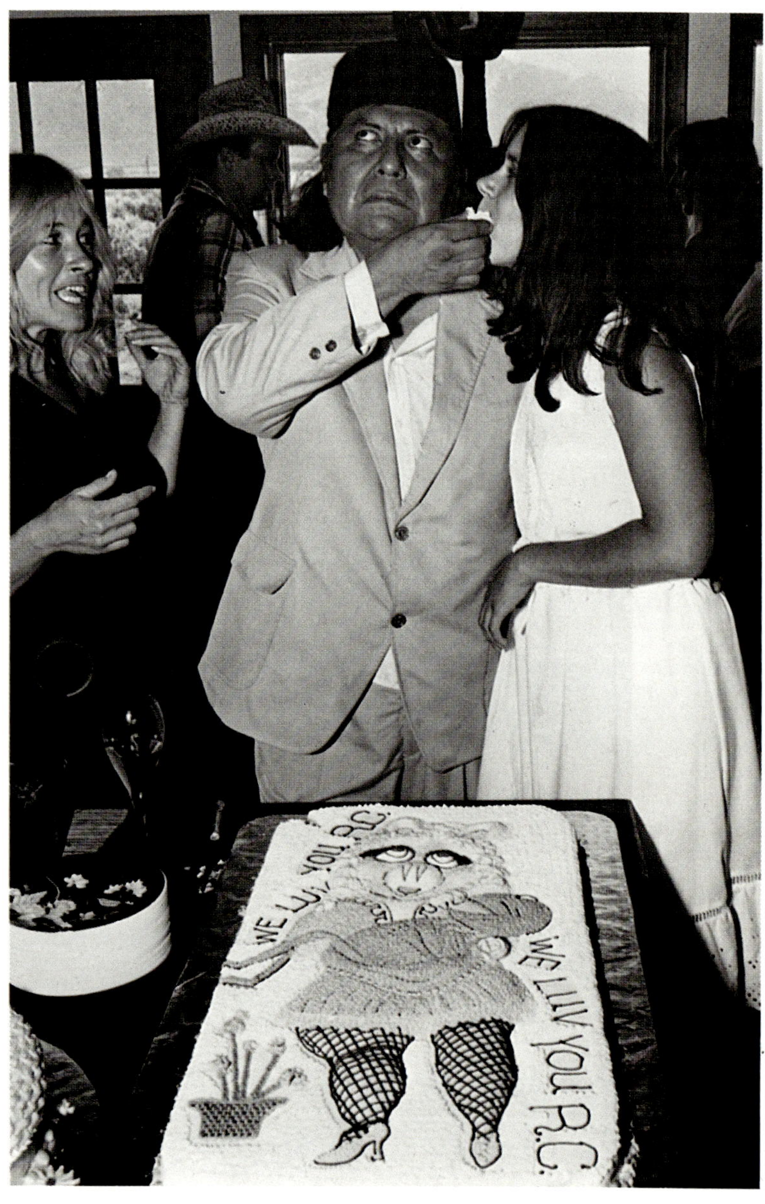

Gorman feeds birthday cake to Tupper Heaton,
Taos, 1981

"Every primitive culture I know has the clown. The Polynesian dances all have the clown at the end, and the Navajo Yei-Bi-Chais are the same. The clown can personify good or bad—not wicked, not Christian suffering and hell, but human foibles, follies."—R.C.G.

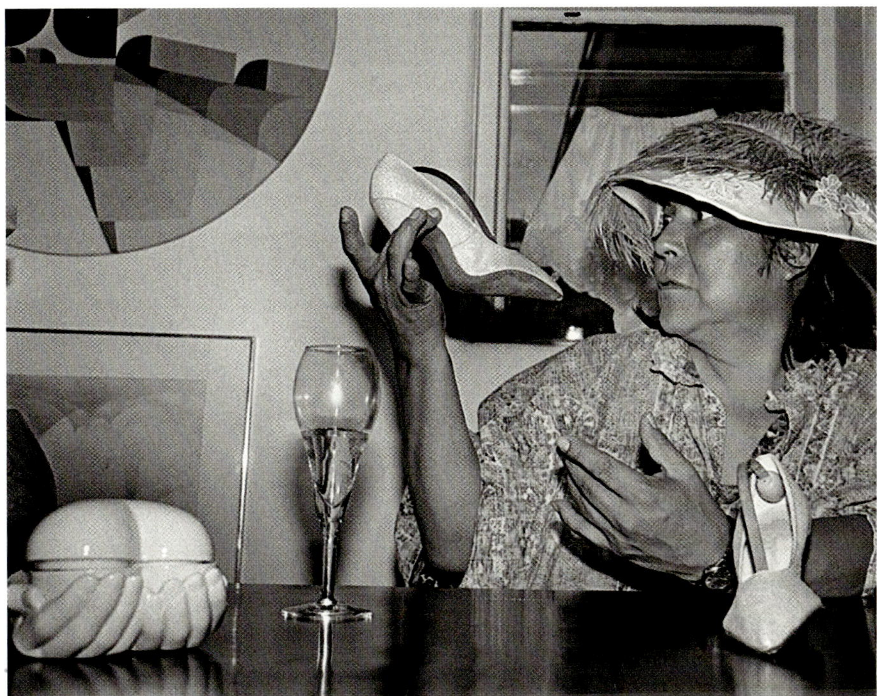

The clown,
Taos, 1981

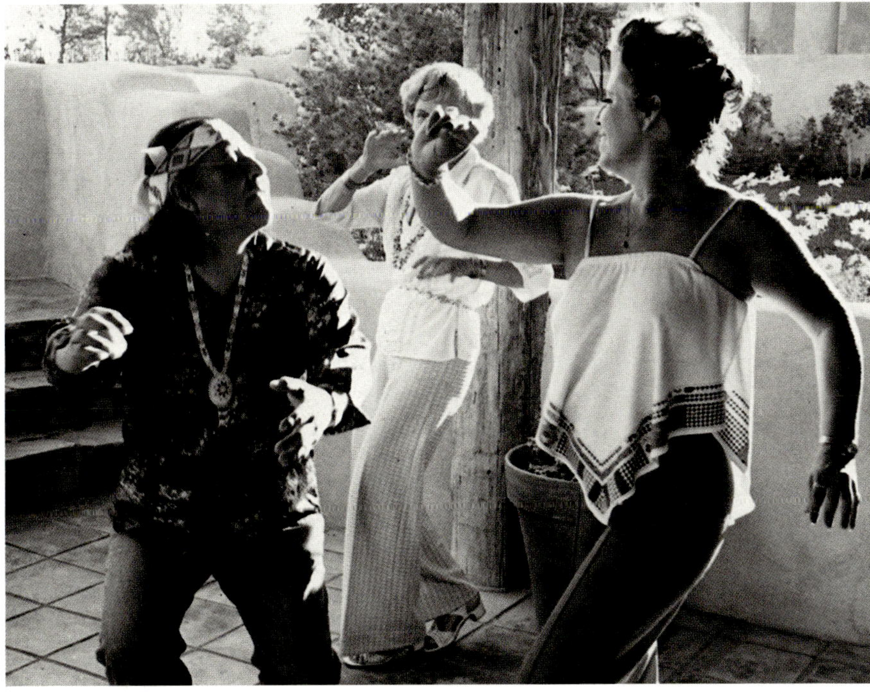

The Navajo Shuffle,
Taos, 1981

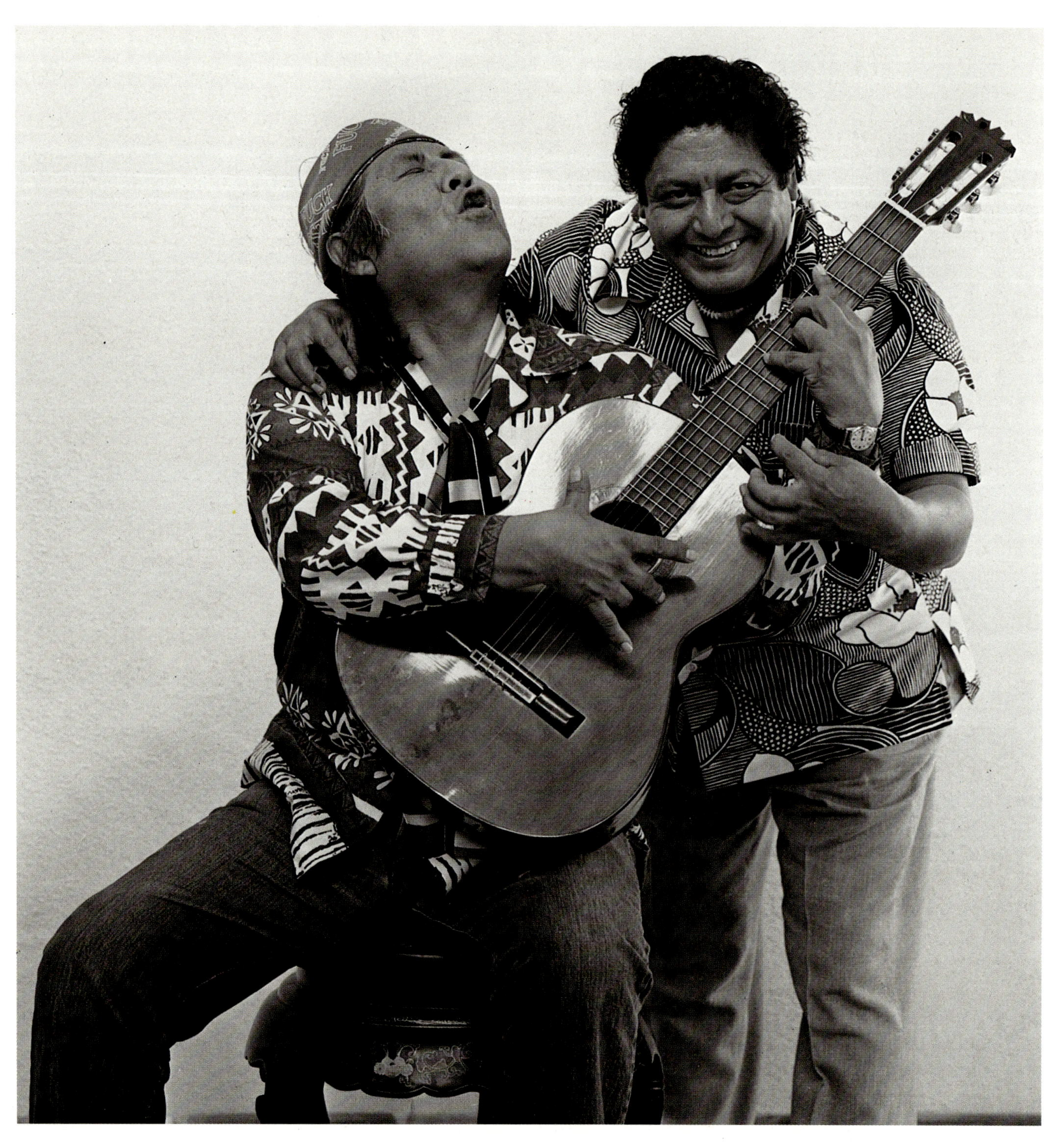

Crooning with guitarist Antonio Mendoza,
Taos, 1981

"Large women have always been my weakness. The fat cat's name is Priscilla."
—R.C.G.

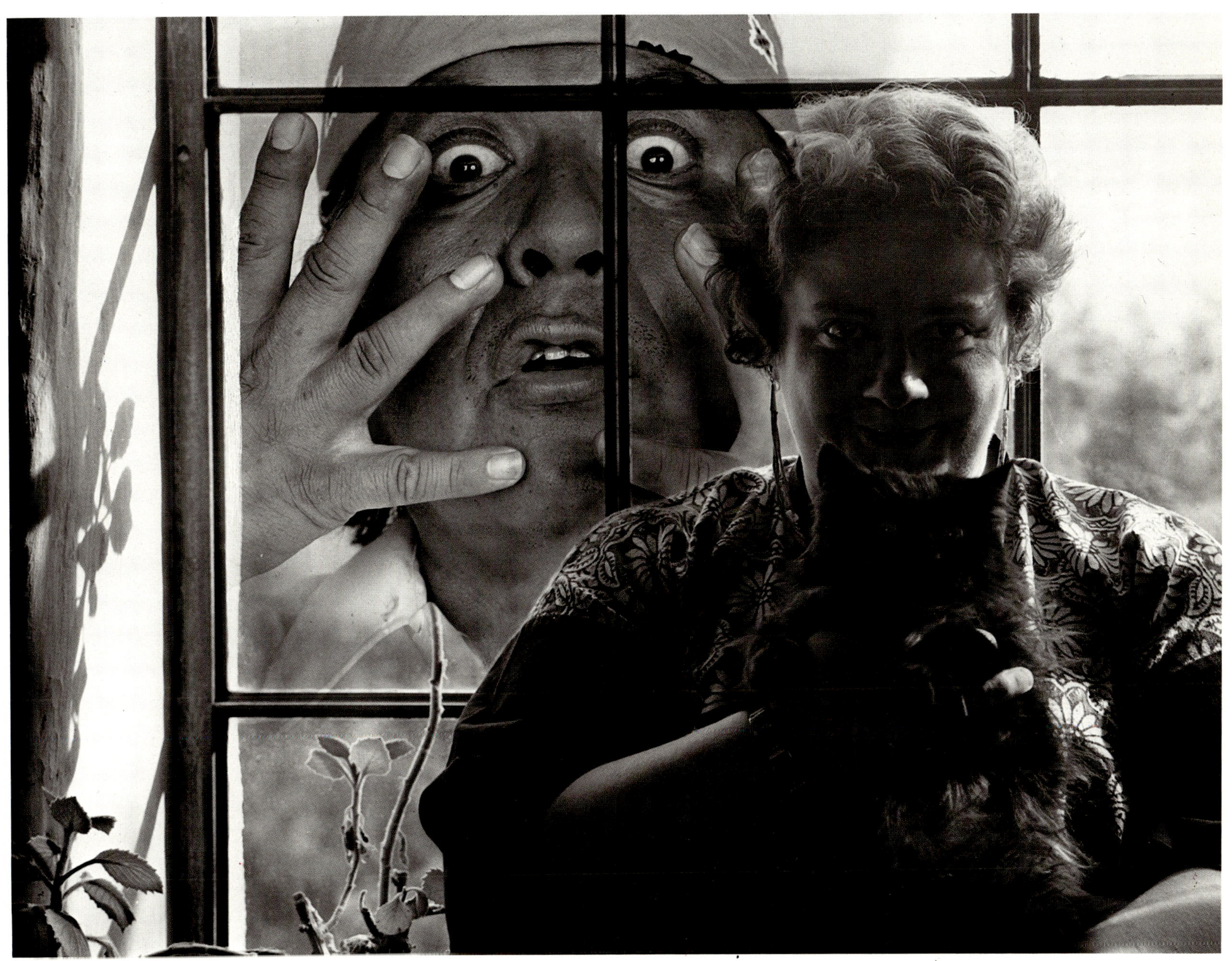

Virginia Dooley,
director of Gorman's Navajo Gallery,
Taos, 1981

"This is Marge Griffin. To me she is Sparkle Plenty. She has the nerve to mix turquoise with diamonds."—R.C.G.

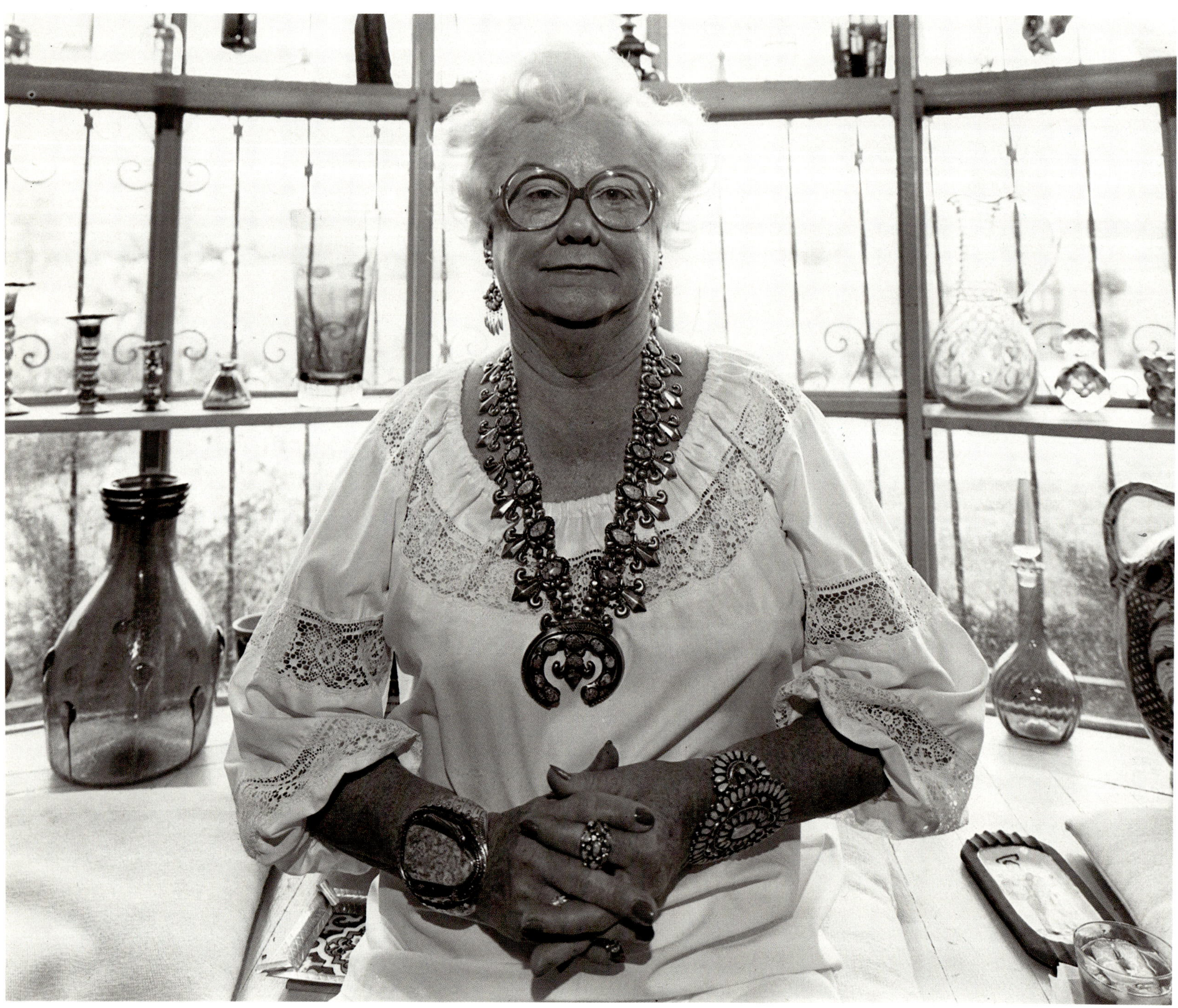

Marge Griffin,
"Sparkle Plenty," Taos, 1980

"When R. C. built his big new house, I gave him a drawing as a housewarming present. When I took it to him, he told me to measure the wall by his swimming pool and tell him what I could do with it! We talked about it some, but the only instructions he gave me were that he wanted a stitched, bas-relief piece with male and female figures on it. 'I don't believe in telling an artist what to do,' he said. 'Just do it.'

"I worked on the project for two or three months. He was gone most of the time in Japan. When he got back, I asked him how his trip was. 'Oh, the same short people, same old temples.' What a funny guy he is."—Gary Mauro

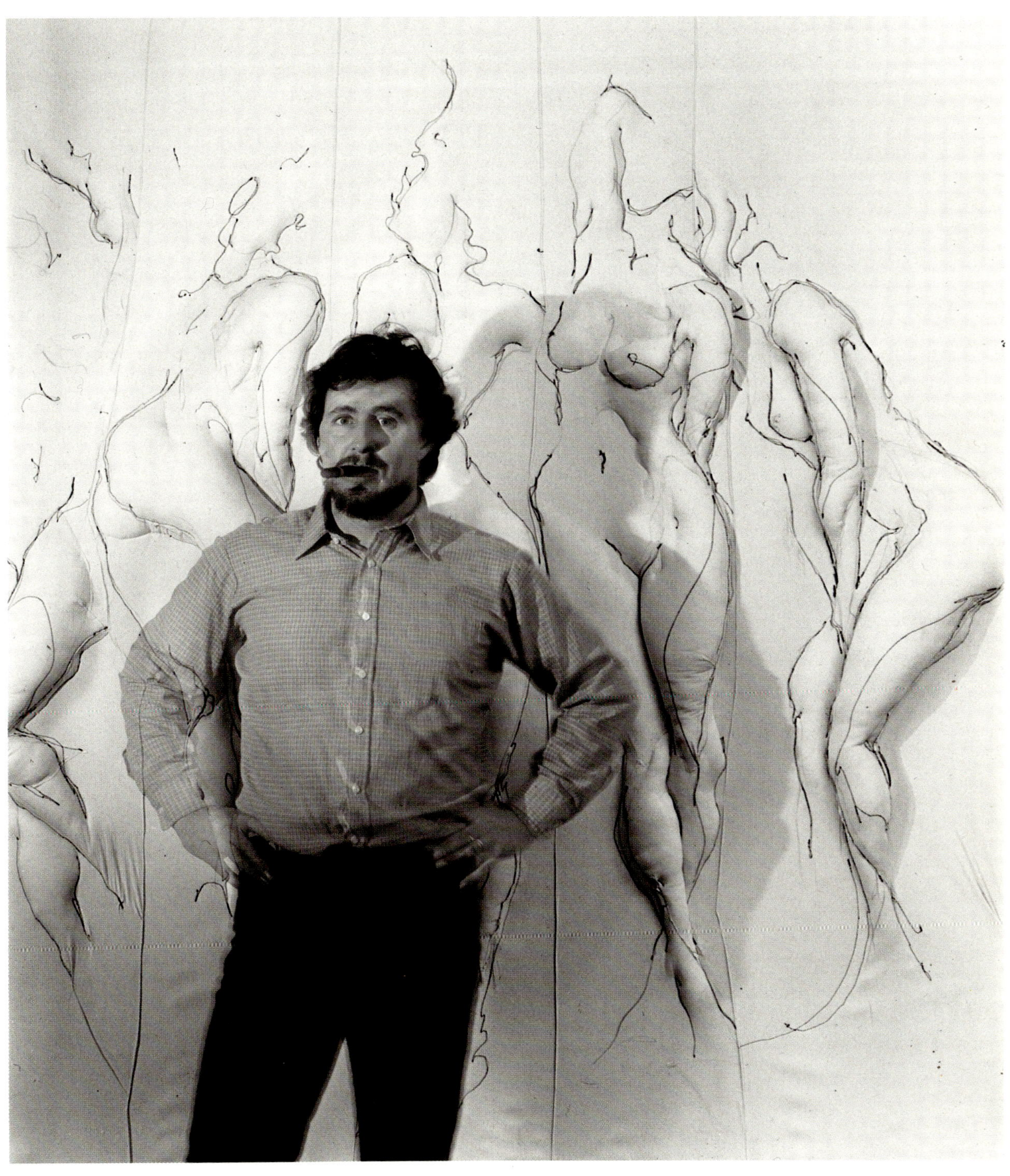

Gary Mauro,
Taos, 1981

In 1979, Gorman moved into his new home, located on a ridge some miles north of Taos, looking out at the sacred Taos Mountain. The house is filled with the trappings of his success: a large, solar-heated, indoor swimming pool; elegant furniture with leather and earth-toned upholstery; the finest of stereo and video equipment; and art from his personal collection of Oriental, European, and local artists. His taste is excellent, and he has drawn all these elements into a whole that is reflective of his zest for life. Yet his sober side is plainly visible, particularly in his love of Chinese porcelains and screens, Japanese doors and sumi drawings. His roots stretch back to the Orient, perhaps explaining his love for its art and food. Yoko Saito, one of his favorite models, is Japanese.

He has built and furnished the house so that it is just as he wants it. His studio is there, his mountain, and all the other things he wants and needs. It is a self-contained center for work, entertainment, and rest. He is still peripatetic, but his pace has slowed noticeably in recent years. Though biographers have placed his birthdate at 1932, his closest friends claim it to be perhaps as much as five years earlier. One can't tell from looking at him; his face is wrinkle-free and has a nut-brown glow.

The comfortable library contains thousands of books on art, biography, Navajo and world history. He has read many of them, and looks forward to some peaceful time when he can read more than ever. As it is now, he rises early, spends the morning working on his art and conducting business on the phone. Then comes a sociable lunch, usually with a half-dozen friends or visitors, prepared by his cook and housekeeper, Rose Roybal. Sometimes he takes an afternoon nap, and he goes to bed early and, he claims, alone.

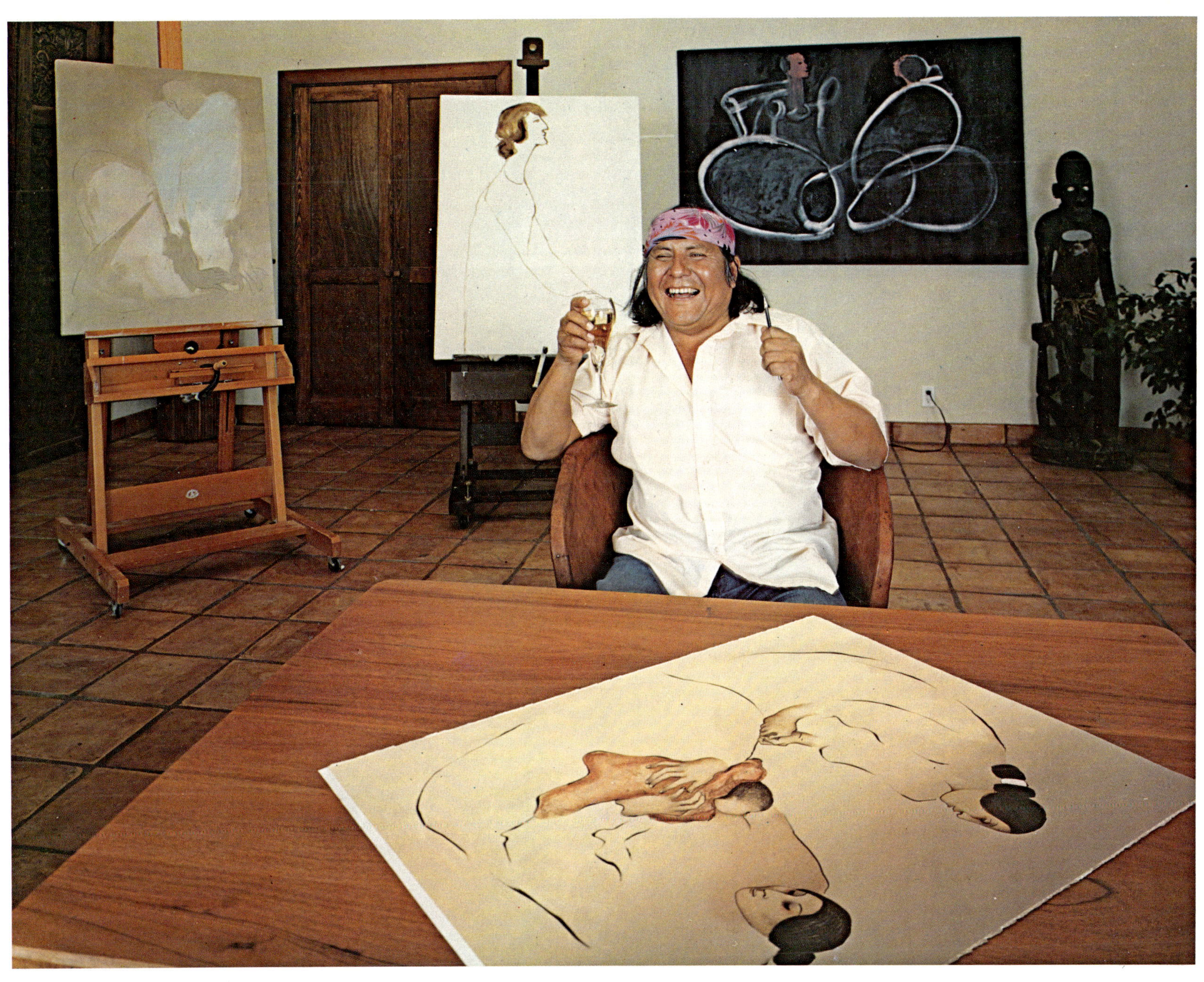

Gorman in his Taos studio,
1981

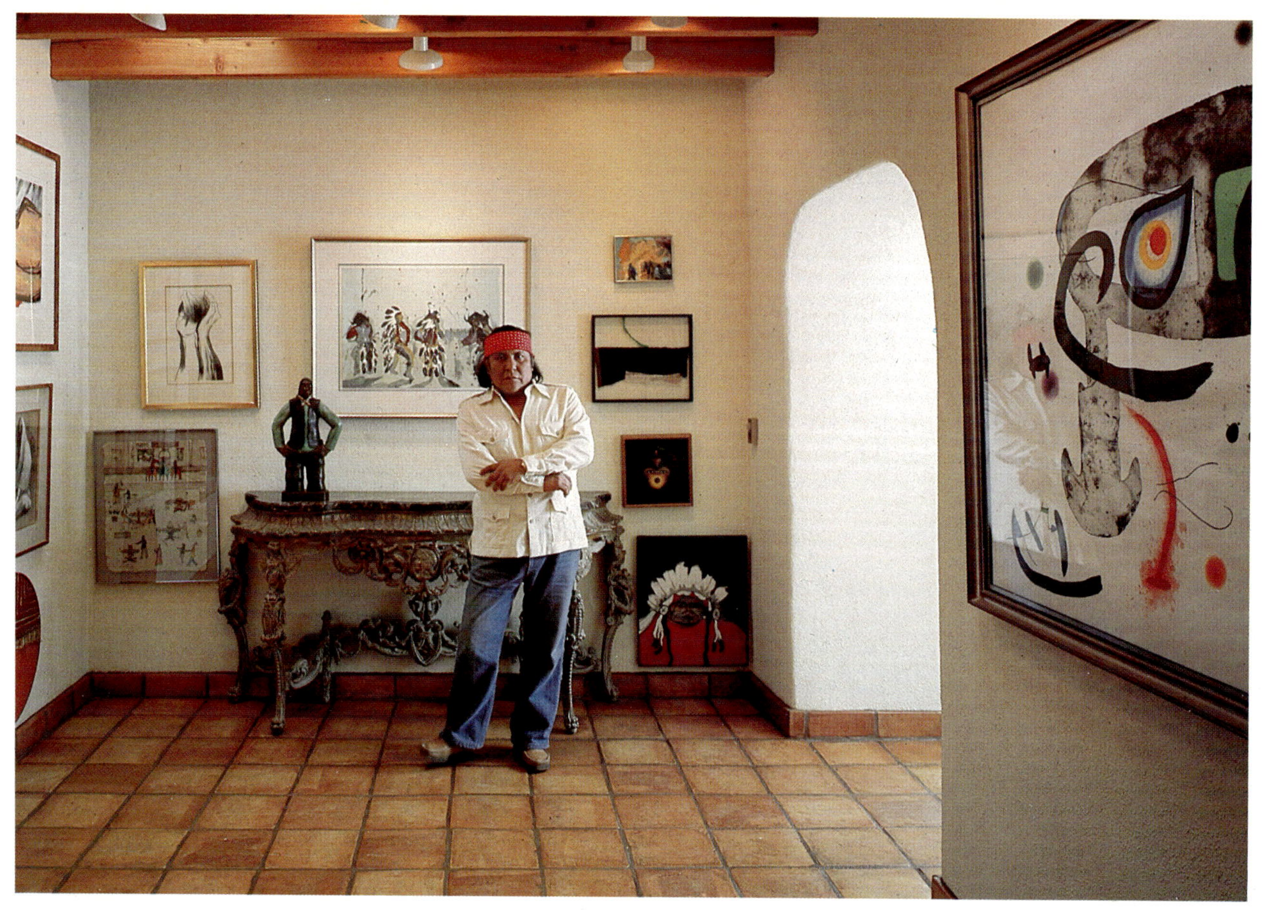

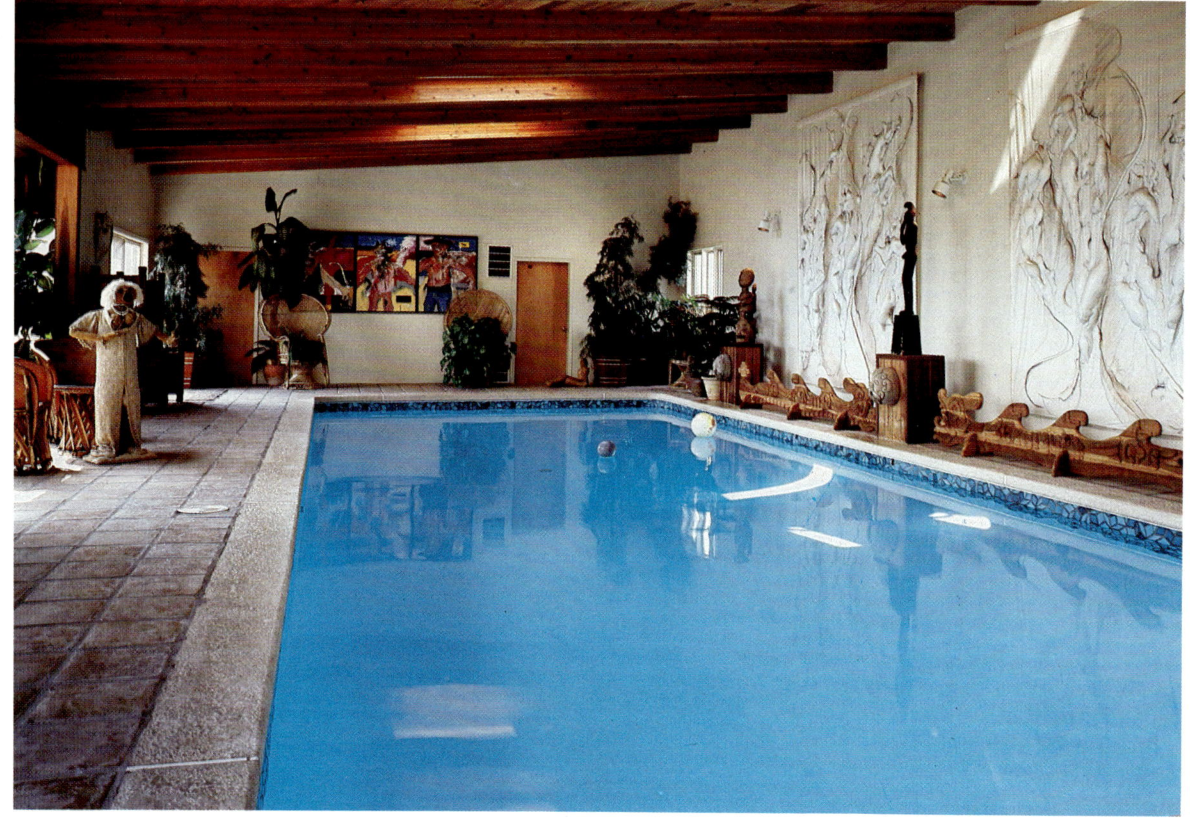

Gorman's home
Taos, 1982

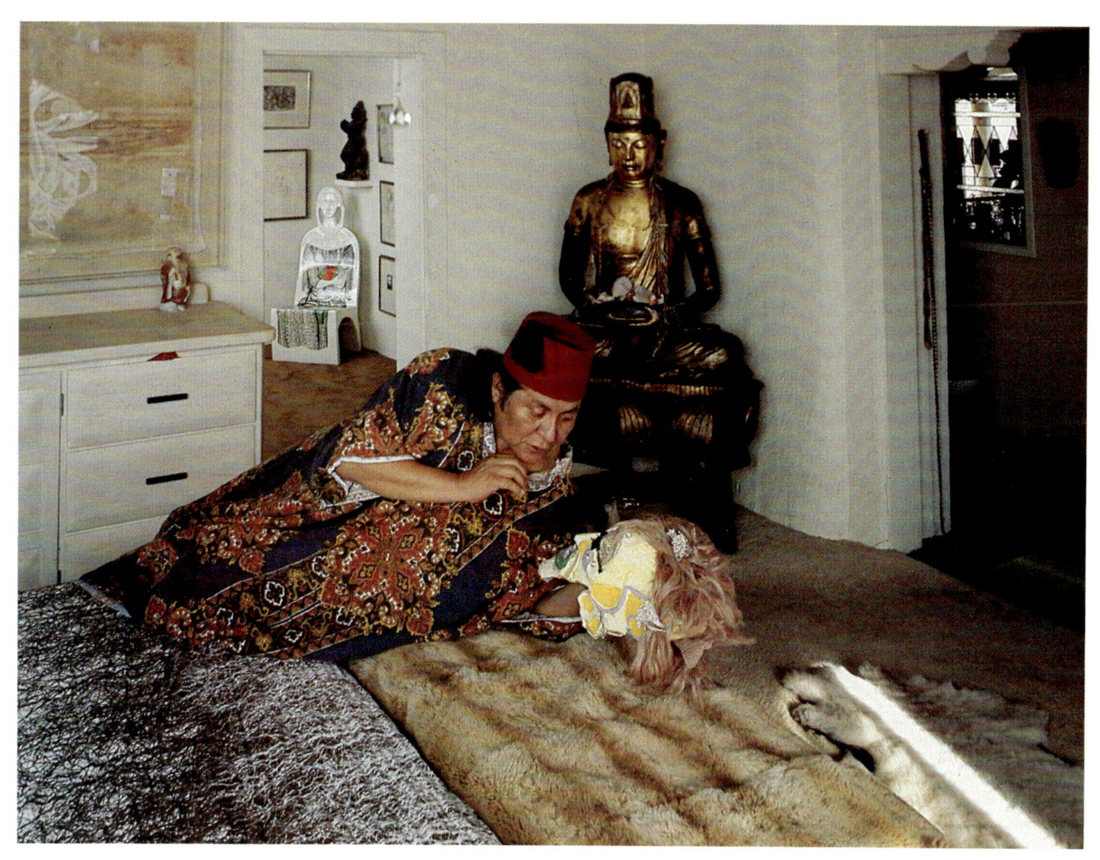

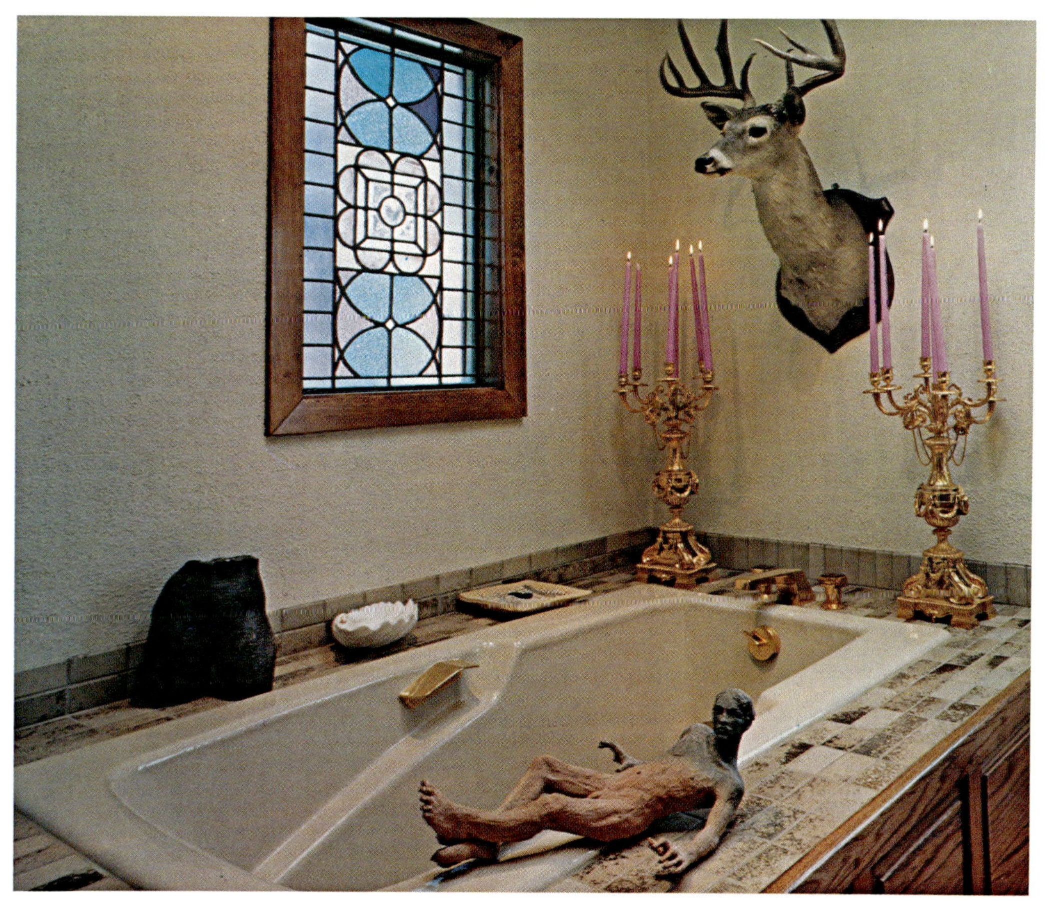

"I lived two different lives. During the school year, I always walked to school, two or three miles every day, and I came home and chopped wood. I did a lot of chopping wood, though I was terrible at it. I had no coordination. In the summer I lived with my grandmother, herding sheep, or sometimes I just followed my father around. He was the first one to give me drawing tablets and crayons, so I guess he was my first instructor. My grandmother was beautiful. She'd ride on a donkey, a white donkey. It was twenty-four miles from where she lived to Chinle. It would take her all day to ride in and bring me something—some meat, or bread, or wild bananas."—R.C.G.

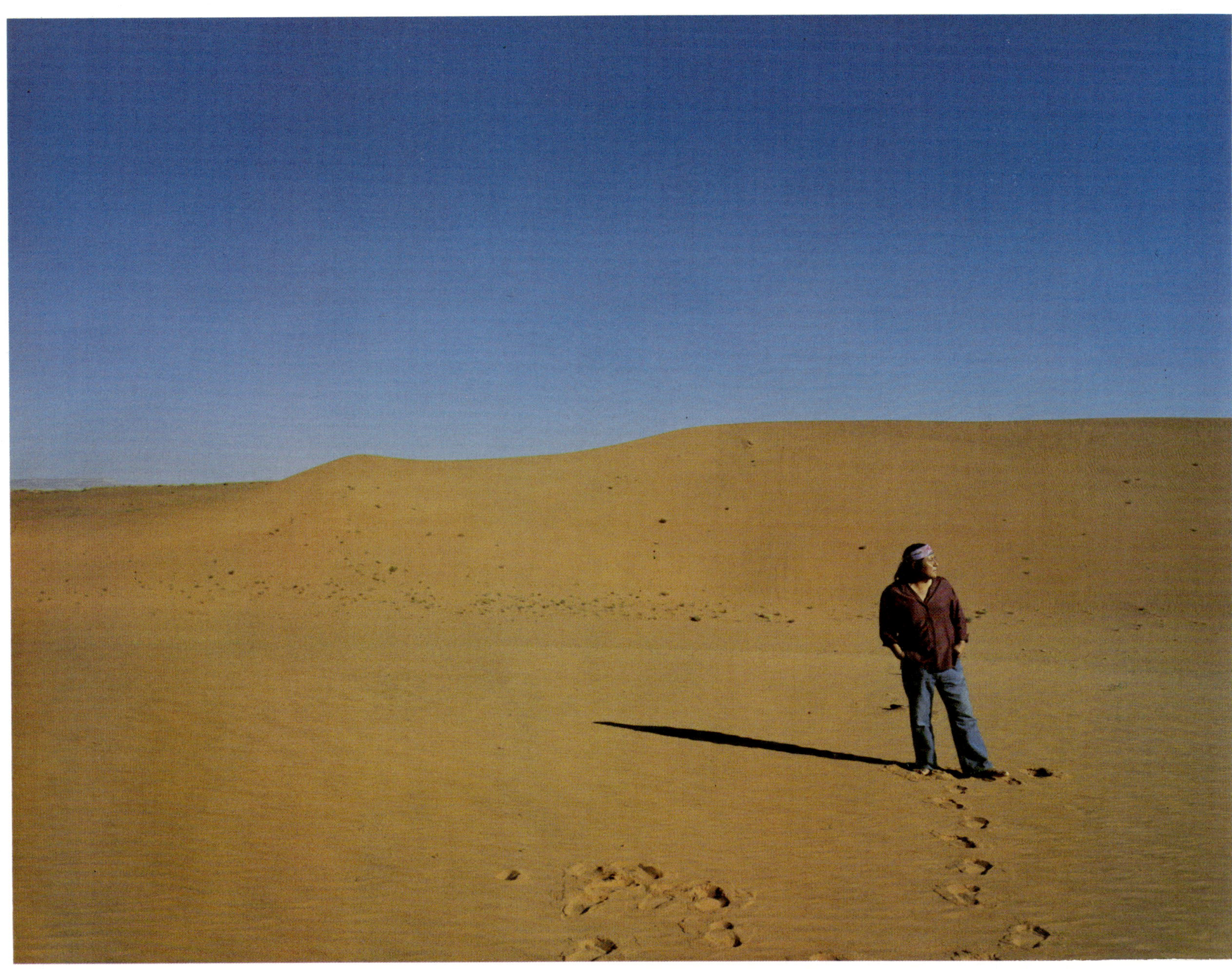

Navajo in the dunes,
Chinle, 1981

"I spent many summers in the canyon with my grandmother, just walking and visiting and watching her pick certain medicinal plants. There was one, it looked like the calla lily, that only she could pluck and suck the nectar from the base of the flower. Only privileged people could taste it, people who knew the ceremony. It was poisonous to anyone else, so I never tasted it."
—R.C.G.

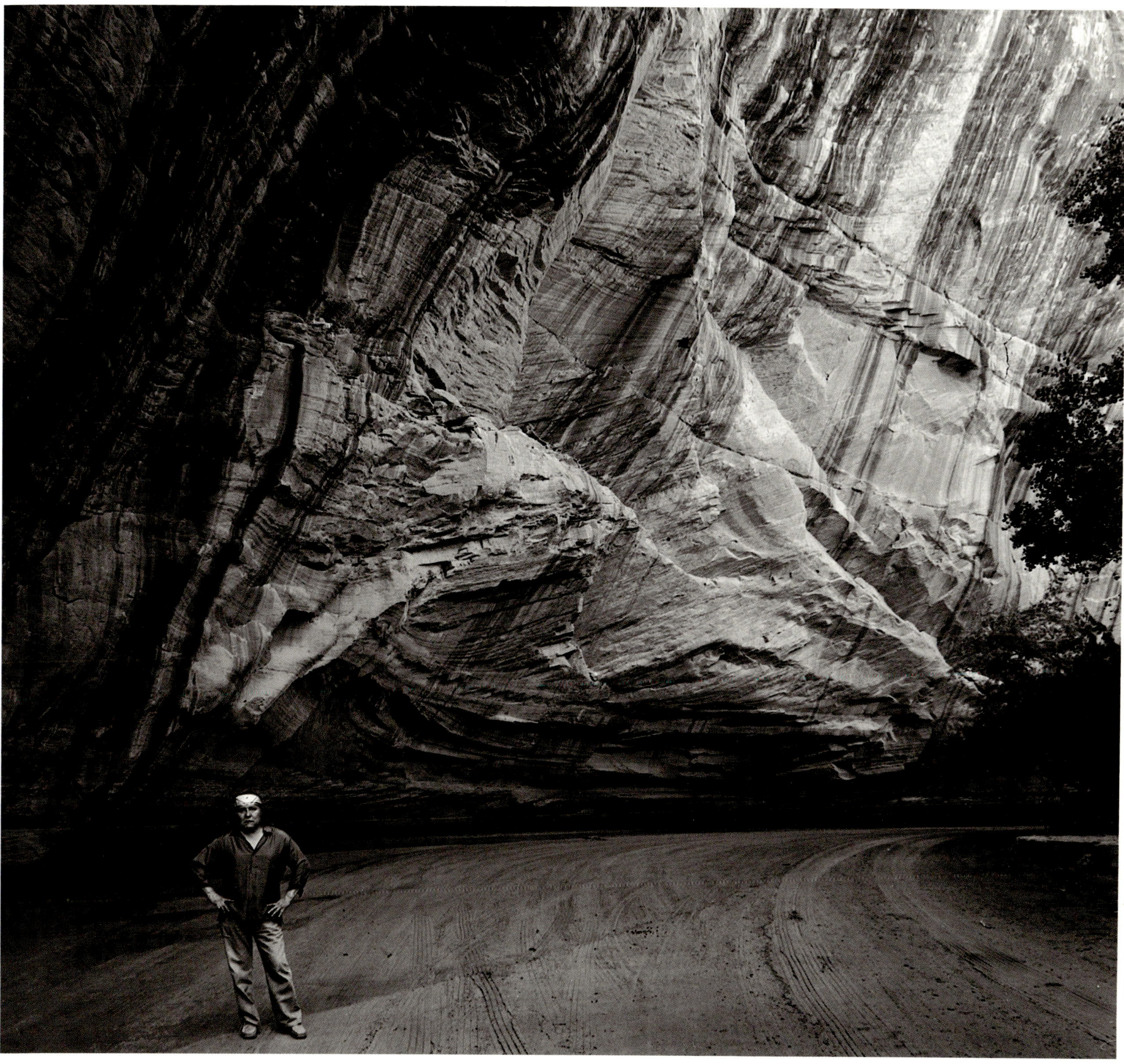

Gorman in Canyon de Chelly, 1981

"I always was in awe of the ruins. I felt there were still people living in them, and I still feel that way. They were built by the Anasazi, not the Navajos. We're much bigger than they were.

"There's magic in the canyon. There's the eerie feeling they're looking down at you. It makes you feel you should have brought a gift."—R.C.G.

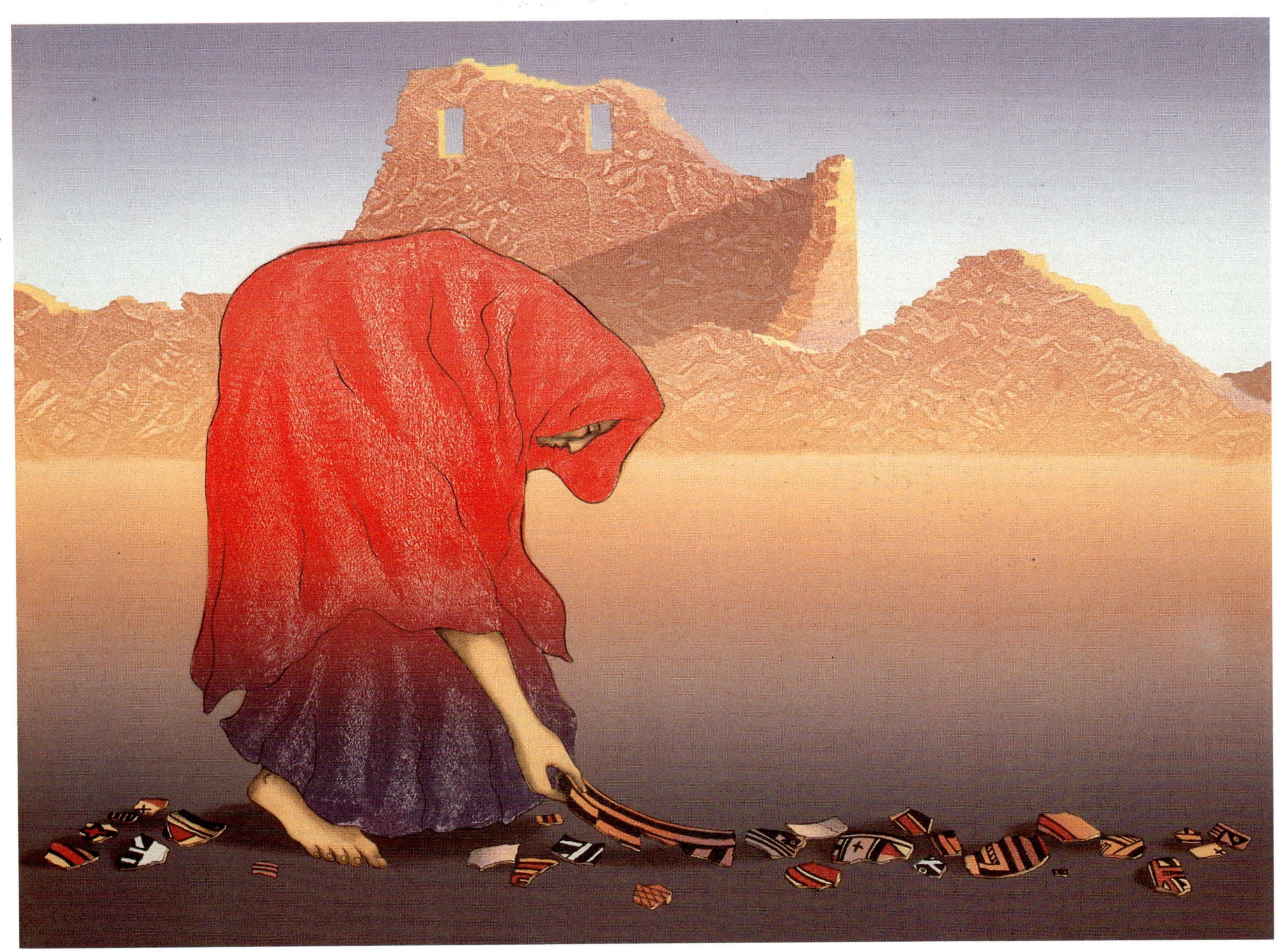

Ruins,
lithograph, Houston Fine Arts Press, 1983

"After exploring Canyon de Chelly, we started up del Muerto, where Gorman's uncle owned a farm. The farm, much to Gorman's dismay, had long been neglected, and we continued twenty-five miles up into the canyon to an Anasazi ruin called Mummy Cave. The day was overcast. Just before we left, the sun burst through, illuminating for about one second only the ruins. The picture was made. Gorman shouted, 'I hope you got that shot, it's been the only one worth taking! Let's go home to dinner.'"—Chuck Henningsen

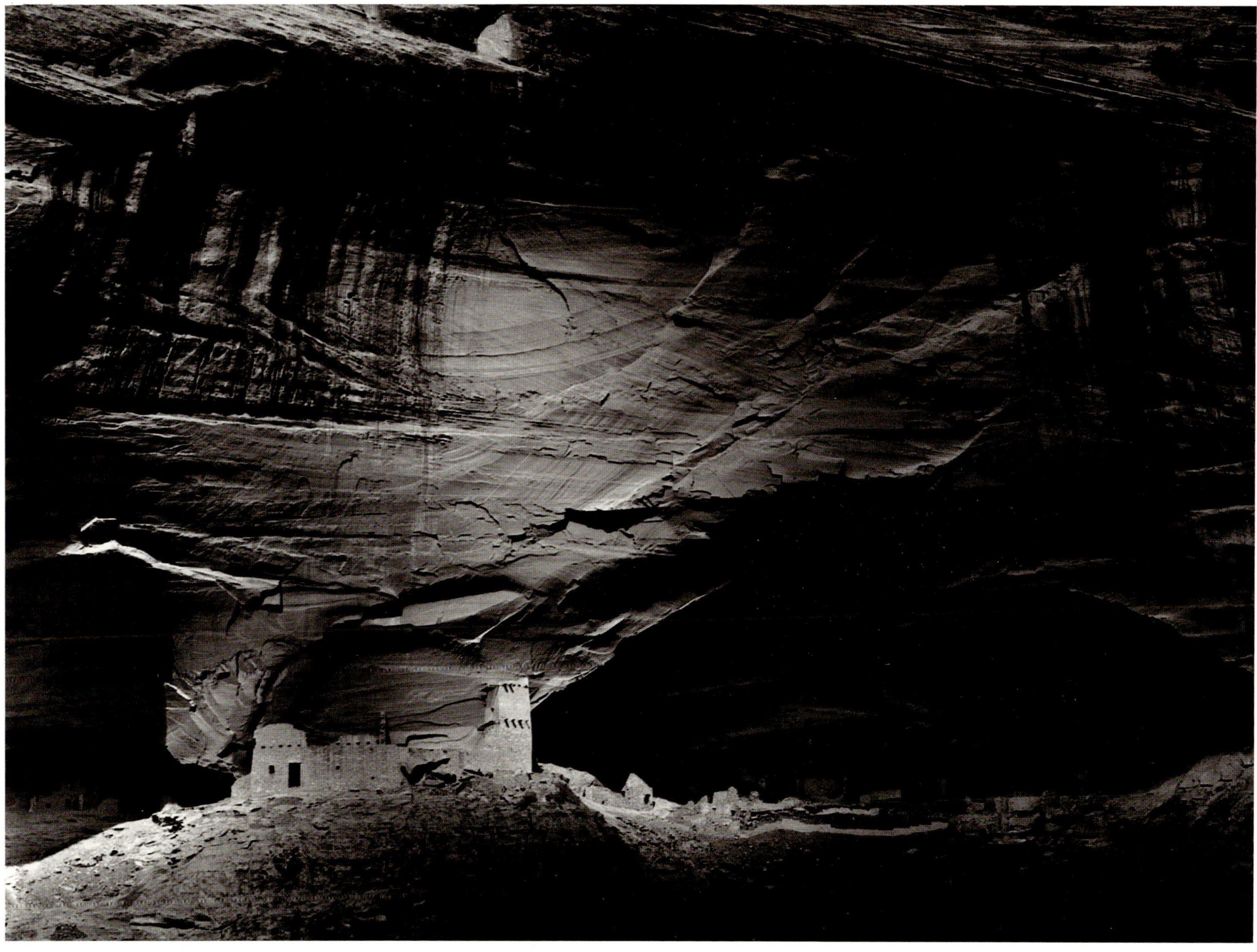

Mummy Cave ruin,
Canyon del Muerto, 1981

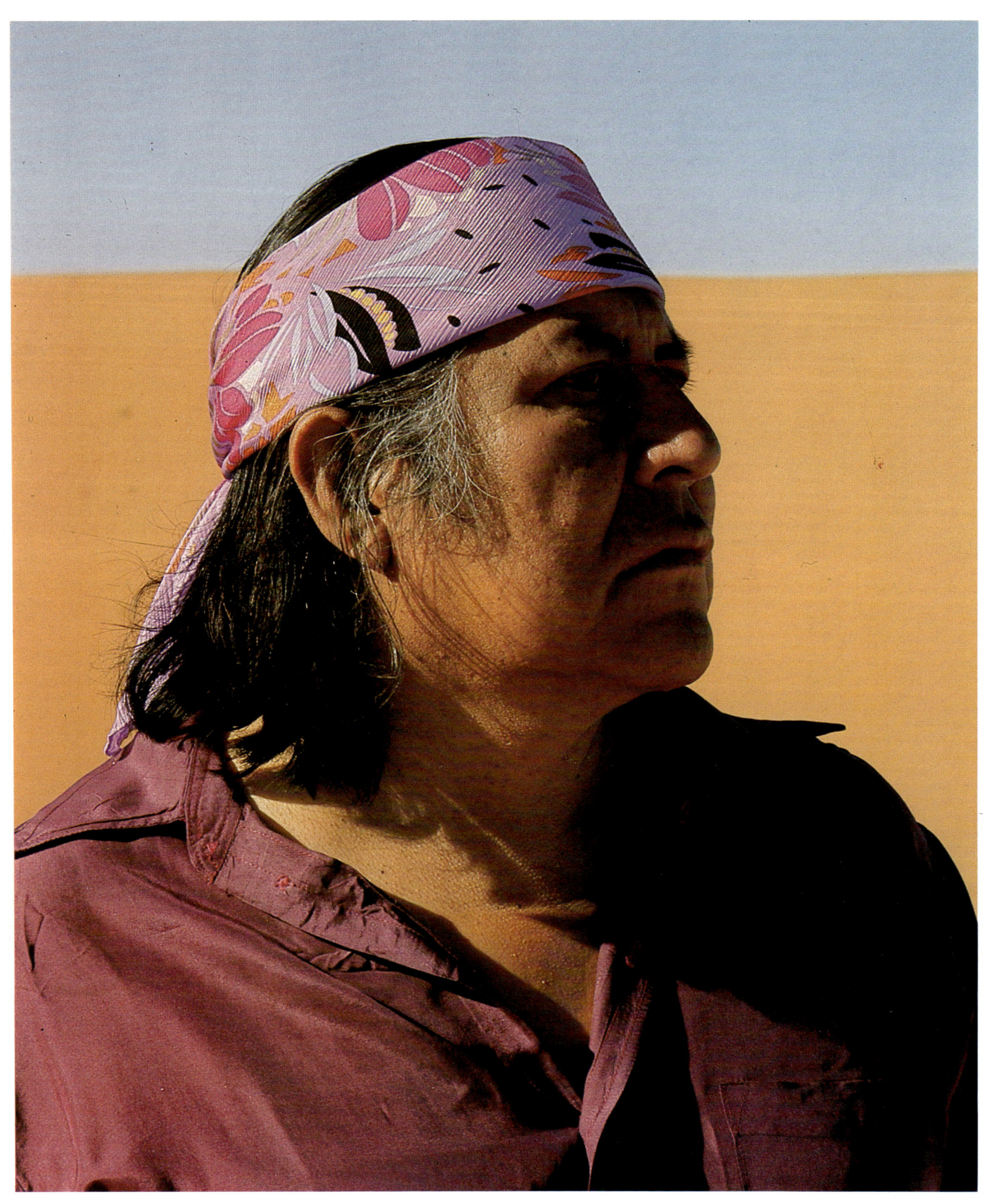

128 Gorman in the dunes near Chinle, Arizona, 1981

This painting is based on the photograph shown on the facing page and is the first self-portrait done by Gorman in fifteen years.

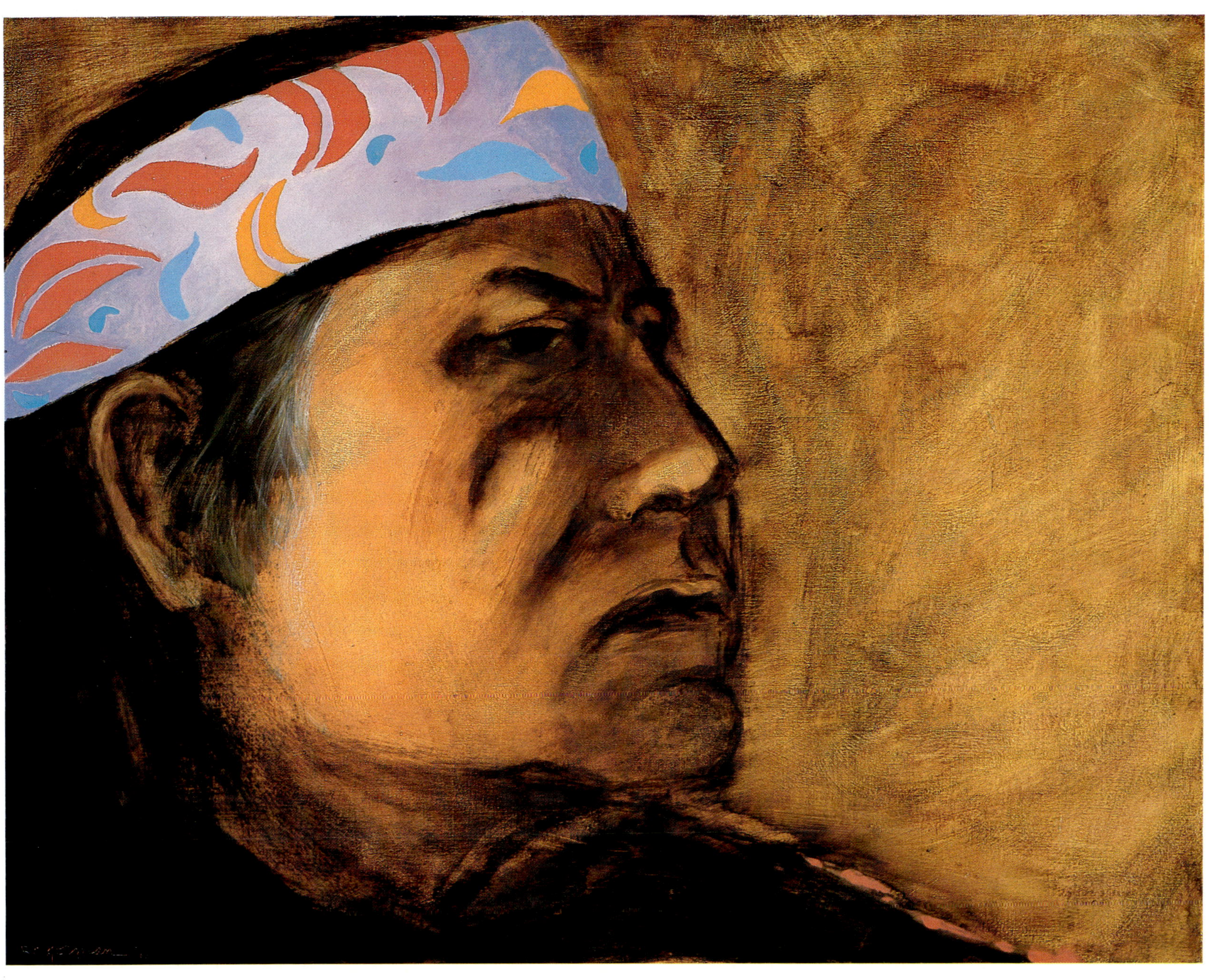

Self-Portrait, oil, 1983

"Sheep have always been our life. We herded them, ate them, sheared them, until the government—Roosevelt and his boys—decided we were too comfortable. There were rich Navajos with 3,000 sheep, and the government cut the herd down to twenty-five, claiming we were overgrazing, and made us keep them within the confines of the reservation. But the Navajos are survivors. We're still here, and he's gone."—R.C.G.

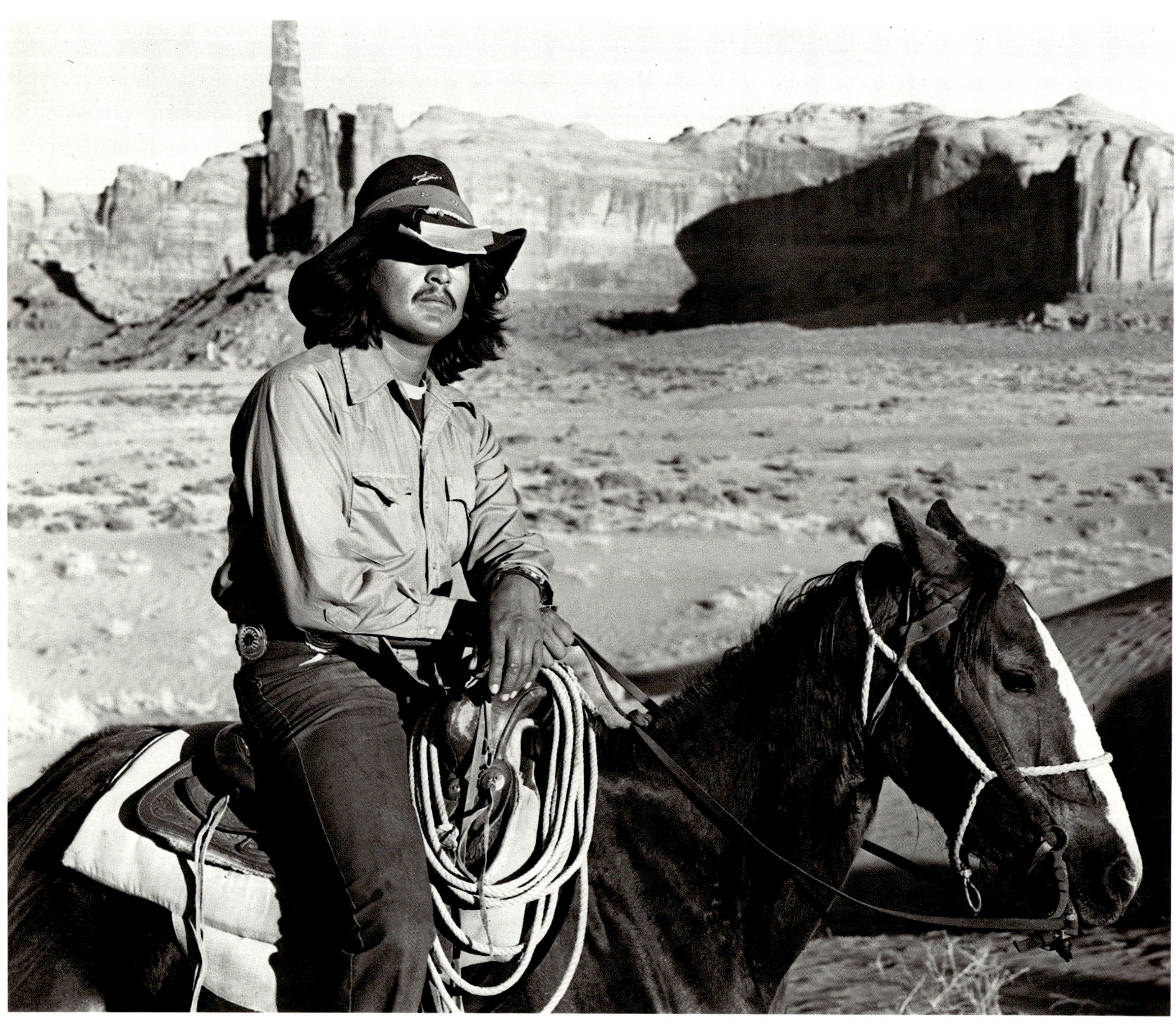

Roy Lee Jackson, Navajo sheepherder,
Monument Valley, 1979

"This reminds me of a Picasso lithograph, *Boy with Goat*. There's a fantastic similarity. I identify with this young nephew of mine, because I did the same thing. I grew up with the sheep. So many Indian children now are raised to be white. So many of them speak only English, and have this ideal of the Christian white image. Indian children must know there's no shame in being Indian. This little boy speaks better Navajo than he does English. So many Navajos think to be successful is to be as white as you can."—R.C.G.

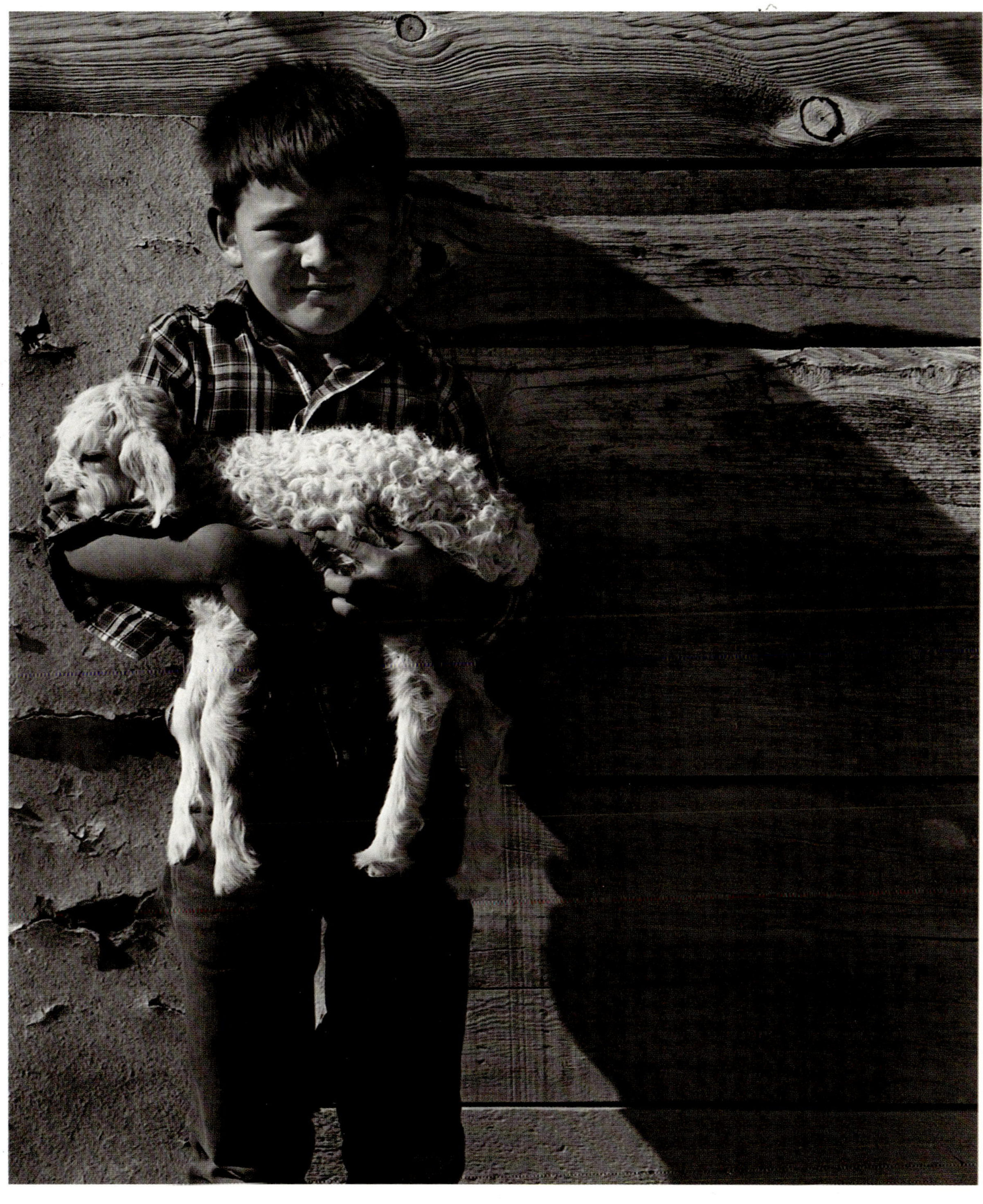

Navajo Boy and lamb, Gorman's nephew,
Black Mountain, 1980

"I raised my brothers and sisters. I was the oldest, which is never any fun. Giving a baby a bottle and changing diapers is never glamorous. My mother worked, my father was away at the wars, so that was my job—shoveling shit. Mother and child is usually one of my stronger images. Those extended fingers and toes . . . it's my idea, I guess, of power in a person."—R.C.G.

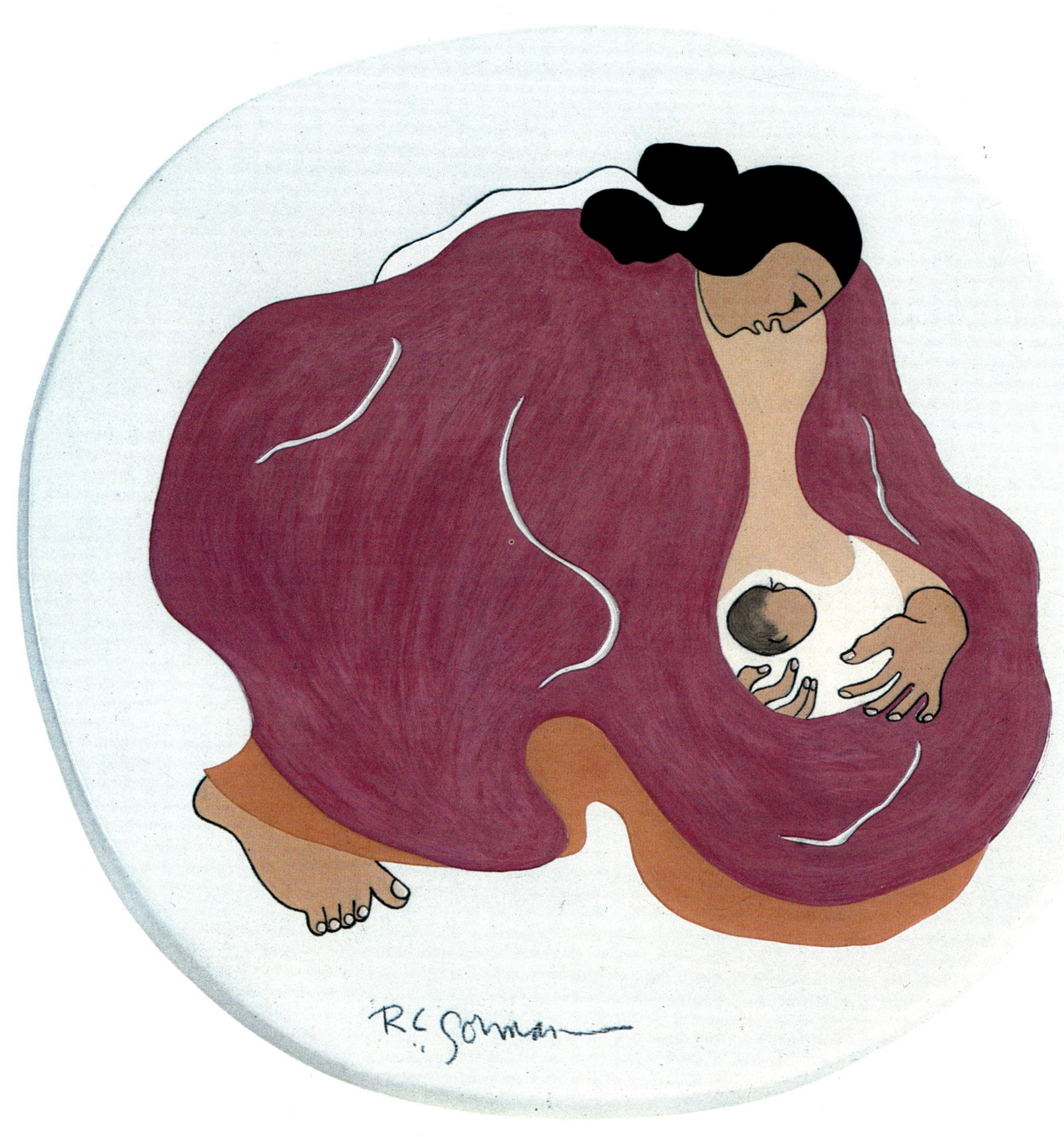

Navajo Woman and Child,
ceramic plate, Grycner Limited Editions, 1982

"I have so many nieces and nephews, and none of them look alike. Way down deep, I feel that's what's going to happen to all Indians. They'll become unrecognizable. I already have blue-eyed cousins. This niece is of mixed blood, part black. She lives with Aunt Mary, who won't turn away anyone. She's the original Navajo old lady who lives in a tar-paper shoe."—R.C.G.

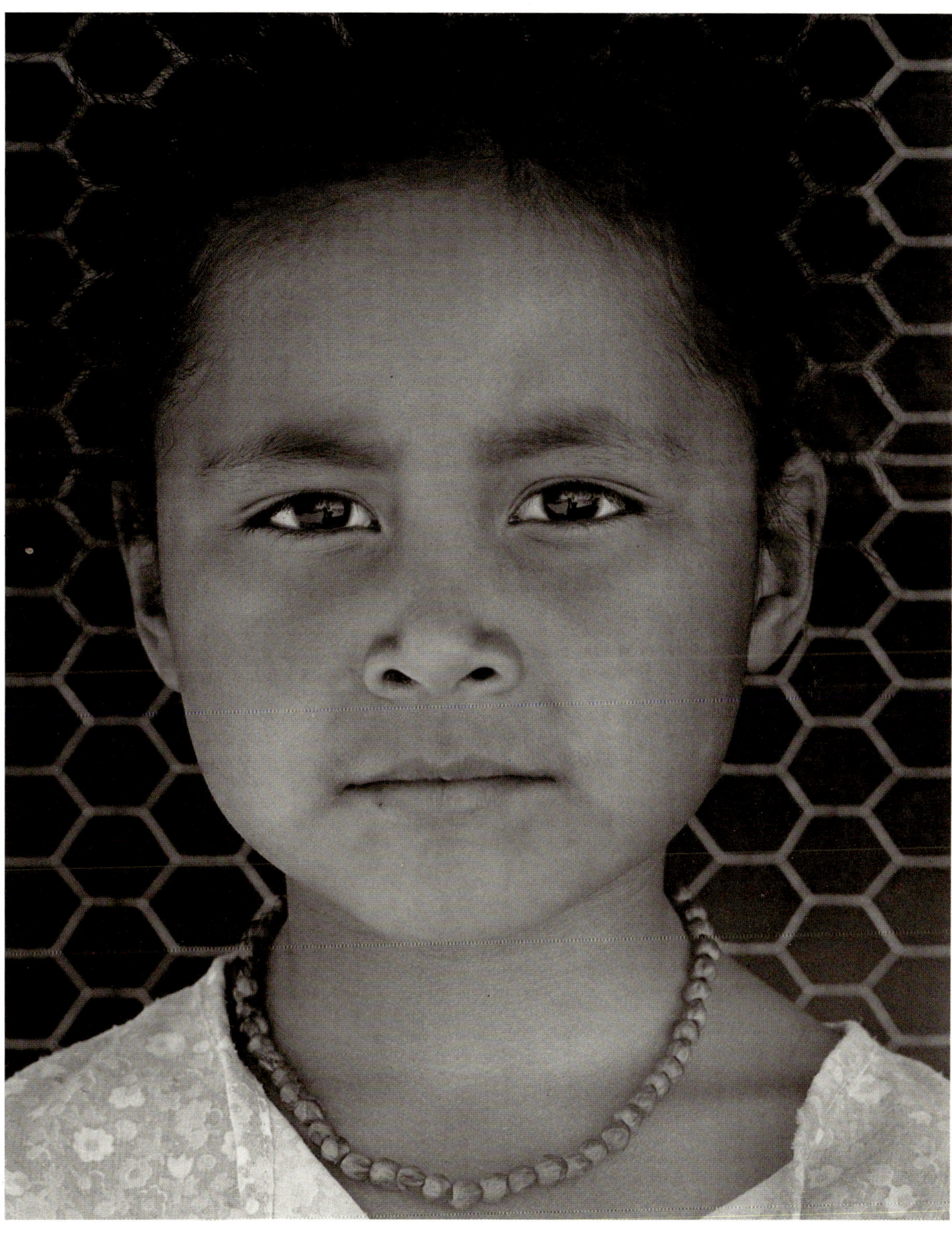

Gorman's niece, wearing juniper berries,
Black Mountain, 1980

"My Aunt Mary has always been a very creative woman. She made her own stoves, built her own homes, and always had time to mold horses and sheep out of clay with me after it rained, when we were herding sheep. She's a very generous woman, even when she can't afford to be. She'll always present you with a gift—wild tea, a little rug she's woven, some fresh mutton, a piece of jewelry. She visited me not long ago, and I saw her sitting on an old stool out there in the driveway, next to my Mercedes. She'd dug a little pit, started a fire, and she was cooking sheep intestines over the fire. That was her gift to me. The car, my swimming pool, those things don't mean anything to her. She was bringing me a part of my home country, to keep me in my place, so to speak."—R.C.G.

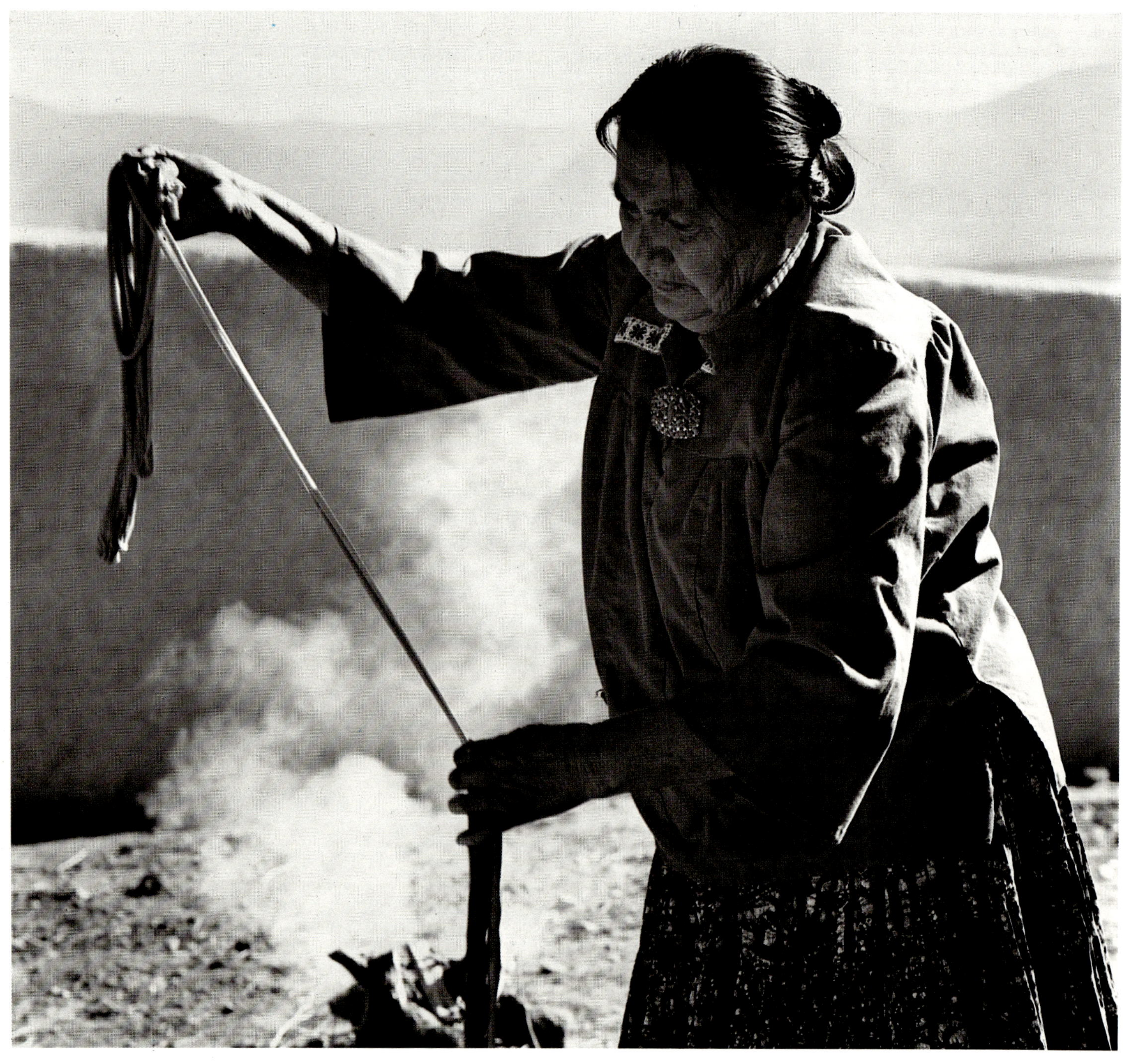

Aunt Mary cleaning lamb intestines,
Taos, 1981

"Everyone loves Aunt Mary, even the chickens that she later serves us for dinner. This is Aunt Mary's chair, which doesn't look like a throne, but it is. She's a queen."—R.C.G.

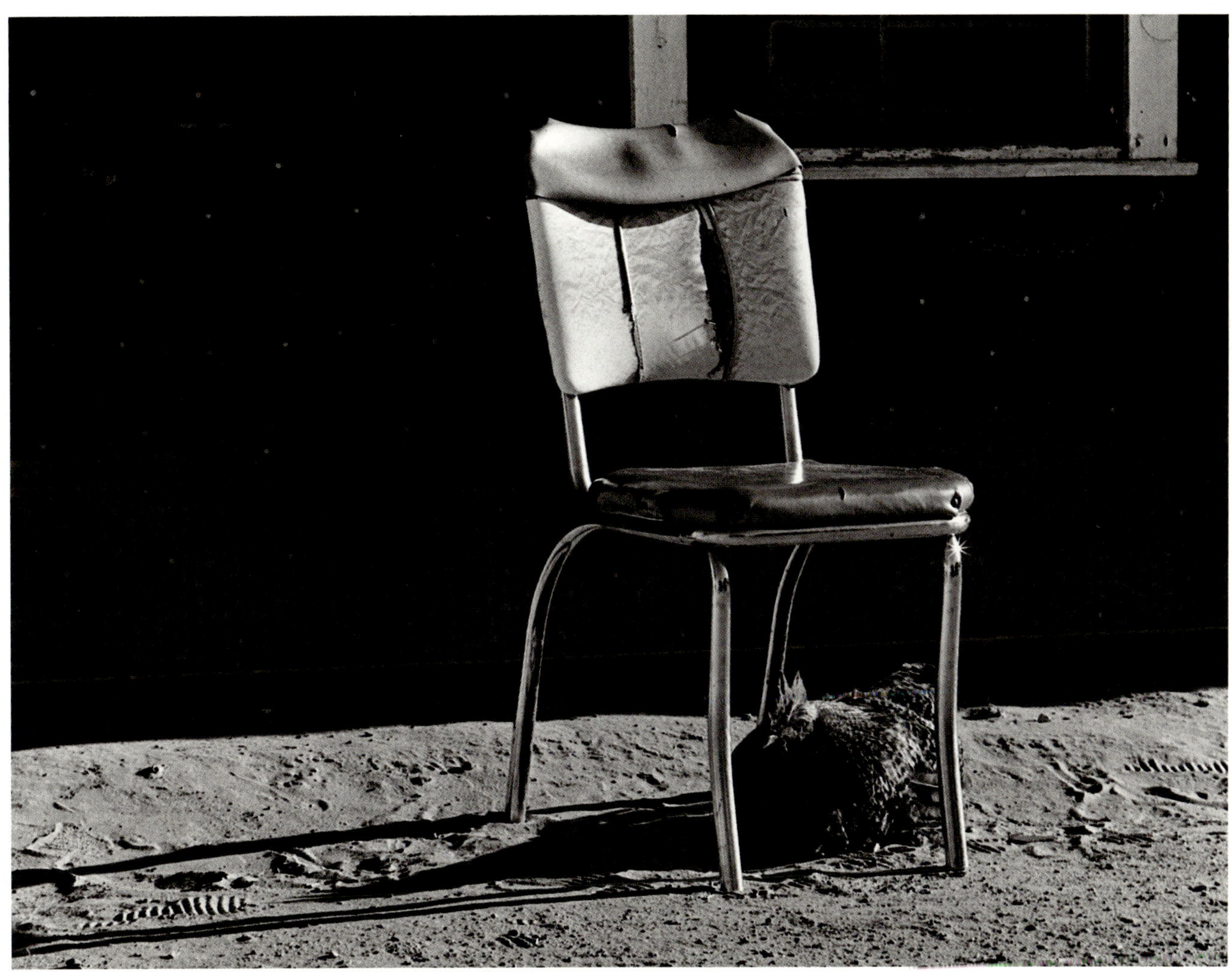

Aunt Mary's chair,
Black Mountain, 1980

"This is Pudgy. I named her that when she was born. I've taken a number of nieces and nephews under my wing. What could I do? My brothers and sisters had so many babies. Maybe in a small way I'm trying to expose them to the fact that the world's large. There's not just one type of people, and they should be able to choose for themselves where they want to be, what they want to do. I have an interest in anyone who's trying to make themselves a little better."
—R.C.G.

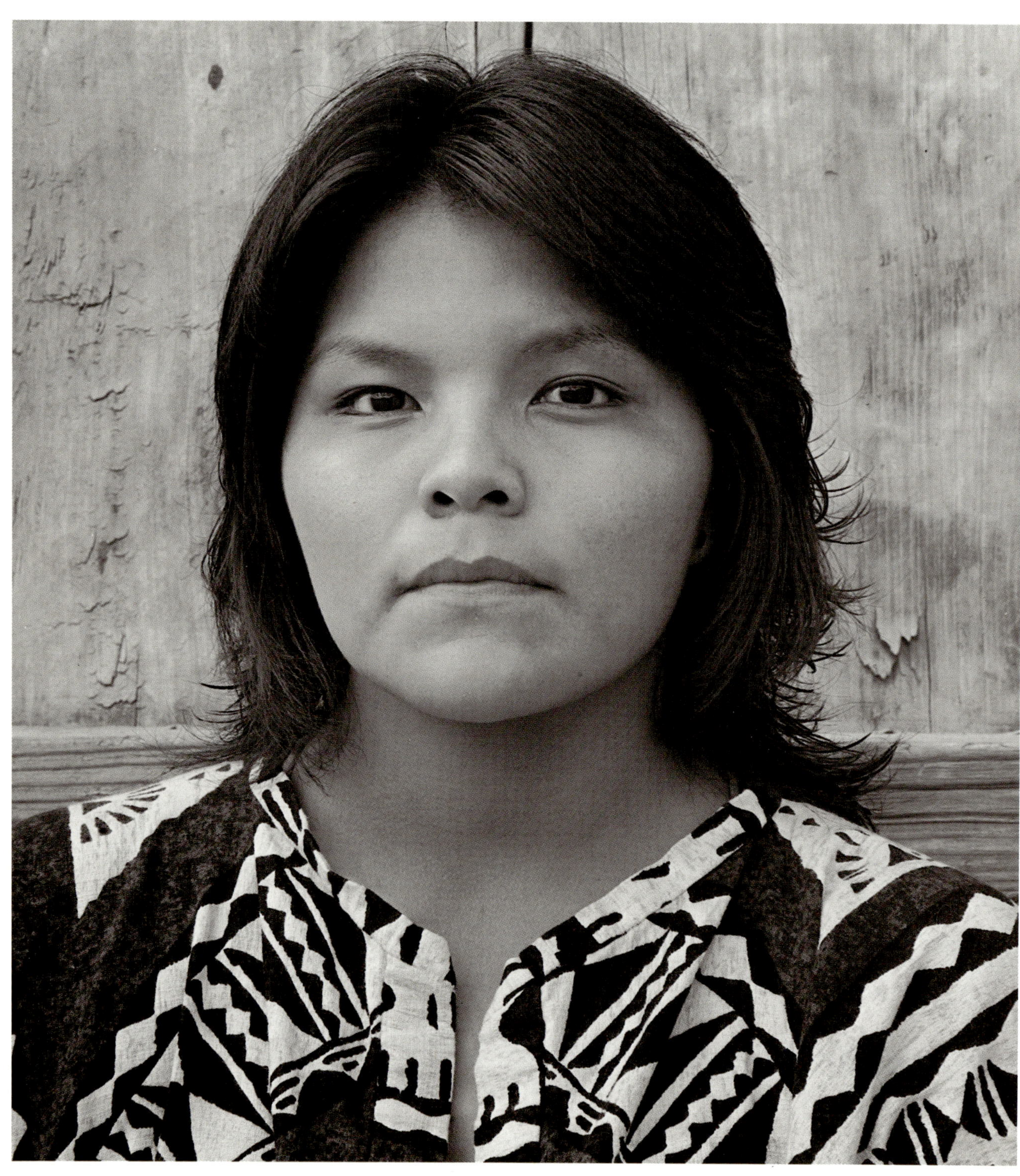

Pudgy Scott, Gorman's niece,
Many Farms, Arizona, 1980

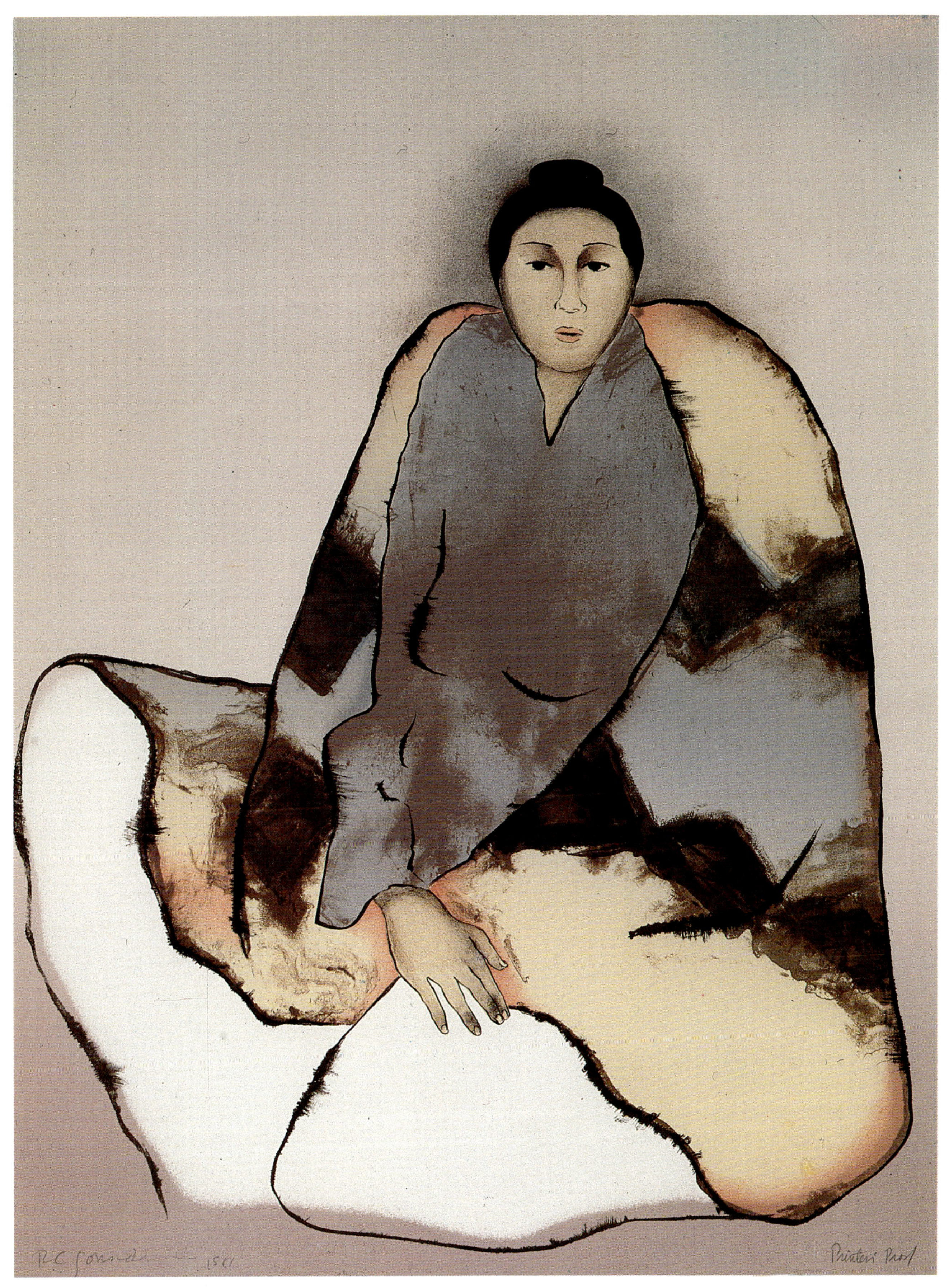

Anna,
lithograph, Origins Press, 1981

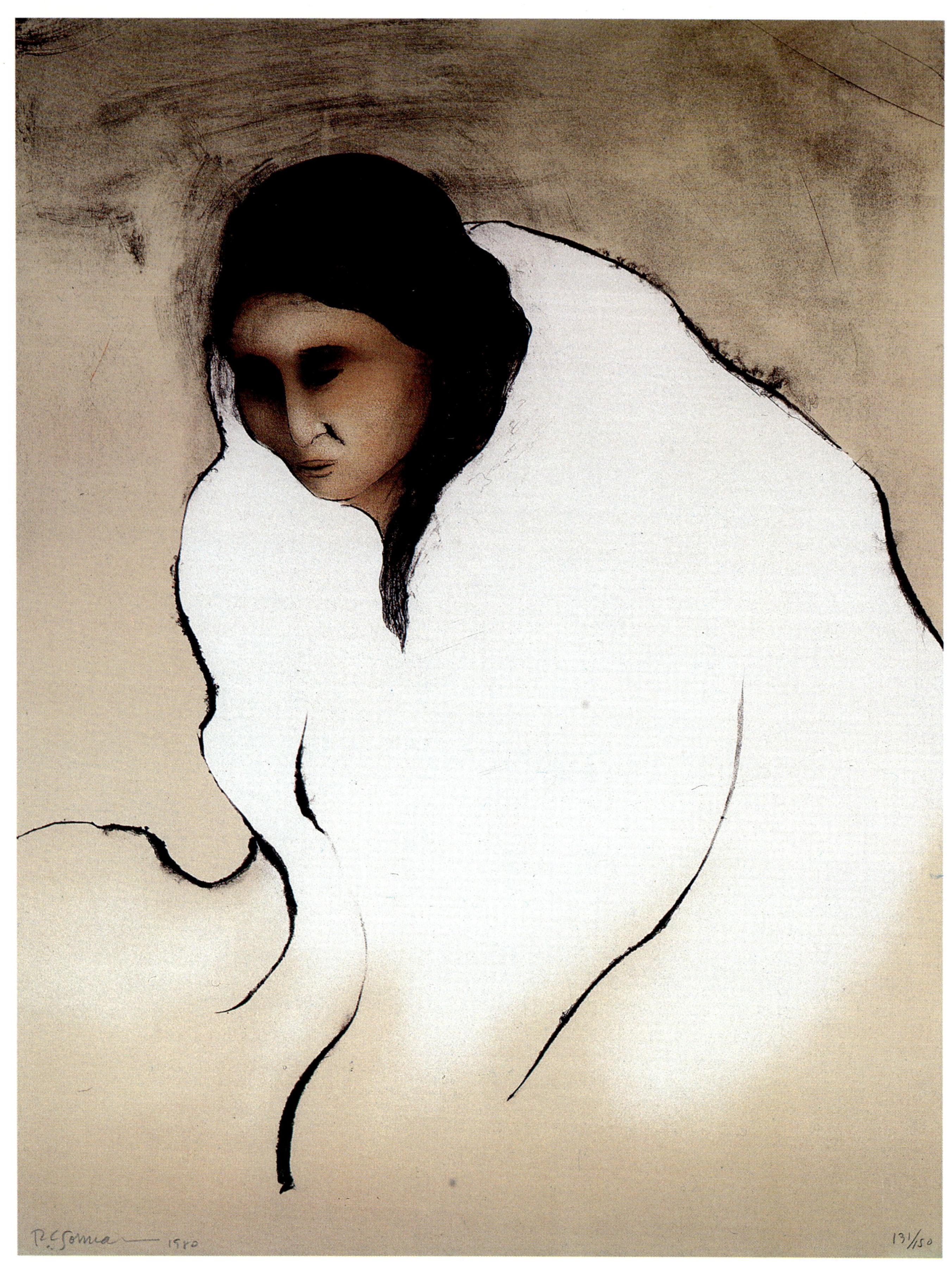

138 **Pilar**,
lithograph, Origins Press, 1980

"Aunt Dolly has all these sons-in-law who buy cars, and when they're no longer usable, they leave them at her place. She's really a powerful woman. She must be one of the early advocates of women's liberation. The moment she had finished having children, she got rid of her weak husband and raised them herself. That's the way she liked it. She's a tough old broad."—R.C.G.

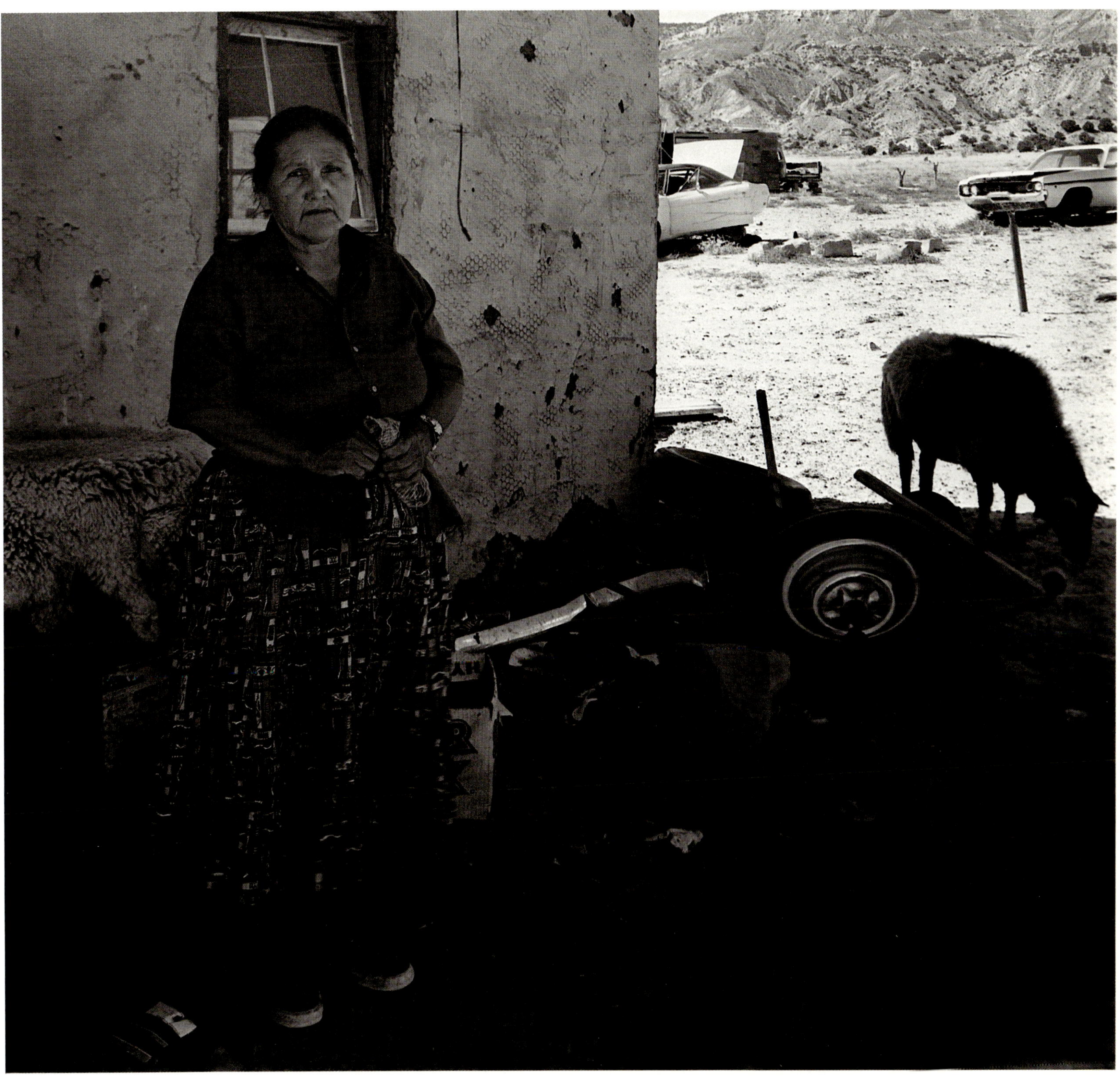

Aunt Dolly,
Black Mountain, 1981

"The plant in front of Aunt Mary is used as a mattress for babies. Behind is piñon, the needles are for medicine, the wood for fuel. There's soapweed down in front. The Navajos found a use for everything."—R.C.G.

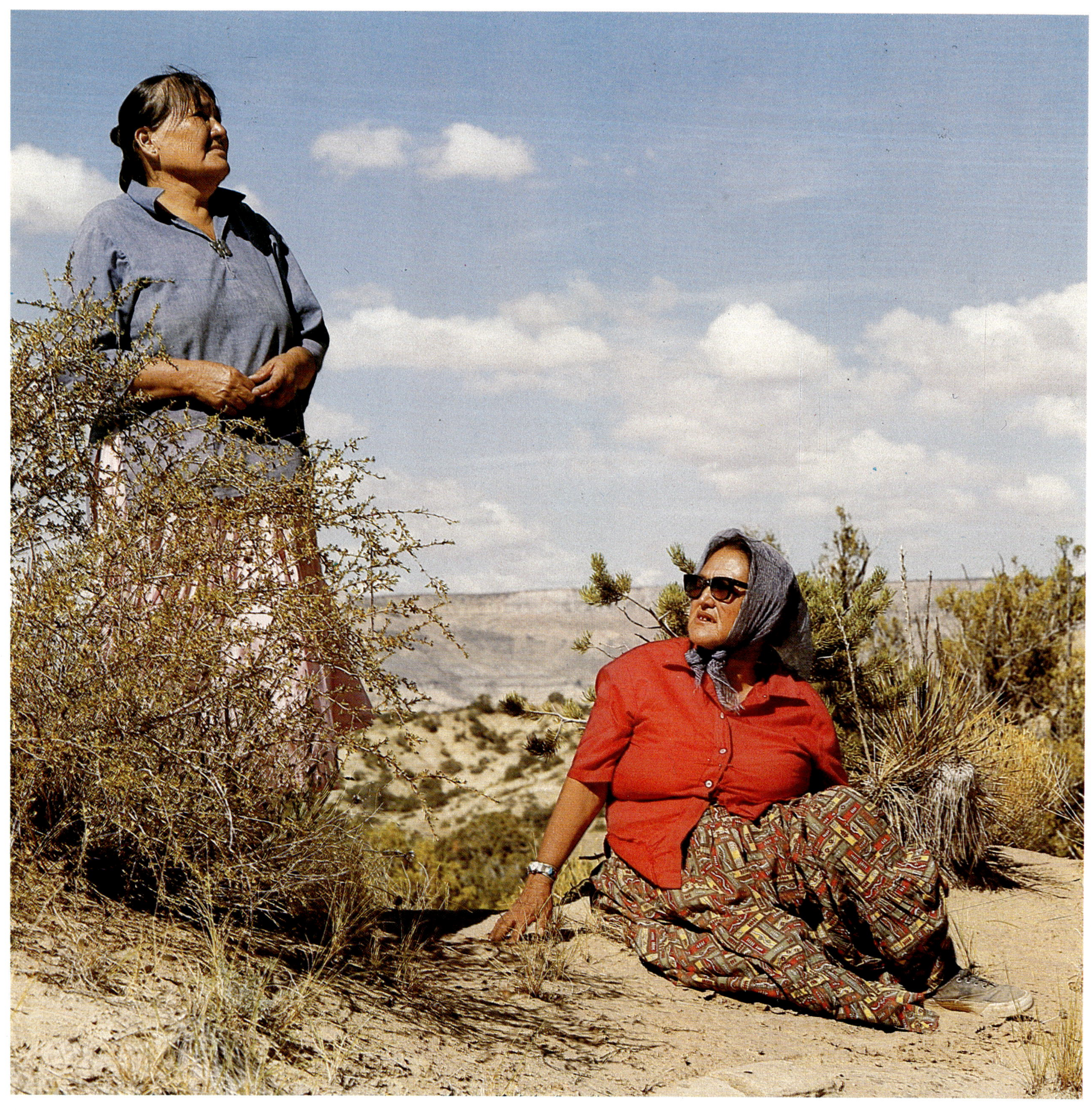

Aunt Mary and Aunt Dolly,
Black Mountain, 1981

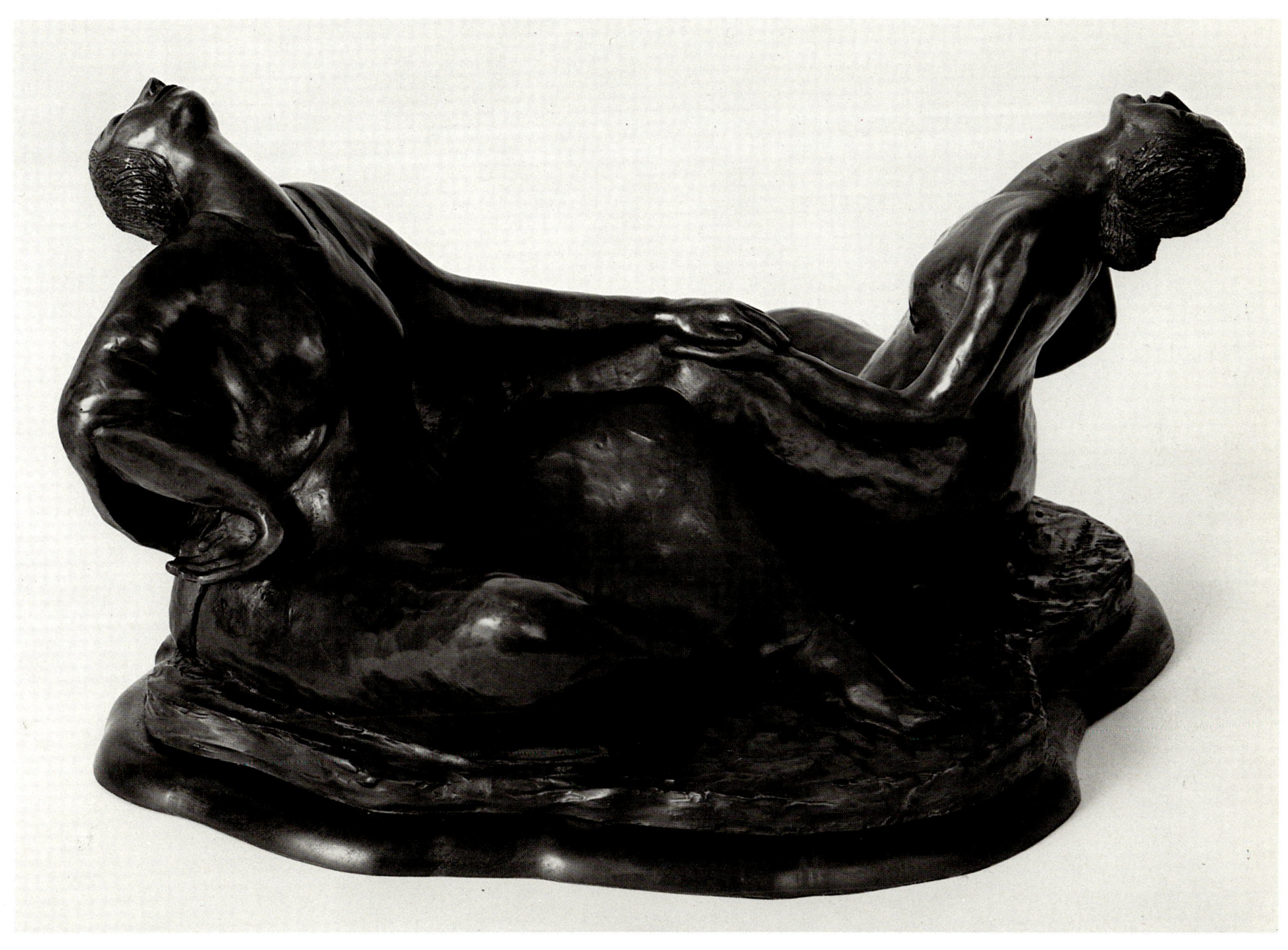

Laughing Sisters,
bronze casting, Editions Press, 1981

Gorman has traveled far from Chinle. Gone is his Navajo dependence upon sheep and the land. No longer must he search out a waterhole or cry because he has nothing to give at Christmas. Gone is the rule of ritual and the seasons. When the weather gets bad, he jets to Hawaii or turns up the thermostat. Instead of hearing the long stories of Navajo legend told in stone hogans, he trades jibes with celebrities and watches his Betamax. As a result of his travels, his readings, and the people he's met, he has become a universal man. Concurrently, his work has become more universal. The faces of his women are less obviously Navajo, more obviously Everywoman.

There's an odd passage, though. The farther he has moved from Chinle and his roots, the deeper he has gone into himself, and the closer he gets to what is Chinle and the Navajo experience. His travels have freed him from having to express himself with the limited tools of traditional Indian art, freed him to express his humanness with all the tools the world has to offer.

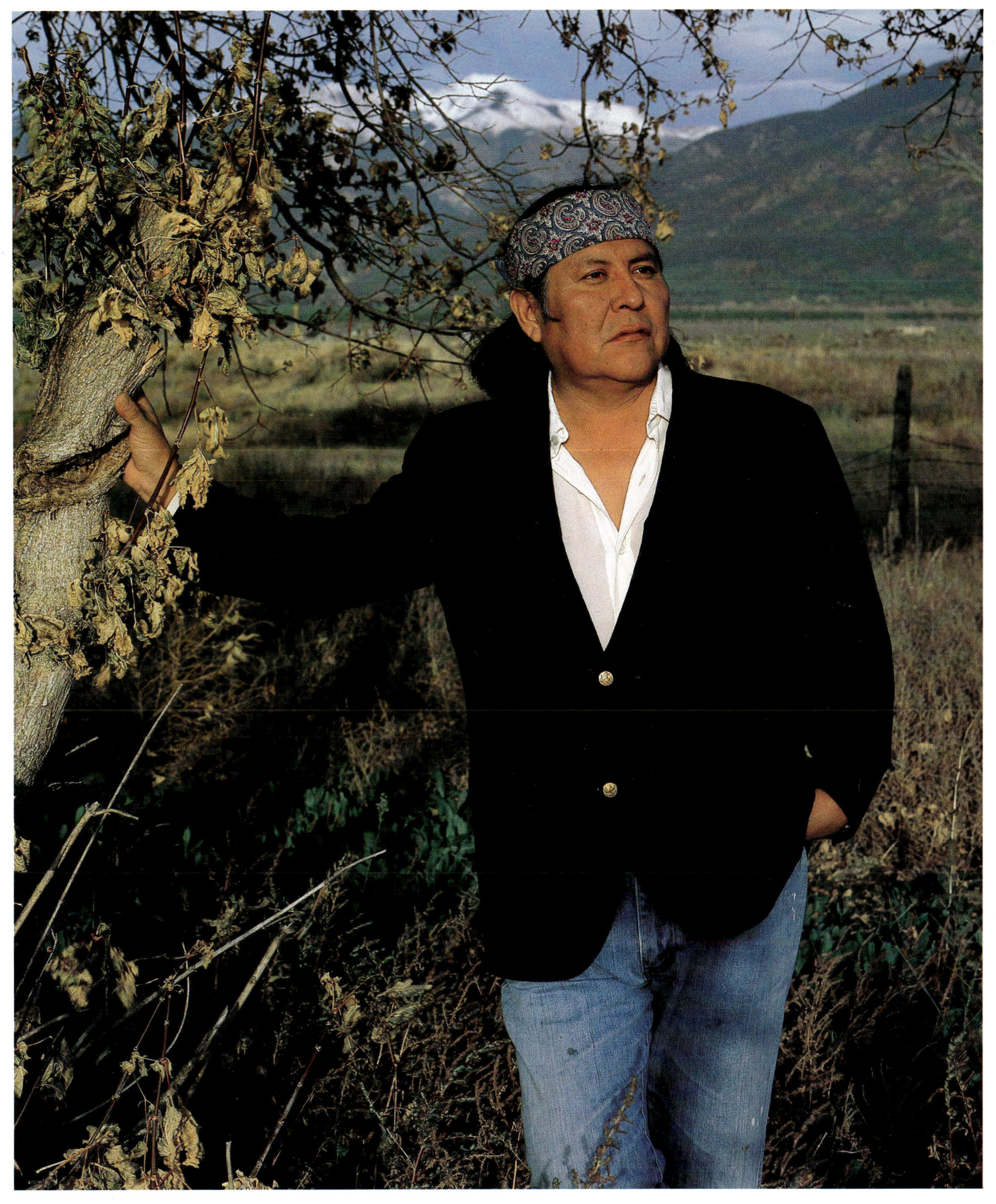

Gorman, Taos, 1982

Designed by Katy Homans
Copyedited by Betsy Pitha
Composition in Times Roman by DEKR
Printed by Arnoldo Mondadori, Verona